BULLIED

BULLIED

What Every Parent, Teacher, and Kid Needs to Know About Ending the Cycle of Fear

Carrie Goldman

HarperOne
An Imprint of HarperCollins*Publishers*

HarperOne

HarperCollins books may be purchased for educational, business, or sales promotional use. For information please write: Special Markets Department, Harper-Collins Publishers, 10 East 53rd Street, New York, NY 10022.

HarperCollins website: http://www.harpercollins.com

HarperCollins®, ®, and HarperOne™ are trademarks of HarperCollins Publishers

FIRST EDITION

Library of Congress Cataloging-in-Publication Data
Goldman, Carrie.
    Bullied : what every parent, teacher, and kid needs to know about ending the cycle of bullying / Carrie Goldman.
       p. cm.
    ISBN 978–0–06–210507–3
    1. Bullying. I. Title.
    BF637.B85G63   201
    302.34'3—dc23   2012005053

12 13 14 15 16 RRD(H) 10 9 8 7 6 5 4 3 2

The names of all victims, bullies, parents, and bystanders who have participated in this book have been changed in order to protect their privacy, unless an interviewee specifically requested that I use his or her real name. The names of all children in Katie's school, with the exception of Katie, have been changed.

The real names of those who wrote public comments on my blog are used where relevant.

The real names of all professionals who spoke to me in their professional capacity—such as authors, psychologists, teachers, lobbyists, scientists, researchers, school administrators, actors, actresses, musicians, martial arts experts, etc.—have been used in the book.

The real names of deceased bullycide victims are used in this book.

THIS BOOK IS FOR MY HUSBAND, ANDREW,
WHO IS MY PARTNER IN EVERYTHING.

Contents

Foreword

Professor Dorothy L. Espelage, Ph.D.
University of Illinois, Urbana-Champaign

After almost twenty years of conducting research on bullying and trying to inform bully-prevention efforts in U.S. schools, why do I find myself so disappointed in the progress that we have made in creating safe schools and preventing suicide ideation and suicide attempts among schoolchildren? Why do kids continue to bully each other on such a regular basis? Why, if our government tells us that we have "proven" school-based bully-prevention programs, are we not moving down the needle of bullying in schools and reducing the likelihood of bully involvement among children and adolescents?

Although I could offer many reasons why bullying in our schools is not reduced, one that is particularly obvious to me is a lack of communication and collaboration among researchers, practitioners (including teachers and administrators), and parents. All too often, scholars conduct their research studies and disseminate their findings to other scholars and rarely attempt to translate their findings into practical solutions for schools. Thus, this academic isolation or elitism leaves the practitioners questioning the commitment of researchers to impart real-world solutions to prevent bullying. On the other hand, numerous books and curriculum are developed by former teachers, concerned parents, and other concerned community members with little attention paid to the decades of developmental, social, and educational scholarship on the topic of peer victimization, aggression, and bullying. As a result, the science-to-practice divides have widened to the greatest we have seen in decades.

Is it a surprise that bullying is not going away? Well, this book, *Bullied,* by Carrie Goldman offers me a sigh of relief. When Carrie first reached out to me to share her daughter's story and her book idea, I was intrigued. I found myself saying, "Okay, you want to talk to everyone that you can about bullying, including scholars, parents, pop-psych authors, and so forth?" I was thrilled. I have to also admit that I was wondering if she could pull it off. She has done just that.

She offers a book in which research—practice—and "lived experiences" inform each other. For the first time, I see where psychological and sociological theories of aggression and bullying help explain all of the complicated aspects of Katie's story and stories that ring through the halls of U.S. schools. Carrie places Katie's story into the complex gendered world that we live in and demonstrates the importance of understanding bullying as a gendered problem and one that requires a gendered solution. Katie's story would not have happened if bullying and peer victimization were not understood as peer-driven phenomena where kids encourage disrespectful and mean interactions, where ostracism and humiliation is the ultimate goal.

In *Bullied,* Carrie enlightens us about the instrumental role that adults play in allowing bullying and peer victimization to continue, from homes to school yards to community centers. From this book, it is clear that adults need to spend much more time evaluating their own attitudes and behaviors and how bully prevention rests with everyone in society.

In short, *Bullied* demonstrates how science and practice can work together to prevent bullying. Carrie Goldman has taken the best of what scholars know about the development of bullying in children and has offered a number of insights about how individuals, peers, schools, families, and community members all contribute to this extremely devastating phenomenon and how we *all* have to work together to decrease it. Her writing style and storytelling leave the reader appreciating the importance of using research to identify real-world solutions to bullying but also understanding that research can be improved by understanding the "lived" experiences of children and their families. She should be applauded for taking the risk to write about Katie's story and doing it in a way that narrows the research-practice gap. Thank you, Carrie, for inspiring me to continue to prevent bullying!

Introduction

In November 2010, I wrote a post called "Anti-Bullying Starts in the First Grade" for my blog, *Portrait of an Adoption*. I was concerned because my daughter, Katie, was upset about being teased for carrying a Star Wars water bottle. Apparently, Star Wars was only "for boys."

It was the post that launched a thousand Geeks. Comments poured in so fast that they crashed the entire ChicagoNow server. Katie's story appeared on international and national news shows. Radio talk shows had a field day with the story, and hundreds of bloggers wrote posts about the Star Wars teasing. A Facebook event was created in support of Geek Pride and Katie, and over thirty-five thousand people participated. Feminists, Star Wars fans, adoptees, adoptive parents, former victims of teasing and bullying—all jumped to a young fangirl's defense.

Why did the article strike such a responsive chord? Because in a time of heartbreaking headlines about cyberbullying, my child experienced a refreshing new phenomenon—a term I am calling "cyber-supporting." People were hungry for a bullying case that offered hope of a happy ending, and Katie's situation became a Cinderella story. It was then that I embarked on a journey to research bullying in our culture.

Bullying has emerged as one of the biggest problems facing our nation's schools to date, but this is largely due to increased awareness and sensitivity about the consequences of being victimized. The media has created a sense of urgency around bullying, and parents are desperate to protect their children. We are closely tracking bullying and taking steps to reduce aggressive acts. We are counting the victims. A 2010 study by the National Center for Education Statistics found that 32 percent of students between the ages of twelve and eighteen reported being bullied within the six months prior to being surveyed. Of the students surveyed, 62 percent reported having been bullied once or twice a year, 21 percent once or twice a month, 10 percent once or twice a week, and 7 percent reported being bullied *every day*.[1] The 2009 National Youth Risk Behavior Survey found that about one in five teens had been bullied at school in the last year, with nearly half of middle-school students being bullied.

Although far too many kids are victimized, the hopeful news for parents and educators is that some measures of bullying have actually dropped since 1999. Ron Astor, coauthor of the critically acclaimed book *School Violence in Context: Culture, Neighborhood, Family, School, and Gender,* told me, "Starting in 1994, many school violence measures began to drop and have continued to drop. But just because our research shows things have gotten better doesn't mean it's not still a very serious problem. And the subjective category of bullying has gone up."[2] It is hard to believe bullying is down in any form when we read heartbreaking reports of youths taking their own lives in response to peer victimization, a form of suicide known as bullycide. But, as Astor points out, schools are hard at work implementing social and emotional learning programs, and this work *is* paying off, which we must recognize so that parents and educators do not get discouraged and feel helpless to make a difference with bullying. Michael Thompson, bestselling coauthor of *Raising Cain: Protecting the Emotional Life of Boys,* reminded me that while many students encounter normal social pain at school, only about 15 percent of kids suffer trauma as a result of being bullied.[3] Yes, 15 percent is clearly the minority, and it is important to keep that in perspective, but in terms of sheer numbers, it still represents millions of traumatized children. For those children who do encounter significant, severe bullying, the damage is lasting and the implications for a normal social life are devastating.

The arena in which bullying is raising the most concern is on the Internet, because people have brought their aggressive tendencies online. Cyberbullying was not a factor in historical measurements of bullying behaviors, so even though other types of physical and verbal bullying have decreased, there has been a large shift to online bullying. Parents who are intimidated by texting and social-networking sites view cyberbullying as a terrifying new form of bullying, but the truth is that cyberbullying is just a continuation of existing adolescent behavior, played out in a new arena. Approximately 20–25 percent of kids have been bullied online, according to cyberbullying expert Justin Patchin, and this is a conservative estimate.[4] Bullies and victims can trade places at the click of a mouse, and things move so fast online that it is difficult to process information rationally before reacting. For the unfortunate kids who find themselves on the receiving end of massive cyberbullying attacks, the relentless barrage of cruelty can create a sensation of sinking into a black hole of pain.

How exactly does the pain of severe bullying affect the most vulnerable kids? Studies investigating the neuroscience of bullying have found that bully victims experience anxiety, depression, post-traumatic stress, difficulty concentrating, headaches, and stomach pain as a result of being bullied.[5] Studies of early social deprivation show that human beings are hardwired to belong,[6] and nowhere is this more evident than in kids jockeying for social position. And the old adage—sticks and stones may break my bones but words will never hurt me? Not true. Neuroimaging studies have shown that parts of the cortical pain network are also activated when a person is socially excluded.[7] This goes not just for adults but for children as well. The brain of a child as young as thirteen has been shown to react to social pain as if the child were being physically injured.[8] Taunting and bullying hurts, and we have the brain scans to prove it. Even worse, repeatedly being victimized by peers—which is the very nature of bullying, the *repetitiveness* of it—actually alters brain functioning, which increases the victim's sensitivity to future attacks, even causing the person to perceive an ambiguous situation as threatening.[9] Years after the school bullying has ceased, victims are left picking up the wreckage.

The outlook for the most-affected victims is serious, but I believe there is hope that we can continue to reduce the number of victims. Bullying is a learned behavior. Children are not born cruel. Babies in diapers do not assess each other as too fat, too poor, too dark-skinned, too nerdy, too conceited. Born innocent, they start learning stereotypes as soon as they understand language, and we see bullying behaviors in children as young as toddlers. Since preschoolers who display marked aggressiveness have a higher likelihood of being bullies in older grades, the earlier intervention begins, the better the results. It is much easier to inculcate kindness and acceptance into a five-year-old who acts like a bully than into a fifteen-year-old who acts like a bully.

In analyzing Katie's story and that of other children and young adults like her, this book examines the roles that schools, families, communities, retailers, celebrities, and the media play in raising diverse, empathetic, tolerant kids. It draws on the expertise of kids, parents, anti-bullying consultants, authors, social workers, psychologists, teachers, and attorneys to evaluate which actions actually help prevent bullying and which ones are ineffective.

This book is for all the parents whose children are trapped in the cruel winter of bullying, whether your child is the aggressor or the target. *You are not alone.* There are ways to help. One of the goals of the book is to help parents recognize the difference between situations that involve normal social pain and those that involve actual bullying. We parents agonize over our children's pain, even when it is the result of normal social conflict, and it is very hard to learn to restrain ourselves from rushing in unnecessarily. A helicopter approach inhibits the ability of children to develop good conflict-resolution skills. Ironically, in trying to protect them, we may actually set them up for future harm if we rescue them every time their feelings get hurt. Fortunately, there are concrete ways to determine whether or not a child is actually involved in a bullying relationship, and I will provide sample scenarios.

This book is for all the children who have witnessed cruelty but have not known how to help without compromising their own safety. It is for all the kids who act as bullies and want to change their own behavior. *You are not alone.* At some point in our lives, we have all been in at least one of the above-mentioned roles.

Finally, this book is for all the children who are being victimized. It is for the child who cries in the night because she fears what the next day at school will bring. It is for the young man who hides his true sexual orientation because he dreads what his college roommate will do to him. It is for the stuttering child who elects silence over speech, and it is for the overweight child who is afraid to unpack his lunch in the cafeteria. It is for the geeky girl who does not yet know that she will grow up to be a respected physicist, and it is for the little boy who wants to wear a sparkly dress. It is for the child with autism who is bullied on the playground and does not understand the insults but knows something is wrong. It is for the child who is mocked because her skin is a different color, and it is for the brothers and sisters who worship at an altar that other families fear. To the princess boys and the Star Wars girls, the nonconformists, the marginalized, the ignored and the outcasts, the hidden Jedis of the universe, over and over I offer up these words to you:

You are not alone.

Part One: Katie's Story

Chapter One

Anti-Bullying Starts in the First Grade

In the fall of 2010, my daughter Katie was a spunky first grader. I could always spot her on the playground, because she was the only girl with long blonde hair and a black Star Wars bag. We had recently braved the throngs at Target for our back-to-school shopping, and Katie very deliberately chose a Star Wars backpack and water bottle. She couldn't wait to show it to the kids at school, and she was not fazed by the fact that none of the other girls in her class sported Star Wars gear.

The previous year, I had picked out Katie's backpack for her, a turquoise Tinker Bell bag that had been prominently displayed in the "Girls" section. I had unconsciously drifted into the marketing trap that was successfully laid out for consumers. Some parents actually voice a preference for gender-coded items, such as the dad who told me, "I have three boys, and I like to see the blue section because it makes it easy to find the toys they play with."

But in light of the past year, I wonder, do most boys play with "boy toys" because that is what we offer them? What would happen if, from infancy on, we used a different system? What if toys were organized by manufacturer or by type of toy or by alphabetical order, instead of by assumed gender preference? Katie accepted the Tinker Bell backpack without question in kindergarten, because it was what I presented to her. I now know that I had been living in a box, and

I pulled Katie into the box with me. My rising first grader was the first to break out of the box when she pivoted around midaisle and headed for the "Boys" bags, and I finally had the good sense to follow her lead.

FIRST GRADE STARTED OFF swimmingly, until late in September when Katie told me that a boy in her class, "Jake," had been calling her Piggy. She said it very matter-of-factly, and at first I could not even tell if she was bothered by this. "Well, I love Miss Piggy," I said.

"Mom, he doesn't mean a fictional pig," Katie replied. I looked at her carefully. She met my gaze with steady but subdued eyes.

"What do you think he means?" I asked.

Katie shrugged, and I told her, "Why don't you tell him to call you Katie? That's your name."

Throughout the day, the conversation bothered me. Was Jake calling her Piggy as a comment on her weight? God, please don't let that start at such a young age. Katie is built solidly—not a skinny, lanky girl—but certainly not heavy. Her birthmother and birth siblings are large people, so I know Katie may have a genetic tendency to be a big girl as she grows older. With that in mind, we try to keep a healthy, active lifestyle, and Katie pays very little attention to body image.

Katie didn't mention it again for a few weeks, and I forgot about it. But one night in October, as I was tucking her into bed, she said, "I'm sick. I don't want to go to school tomorrow." My hands grew still on the covers.

"What's wrong?" I asked.

"Jake is calling me Piggy." She started to cry, hard. "And he has other kids calling me Piggy too. We all sit at the same work table."

As a parent, there are few things more heartbreaking than watching your child suffer at the hands of another child. My sweet, vulnerable Katie, weeping because she was afraid to go to school and be taunted. I had recently seen a report on ABC News that thousands of kids feign illness every day due to bullying, and here was my daughter saying she wanted to stay home from school for that very reason.

For a moment, I felt a wave of helplessness, because I could not control what Jake said and did. I imagined parents around the country, feeling the same way, as their children beg out of school for fear of being taunted. What do we do? How do we respond? I found myself beginning the journey that so many of us have traveled.

"Katie," I said, "I am glad you told me. If others are giving you a hard time at school and you can't find a peaceful way to make them stop, then it is important to ask for help. Do you want me to talk to Mrs. Martin?"

"Yes," she sobbed.

"Okay, I will call her tonight, as soon as I go downstairs. Don't worry, we will figure it out. It will get better." She calmed down and put her head on the pillow. My stomach felt jittery as I walked out of her room, and I paced the house for a moment to let the nervous energy dissipate before making the call to Katie's teacher.

Jake had been in Katie's kindergarten class the previous year, and they had occasionally clashed, but by the end of the year, they were close buddies. I wondered why they weren't getting along. Now that I thought about it, Katie had rarely mentioned playing with Jake this year.

My phone call with Mrs. Martin went far better than I could have anticipated. She expressed real empathy for Katie's pain and vowed to talk to Jake the next day. She said she might switch Katie to another table to give her a new group of kids to work with and would monitor the children closely, and she gave me her personal email and cell-phone number so that I could contact her at any time.

In the morning, when Katie was well rested and content, I talked with her about the possible motivations behind Jake's taunts. "Katie, one of the reasons that kids taunt one another is because they don't feel secure. I suspect that Jake sometimes feels very alone. Maybe he picks on you and rallies others to join in because he feels different himself, and this is the only way he knows how to act on those feelings. Who knows? It doesn't make it right or acceptable for him to call you mean names, but it might help us understand why he is doing it."

We walked to school, and Katie jogged off to play briefly with her friend Kacie, who was in her class last year but in a different class this year. I happened to see Jake standing by himself and made a split-second decision to approach him. There were no other kids around; school hadn't started, and I wanted to talk to him. I did not want to make him apologize; I certainly did not intend to scold him. I simply wanted to inform him how his words were affecting Katie and ask him to treat her with respect.

"Jake, Katie tells me you have been calling her Piggy," I began. "Is that true?"

He looked at me and then looked down. "Yeah," he said.

"You and Katie are friends, and you've had fun playing together in the past. When you call Katie Piggy, it makes her sad. She didn't want to come to school today because she was upset about being called Piggy, and that made me feel very sad too."

He listened but didn't respond.

"Call her Katie. That is her name. Just like she calls you Jake, because that is your name. Okay?"

"Okay," he mumbled.

"And have a good day at school," I told him.

During my walk home, I hoped that approaching Jake had not been inappropriate. What if I had made things worse? Was first grade still young enough for me to talk to Jake without triggering a backlash for Katie? I wasn't sure if Jake even realized how much his words were hurting Katie's feelings. Fraught with anxiety, I worried throughout the day. After school, Mrs. Martin told me that she had spoken with Jake, and Katie reported that the day had progressed without incident.

A few days later, Katie came home and showed me that Jake had slipped a letter into her backpack. It was an apology note that he had written, all of his own accord. I felt genuine warmth for this little boy as well as relieved that, in this situation, everything had turned out okay. I talked about the experience with some of my closest friends, mostly because I was worried that Katie would retain some concern about her body image. Fortunately, she was very resilient and moved on, but I had a glimpse into the ugliness that many children must experience. For Katie, however, the taunting had ceased.

And then one November morning, Katie pulled her Star Wars water bottle out of her lunch bag. "I don't want to bring my Star Wars water bottle. It's too small."

"But you love that water bottle," I protested.

Katie repeated that the water bottle was too small and searched through the cupboard until she found a pink water bottle. "I'll bring this," she said.

I was perplexed. "Katie, that water bottle is no bigger than your Star Wars one. I think it is actually smaller."

"It's fine, I'll just take it," she insisted. I kept pushing the issue, because it didn't make sense to me. Suddenly, Katie burst into tears.

She wailed, "The first-grade boys are teasing me at lunch because I have a Star Wars water bottle. They say it's only for boys. They say it at my locker when I unpack my bag, and they say it at lunch and at recess. They laugh at me."

Such a tender young age, and already Katie was embarrassed about the water bottle that brought her so much excitement and joy a few months ago. Is this how it starts? I wondered. Do kids find someone who does something differently and start to beat it out of her, first with words and sneers? Must my daughter conform to be accepted?

The confusing part for me was that I knew those first-grade boys. They were not simply random cruel boys bullying my baby. They were good kids individually, and Katie often played happily with them. But when you put the boys together in a pack, maybe they started to feel vulnerable and insecure. Maybe they bullied others to get laughs out of one another. Maybe they did it because if they were busy taunting Katie, nobody would taunt one of them. Maybe they did it because they wanted her attention and had limited social skills at this age. Maybe they did it because they didn't even know how she was feeling.

I was not even sure how to define Katie's experience. Was it just teasing? Curious, I logged onto the Internet and did a little research. To my surprise, Katie was experiencing two types of bullying: verbal taunts and relational bullying. According to Dan Olweus, one of the foremost authors of bullying research, what was happening to Katie was a form of bullying because (1) the comments made to Katie were negative and unwanted; (2) the taunting was happening repeatedly; and (3) there was an imbalance of power (multiple boys versus one Katie). Bullying occurs on a continuum, starting with milder incidents such as those experienced by Katie and potentially leading into severe, prolonged tormenting. In the absence of intervention and social change, it would not be unusual to see these same boys escalating their attacks as they head into middle school. Like with so many things, it appeared that early intervention now would translate into prevention later. To dismiss the taunting as "boys being boys" or as "a schoolyard rite of passage" would send the message that the behavior was normal and acceptable.

What really saddened me was that Katie wanted to compromise who she was in order to fit in. Some kids might lash out and become aggressive when they are picked on, but Katie chose to shut down and try to minimize the attacks by not attracting attention. "Katie, it is okay to be different. Not all girls need to drink out of pink water bottles," I told her.

"I'm already different," Katie lamented. "Nobody else in my class wears glasses or a patch, and I don't know anybody else who's adopted. Now I'm even more different, because of my Star Wars water bottle."

I did not force her to take the Star Wars water bottle, because it was not my decision to make. But I urged her to stay true to herself and said I hoped she would soon feel ready to resume carrying the Star Wars water bottle.

The next day, I sat at my computer, preparing to write a post for my blog, *Portrait of an Adoption*. The upcoming week was Anti-Bullying Week at the schools, and it seemed like an ideal time to write about Katie's Star Wars experience. I recounted the story, published it under the title "Anti-Bullying Starts in the First Grade," and sent it to Katie's principal, Kate Ellison. She forwarded it on to the teachers and staff at the school. Two days later, one of the school's PTA co-presidents, Evan Girard, called me to ask for permission to post the article to the school Listserv. "Sure," I replied, and I was really glad to see that the school's leaders were actively sharing the story and fostering discussions.

That evening, a few readers posted supportive comments for Katie. I chuckled because the comments were all from female Star Wars fans. They were obviously responding to the part in my post where I had written, "I would love to be able to show Katie that she is not alone, that other females appreciate Star Wars. If there are any female Star Wars fans reading this, please feel free to show your support for Katie. I will let her read your messages or comments, and I think she will be surprised by what I suspect is a vast number of female fans."

I spent a few minutes writing a thank-you comment to each of the nine women who had written kind comments to Katie, scanned my email, and logged off. It was time for bed.

Chapter Two

The Littlest Jedi

A couple of days later, while sitting outside Katie's ballet class, I glanced at my phone to see if there were any new responses to the post. The page was unusually slow to load, and I wondered if it was my connection or a problem with the ChicagoNow server. Impatiently, I tapped my phone, and the page finally pulled up. To my astonishment, there were two hundred comments on my post. Where was all the traffic coming from? Even as I looked at the page, I saw the comments number switch to 201, then 202, and the "likes" number was increasing by the hundreds. And then the server crashed. Something unusual was going on, but I would have to wait another hour before I could look into it. When we returned home, I headed straight to the computer and logged on. There were now four hundred comments on my tiny, unknown blog, with more pouring in by the minute.

As I rapidly scanned through the first few pages of comments, I noticed a theme. Women, hundreds of women, were writing to Katie. Girls, teens, young, middle-aged, and old women—all were racing to log in and share with my little girl their own experiences of being teased. The commenters had learned about Katie from a popular Geek Girl website called Epbot.com run by Jen Yates. One of the mothers from Washington Elementary School had forwarded my post to Yates earlier that day. The Epbot readers had a long history of feeling different and were frequently bullied as young girls for being geeky or tomboyish. We started reading their comments after dinner and soon grew lost in everyone's stories. We read one last message before heading upstairs to bathe Katie and her little sisters, Annie Rose and Cleo.

Dear Katie,

When I was in grade school, I had a Return of the Jedi lunchbox with a thermos that had an Ewok on it, and I took that to school every day. I was so proud of that lunchbox (in fact, I still have it). The boys made fun of me too, Katie, not just because of the Star Wars stuff, but because I looked different too. They said all sorts of awful things to me, and it did hurt my feelings, but it never made me stop loving Star Wars. Honestly, it was really hard to learn to not care about them, but I worked hard at it (even cried about it at home), and eventually, when I got a bit older, I made friends with the boys who teased me . . . because we all loved Star Wars.

Much love to you!!

Zaika

The Geek Girls from Epbot were quite effective at spreading the word about the little first-grade girl who was taunted for carrying a Star Wars water bottle. Within a few hours, comments began pouring in from a new group—men who were touched by Katie's plight.

Dear Katie,

I'm just a boy but I've grown up a lot. I've been picked on for being adopted, being girly, wearing glasses, being heavier than other kids, and for being smarter than other kids.

But all those kids who bullied me have not amounted to much, and I'm living a pretty great life. I'm doing what I want, making good money, and being happy.

You sound like a terrific person for liking what you like and for being so brave. The world needs more people like you, and we're all glad you're just who you are.

Paul

One reader created a Twitter hashtag, #maytheforcebewithkatie, to allow interested parties to follow Katie's story more easily. NASA jumped in, tweeting "Come on, boys, Star Wars is for everyone." Bonnie Burton, senior editor at www.starwars.com, tweeted about it, which caught the attention of Geek Girl celebrities, including Alyssa Milano and Felicia Day. Alyssa Milano tweeted that she was sending a "virtual hug" to Katie.

Felicia Day, an actress, Geek, and gamer with nearly two million twitter followers, took the extra step of writing a supportive comment to Katie on my blog post, reminding her that "each of us in this world is totally unique, like a snowflake, and to try to be like other people means wasting what's special about yourself." I contacted Felicia Day a few months later, interested in why she had responded to the story. Day shared that she had been homeschooled as a child, which made it hard for her to relate to other kids. "I definitely felt ostracized sometimes, because I didn't share all the same interests as the other kids. I liked video games, I liked old black-and-white movies, I was really into doing math. Other kids had a hard time connecting to me outside whatever interest brought us together, like ballet or violin." Day encountered exclusion frequently, and it "definitely made me more self-conscious than I naturally would have been, more hypersensitive to what people thought of me."[1]

Felicia Day was not the only science-fiction actress who wanted to lend her voice to an anti-bullying message. Catherine Taber, the actress who voices Queen Padme Amidala for *Star Wars: The Clone Wars*, wrote a message to Katie, reassuring her that "Padme would tell you to be proud of who YOU are and know that you are not ALONE!" Taber, who found out about Katie from the Epbot.com post, was one of the first to take action. "I felt a whole bunch of emotions when I read the story," she told me. Taber, who also wore thick glasses in the first grade, sent us a photo of herself as a bespectacled child. Playing Padme on *The Clone Wars* has affected Taber's views on bullying, because "Padme does not like or tolerate bullies. She is all about doing what is right, even if that means standing up to someone bigger and stronger than her. And she knows the value of enlisting the help of others when the 'bully' is too big for her to handle alone."

Taber alerted her *Clone Wars* cast mates to Katie's story, and shortly thereafter I received an email from Tom Kane, the actor who voices Yoda for *The Clone Wars*. Tom Kane felt a special connection with Katie because he has adopted five of his eight children. Several months after we first met, Kane explained to me, "I was a kid who didn't have a lot of friends when I was younger. And because I didn't have a lot of friends, I empathized and identified with kids who were bullied, although I was not a target." Kane was somewhat immune to bullying because he was always the biggest guy in the room, and that intimidated other kids. He would use his size to defend kids who were being bullied. "If I said 'cut it out,' the bullies would stop," he recalled, adding "That's what I like about Yoda—he defends the defenseless." Kane did admit, "I can see how big people can start to feel a sense of entitlement. As an adult, people always defer to me when I speak, because I am a tall, big guy, and it's easy to feel like, 'hey, I'm the big man on campus.' But it is a choice you make, and you have to be responsible for your behavior."[2]

The Star Wars community came out strongly in support of a little girl's right to be a fan. One man dressed as Darth Vader made a YouTube video for Katie, affirming that Star Wars is "for everyone." James Arnold Taylor, who voices Obi-Wan Kenobi in *The Clone Wars*, sent us a privately recorded message. Among his advice was, "forgive those who told you that Star Wars is only for boys" and "be sure to eat your vegetables." One enthusiastic reader created a Facebook event to be held on December 10th called "Support Star Wars and Geek Pride for Katie," and over thirty-five thousand people "attended." The Facebook page became a place for people to share their own stories and find a community of likeminded Geeks. Carrie Gouldin, who owns ThinkGeek.com, contacted us on behalf of all her "proud Geeks" and shared a link to all the supportive comments coming in on her company's page.

As the emails poured in, my husband, Andrew, and I experienced overwhelming gratitude for the kindness of strangers. Gratitude, but also a feeling of angst. Who were we to deserve so much support from the world? Why was our daughter's story the one that struck a responsive chord, when surely there were so many others who had suffered far more than Katie at the hands of bullies?

I then understood that Katie herself was simply an arbitrary subject. She represented any child, every child. Katie put a human face on the idea of a bullied child, and people could respond to a human face. When people wrote comments to Katie, they were writing them to all children; they were writing comments to themselves in the past, to the teased and taunted geeky girls they had been decades ago.

The issues raised in Katie's story touched a universal nerve, prompting men, women, and children to write to us from Bulgaria, Mexico, Colombia, Canada, England, Israel, Sweden, Ireland, Spain, Afghanistan, Australia, Dubai, Japan, and on and on. We heard from people young and old, male and female, privileged and poor, all affirming an anti-bullying message. The comments, thousands of them combined from various blogs around the world, tell a story. They tell us that we are not alone, that teasing, pain, and, ultimately, resilience, are all part of the human condition. They tell us that someone cares. When men wept at the image of my daughter being taunted on the playground, it was because they pictured their own vulnerable daughters in her place. Katie happened to be a very sympathetic character, this child who was an adopted, glasses- and patch-wearing, Star Wars–loving first grader. The response to Katie's story was symbolic of the public's attitude toward bullying. It was time to step in early and turn things around.

Chase Masterson, the actress who played Leeta in the final five seasons of *Star Trek: Deep Space Nine,* spent an hour on the phone with me, describing her own strong response to hearing the story. Masterson had been severely bullied as a child, and the memories were fresh as she talked, punctuated by silences in which she gathered her thoughts. "My dad was in the army, and I was all over the place. I landed in Texas, and I was a strange Geek Girl who loved math and science. At that time, being a smart girl in Texas did not get you dates. I felt really outcast. I was 'Other.'" Masterson was termed "painfully shy" by her junior-high-school drama teacher, and she felt as if she would never break into the mainstream of popular kids. Of that time, she said, "It is hard to see the big picture when you are young—all that mattered was what lunch table you got to sit at. I was actively made fun of by some pretty mean kids in the popular group, and it was humiliating. Back then, I just wanted to die." We talked about how kids who are victims often believe the bullies and begin to feel worthless, and Masterson commented that she really struggled with self-acceptance.

Masterson is very close friends with Peter Mayhew, the actor who played Chewbacca in the original Star Wars trilogy, and she put me in touch with him. Mayhew himself knew what it was like to be different, having stood out from his peers all his life due to his seven foot three height. The actor told me, "Everyone commented on my size. I could hardly hide it. My older brother and his friends helped protect me from the taunting. They were my security blanket; nobody knew I was the younger one."

Mayhew found inner strength from his mom, who taught him that his height was a gift. Today, Mayhew and his wife, Angie, are passionate about bullying prevention. In 2011, they published an anti-bullying children's book called *My Favorite Giant,* in which Peter describes how we are all more the same than we are different. The book is designed to teach acceptance to young audiences. Mayhew's message of acceptance is representative of the *Star Wars* family, and even George Lucas's own daughter, Katie Lucas, struggled with feelings of isolation as a child. In a very touching gesture, Katie Lucas sent a letter[3] to our Katie, sharing her own history of being bullied.

> *Katie, my name's Katie too!*
> *And I'm adopted.*
> *AAAAND I wear glasses!*
> *AAAAAAAAAND I had an eye patch until I was 6!*
> *I was bullied a lot when I was younger—for being a girl, for liking Phantom of the Opera and Buffy, for being George Lucas's daughter!*
> *It's hard to be different, but it's also exactly what YOU ARE. Don't deny it—you are absolutely perfect just the way you are. No matter what anyone says.*

Don't you like not being like everyone else? I do!
You're special. Let yourself be special and be happy
that you are! Not a lot of people get to be so passionate
about the things they love.
Growing up, every single person in my class thought I
was weird, EXCEPT for one boy, who is STILL my best
friend. He loved Buffy and Phantom of the Opera too! He
didn't care who I was, or what I liked, he liked me for me.
Someday, you will find a friend just like mine and the
bullying won't matter so much anymore.
Always be yourself, and be proud of who that is!
Good luck and May The Force Be With You!
Katie Lucas

Katie Lucas's words of comfort showed us that nobody is insulated from feeling "Other," no matter how famous or connected her family may be. It surprised me how many of the actors and actresses associated with *Star Wars* had personal encounters with being teased, taunted, or bullied. I spoke several times with Ashley Eckstein, who does the voice of Ahsoka Tano for *The Clone Wars*, and she laughed as she told me, "Oh, I got so many taunts when I was the only girl on the T-ball team! But my parents taught me that I could prove I belonged there by being the best at what I did. One time the team put me on the pitcher's mound, and while everyone was laughing at me, I won the game and got their respect. Now I tell kids—what are your strengths? Don't focus on your weaknesses." Eckstein brings that attitude into her portrayal of Ahsoka, using the little Padawan's small size as an asset.

Eckstein's *Clone Wars* colleague, James Arnold Taylor, also needed to develop coping skills at a young age to fend off taunts. Taylor, who voices Master Jedi Obi-Wan Kenobi, stands five foot four in real life. Taylor told me frankly, "I often mentioned my height first, and that removed the power from other people to make fun of me. I'd say, 'Yeah, I can't reach that top shelf, but you can, and I'll entertain you while you're doing it.' I found my talents—I could use voices and humor, and I even befriended the bigger guys so they could protect me. I enlisted the bystanders to become positive influences." Taylor is a great example of a person who acted upon the classic advice "embrace the things that make you different." He accepted his height and owned the very characteristic that potentially made him a target. "My mom was a single mom raising three kids, and because of the trials early in my life, my natural instinct was to make everything okay and entertain people. But when I talked about being short, I made sure to entertain without being self-deprecating." Taylor is funny, but also a warm, bighearted guy. When the conversation turned to the seriousness of bullying, he simply stated, "I believe that we all have strengths in our hearts. We want to love and be loved and search our hearts for a way to communicate and find common ground."[4] I found it interesting that Peter Mayhew was taunted for being too tall and Taylor was ridiculed for being too small. Life can be harder for those at the edges of the bell curve.

The more I got to know the people in the *Star Wars* community, the more impressed I was by their generosity of spirit. When I mentioned to one employee at Lucasfilm that 50 percent of the kids at Katie's elementary school qualify for free or reduced-cost lunch due to low family income, she spoke with Lucasfilm's partners at Lego and Hasbro. Two weeks later, dozens of boxes of Star Wars toys quietly arrived at Katie's school, just in time for Christmas. There were no photo opportunities, no cameras. The school's social workers spent hours sorting toys to donate to the neediest families.

ON TUESDAY, DECEMBER 7, 2010, Andrew and I left our three-year-old daughter, Annie Rose, and our six-month-old baby, Cleo, with his parents so we could take Katie to a special screening of three new *Clone Wars* episodes in Chicago. Kathy von Beuningen, a member of the 501st Legion, a Star Wars costuming organization, had made Katie a beautiful Princess Leia costume, and we helped Katie change into it. Before the screening began, Tom Kane stood in front of the audience and hosted a few rounds of Star Wars trivia. Charismatic and well spoken in front of the crowd, he filled the room with warmth and enthusiasm. It was funny to imagine this six foot five man as little Yoda. To Katie's delight, we were seated right next to Tom, and when he returned to his seat, Katie jabbed him in the ribs and said, "Good job, Yoda!" in her jaunty little way.

Attending the *Clone Wars* premier served an interesting purpose for me. It gave a human face to the cybersupporters of Katie. We saw real people who proudly identified themselves as Geeks. There are countless clubs and organizations out in the world, and I have witnessed the great unifying power of common interests. I have seen waves of emotion shared by people at musical concerts. I have seen sports fans literally go nuts over the outcome of big games. I remember when my husband and I were lucky enough to be attending the White Sox game where Mark Buerhle pitched a perfect game and the energy connecting the fans was awesome.

But until I wrote the anti-bullying article, I had underestimated the power among the self-named Geeks, nerds, Star Wars fans, and science-fiction fans. They can cheer with the best of the sports fans. Aided by the speed and ease of social media, the Geeks were the ones who sent Katie's story zipping around the globe. Without a doubt, they have been the most vocal supporters of Katie's preference for "boy toys." Their voices are passionate and compassionate. As Katie's story went viral, the Geeks led the cybersupporting effort and left thousands of comments. Their words collectively told the story of a group of people who were marginalized during their childhoods for being nerdy and for being girls who liked "boy interests."

What struck me was how those individuals who were once so isolated are now part of a very tight community. They have found one another; they are plugged into one another, and they have one another's backs. Now they have Katie's back too. The Geeks have adopted Katie, taken her by the hand, and offered to escort her through life as a girl who likes Star Wars. At the screening, I felt the love and support of the other people. I could see their faces and hear their voices. They smiled upon my little girl and complimented her on her Star Wars costume. She was accepted and celebrated for being different. She was The Littlest Jedi.[5]

Chapter Three

Our Local Community Response

In concurrence with the Facebook event that had been created called "Support Star Wars and Geek Pride for Katie," our elementary school principal, Kate Ellison, decided to hold a special day at Katie's school, but she wanted to make it even more inclusive. After discussing the issue with school leadership, she declared Friday, December 10, Proud to Be Me Day and invited students to wear or bring anything that represented a special interest of theirs, regardless of gender, age, or ethnicity. Ellison's reaction to the entire situation reflected compassion. She took what could have been construed as a negative event and turned it into a teachable moment. As Mike Robey, the assistant superintendent for our school district, put it, "Kate is a social worker by training. Her background is really important to us. She gets relationships and kids."[1]

Washington Elementary is a unique place that represents a special cross section of our city. We live in Evanston, a liberal college town that is the home of Northwestern University, located about twenty-five minutes outside of Chicago. Evanston is a community unlike most other small towns, because it represents the very diverse population of a much larger city. There are the usual unfortunate side effects of this: Evanston does have the stereotypical socioeconomic segregation that occurs in large cities. As with many communities where there is self-segregation, it largely falls along racial lines.

When you have children originating from different walks of life, the situation can be ripe for fear, ignorance, and bullying.

But Katie's school is different. For one thing, there are a few parts of Evanston that represent the very best in managing a diverse population. We happen to live in one of the pockets of Evanston that is not homogenous. Our neighbors are Caucasian, African American, Latino, Indian, you name it. This diverse atmosphere is evident when you walk through the halls of Washington Elementary. All signs and communication are written in both English and Spanish. Katie is in a two-way immersion program, and she spends most of her day in a Spanish-speaking classroom. In addition to many Latino children, the school has a large number of African American students.

Children from different backgrounds who continually spend time together are less likely to fear one another's differences. In this case, familiarity breeds friendship, not contempt. When I asked Katie about the boys who taunted her, she told me that it was not the boys from her class who knew and accepted her. It was first-grade boys from other classes who had not spent as much time with Katie and had not developed respect and understanding for her preferences.

As evidenced by Katie's own experiences, however, the diverse, accepting environment at Washington doesn't mean the school is free of bullying. As I mentioned earlier, I was initially hesitant to use the word "bullying," due to the stigma attached to it, and instead labeled what happened with Katie as teasing. But after reading *The Bully, the Bullied, and the Bystander,* I reached out to author Barbara Coloroso to ask some questions. Coloroso pointed out that teasing is done without intent to harm, between friends or family members. It allows the teaser and the person being teased to easily swap roles. If someone teases you and you do not like it, the teaser will be able to tell by your body language and your expression and would stop. "For example," Coloroso asked me, "if you teased me about my white hair, and I happened to be having a rough day and did not feel like being teased, and you saw my expression fall, what would you do?" I would apologize, I told her, for hurting her feelings unintentionally. "Right," she confirmed, "because you were only teasing.

The boys were taunting Katie, because they kept it up when she was clearly not laughing along with them."[2]

When I wrote about my daughter's tears from taunting and teasing, the most important outcome was that the adults at the school *cared*. In my interviews with bullying victims over the past year, I have often heard that the adults in the schools did nothing when confronted with the information. As Edward, a student who was severely bullied, explained to me, "The school just told the bullies (there was the ringleader and his cronies) to stop, but they never listened. Bystanders generally cheered them on or even joined in." If children do not expect anyone to help, they will continue to suffer in silence. Why would a victim risk telling an adult and attracting further wrath from the bullies if he thinks the adults won't do anything to help? One victim, Alexis, told me, "When my father would talk to the school, everyone knew it. And the teasing only got worse for a little while before it leveled back out to its usual torment." Or sometimes the adults would misinterpret the situation, as evidenced by Eric's experiences: "I would get in trouble for trying to defend myself because the bullies would tell the teachers I started a fight, when they had in fact come after me first." These problems are some of the biggest deterrents to children reporting incidences of bullying. They need to feel that someone will listen to the whole story and care enough to take effective action.

On the evening my anti-bullying article was posted to the school's Listserv, I began receiving supportive emails from parents, some of whom I had never even met. I am sure there were some parents, particularly of little boys, who privately thought what happened to Katie was no big deal, but I never heard anything rude from them. They responded with respect for Katie's feelings, which is the fundamental reason why Washington has a positive community. Respect is the answer to bullying, whereas dismissiveness contributes to bullying. A dismissive school would have blown off the whole incident as an example of "boys being boys" or "it was just harmless teasing." But our school is the "feelings school," and it used Katie's experience as an opening for discussions.

Trudy Ludwig, activist and bestselling author of anti-bullying books, has found a way to describe bullying behavior without labeling the perpetrators as bullies. "I say that they put on a 'bully hat,' and they act like a bully while wearing the bully hat. But this means that they can take the hat off and change."[3] One of the many things I have learned about bullying is that it is very fluid. Some of the same boys who were making fun of Katie have themselves been victims of bullying. There is a term—bully–victim—for individuals who engage in bullying behavior and are also frequently victimized by others. Thirteen-year-old Emily is one such example, and she told me, "The other kids first started to pick on me because I had different interests than most everybody else. As it progressed, they started to nitpick and do whatever they knew would bug me. I tend to respond with aggression, which gets me into trouble for attacking other kids. I feel like nobody cares or like there is something wrong with me." Studies show that kids who are bully victims experience higher levels of depression than kids who are primarily just bullies or primarily just victims.[4]

Any child can wear the bully hat, and take it off, and put it back on. Your child, my child, your best friend's child—Trudy Ludwig advised me not to assume based on one incident that a child is always a victim or always a bully. She said it is common for a child to play the role of bully, victim, and bystander, all in the same month, same week, or even the very same day. I have seen this even with my own kids. Katie, universally known for being on the receiving end of the taunts, is pretty skilled at dishing it out to her younger sister. I have seen her play the aggressor plenty of times when she is trying to get a rise out of Annie Rose. On the flip side, I have seen Annie Rose reduce Katie to tears.

As Ludwig pointed out, "Kids make mistakes, and our job as adults is to make sure the kids don't keep making the same mistakes over and over again."[5] Every kid, every person, every parent and teacher, physician, nurse, electrician, janitor, every major-league athlete—we all make mistakes. The real question is, how do we handle mistakes when they happen? Do we hope nobody saw what happened and continue as before? Do we try to cover it up and just make things worse? Or do we stop, own up to the mistake, and look for a way to right the wrong that has been done? We as parents are very quick to be outspoken when our kid is the victim. Let us be just as visible when our child is the aggressor.

It can be confusing for parents when their child is involved in a conflict. There is a lot of misunderstanding about what comprises normal fighting and what comprises actual bullying. One-time disagreements are not the same things as repeated actions against a target. At the Washington PTA meeting about bullying, one mom said, "Look, I certainly see misbehavior occurring on the playground, but I wouldn't say I see a lot of bullying." And principal Kate Ellison concurred, "It is true that we do have relatively little bullying here. We get office referrals for kids being disrespectful or defiant, sometimes for one-time fights, but bullying is not too common at Washington. We added 'Be Respectful' to our core Washington Ways in order to address the respect problem." Unsurprisingly, adding Respect to the core expectations for behavior at school is probably one of the reasons that bullying is uncommon there.

Another Washington mom told me, "Sometimes my daughter gets all upset because her best friend is ignoring her, and the next day, they are glued at the hip. It is just as exhausting for parents and teachers to watch the social drama as it is for the kids to live it." As parents of school-age children know, friendships and alliances can turn on a dime. I recalled the advice of Rosalind Wiseman, bestselling author of *Queen Bees and Wannabes*: "Sometimes your daughter will be the dumper, sometimes the dumpee. When your daughter is on the outs with her friend, discourage her from demonizing her friend or the friendship by focusing only on the negatives, and don't you do it either, because where will you be when they are back together next week?"[6] Like Ludwig, Wiseman counsels that it is important to give kids second chances. As parents, we understandably develop negative feelings toward kids who mistreat our sons and daughters, but it is best to readjust these opinions, because children's friendships regularly realign. You might end up in a bitter conflict with your child if you are unable to embrace her burgeoning friendship with a former enemy.

Fortunately, the attitude toward social conflict at Washington is a healthy one, with a strong focus on directly addressing issues and concerns. The parent community is involved; the teachers are connected to the students; and the principal sets the right tone. By contrast, a week or two after Katie's Star Wars story went public, I was contacted by another author, Emily Rosenbaum, whose son Zachary was having a similar taunting experience. Zachary's first-grade classmates had made fun of him for bringing My Little Pony to show-and-tell (according to the six-year-old toy gods, My Little Pony is only a "girl toy"). In a subsequent article for *Ms.* magazine, Rosenbaum wrote, "When the teasing starts, adult response is crucial. While Katie and Zachary had similar experiences at school, Goldman and I had remarkably different ones when we tried to address the problem. My child's teacher put a stop to the individual instance of teasing, and that was the end of it, but Goldman's community took the teasing as a call to action."

In an effort to rehabilitate Zachary's image at school, Rosenbaum encouraged the boy to bring a Harry Potter book to the next show-and-tell. I told Katie about Zachary and explained how sad he was feeling about being taunted. Katie, having been the beneficiary of an outpouring of affirmation and support, wanted to spread the love. I looked up Emily Rosenbaum's phone number on my cell phone, and Katie left the following message for Zachary: "I am Katie. I like Star Wars, and you like My Little Pony. That's great. I know other boys who like to play with My Little Pony, and it's great, and umm, May the Pony Be with You!" she finished proudly with a giggle.

Part Two: Kids at High Risk for Peer Victimization

Any child can be the target of taunting and bullying, and plenty of parents have watched in agony as their seemingly well-adjusted, well-accepted children have inexplicably fallen from the grace of their peers. But while it is true that any child can be singled out, there are certain groups of children who are at higher risk for peer victimization.

Who is at increased risk? The kids who are different—children who are heterosexual but challenge gender norms; children who are gay, lesbian, bisexual, and transgender; children who have different physical appearances; children who receive special education; children who qualify for free or reduced-cost lunch; children who practice a minority religion; children who have atypical family structures—these kids are more likely to draw unwanted negative attention. The following five chapters are devoted to these high-risk groups, sharing their stories and my research about their experiences.

Chapter Four

From Geek Girls to Sluts: What Does It Mean to Be a Girl?

Geeks and nerds have been the targets of bullying for decades. Female Geeks, in addition to being considered uncool, have historically had to deal with a whole additional layer of prejudice, because the mainstream belittled their contributions to male-dominated fields. Little girls with geeky passions needed to be very persistent about following their "boyish" interests. Rosie, for example, wrote to Katie, "When I was younger, I got picked on by boys and girls. I went to space camp instead of cheerleading camp, and my mom liked to take me to the science museum instead of the nail salon. Guess what? Now I'm in school to be a DOCTOR!" Unlike in generations past, however, there is now an entire Geek Girl movement that empowers girls like Rosie. These geeky women have proudly made their way into technical fields, but they easily remember the sting of being taunted. Holly, who is a generation ahead of Rosie and two generations above Katie, wrote to us that "Kids were mean to me sometimes, too, because I liked Star Wars and *Star Trek,* and no other girls did. (I had to wear glasses too!) But you know what? Those shows inspired me to become an engineer and now I work at NASA!" Geek Girls are extending the hands of mentorship and support to young Geeklets, urging them to stick it out.

What is a Geek Girl? She is a chic intellectual, often working in the fields of science or math, proud of her recreational interest in games, fantasy, comic conventions, chess, and science fiction. She celebrates a girl's right to excel in areas outside of pink. The Geek Girl movement has taken ownership of the image of a nerdy, shy, bespectacled bookworm and empowered the stereotype. This is all good, right? But something inside me hesitates when I see Geek Girls portrayed in the entertainment media as super sexy—such as a big-breasted, high-heeled woman in a skimpy superhero costume—because it feels as if Geek Girls are promoting the widely pervasive idea that you need to be sexy in order to be cool. The sexy factor can at times undermine self-acceptance for Geeks by separating them into the hot Geeks and the not-hot Geeks.

Given that the mainstream decided Geeks were cool once they proved they were sexy, one could argue it was their sexiness and not their geekiness that caught the world's eye. If Geeks should be celebrated first and foremost for their brains, then why do we see a Geek Girl on the cover of a magazine dressed in sexy clothes? She could be a sexy firefighter or a sexy police officer or a sexy astronaut; the emphasis would frankly be on the fact that she is sexy. But if you take away the sexy, would the Geek still be on the magazine cover? This is worth exploring because it represents the bigger issue of the importance of looks in our society, and since physical appearance is one of the most common reasons why kids are bullied, one has to wonder if we are subtly pushing attractiveness even as we package it as acceptance of Geeks. There is nothing wrong with being sexy. Sexy is good. But it gets tricky when you use sexy to gain acceptance, and even more so when you use sexy to sell things, because you run the risk of promoting unhealthy sexualization, especially to children.

But then I see the opposite point of view. You could claim that it is empowering for females to be sexy and geeky. After all, why give up your femininity just because you are a scientist or a mathematician? The female Geek in a short skirt and high heels is refusing to be boxed in by a stereotype, and she is proud of how she looks in revealing clothes. Many girls would label a sexy Geek as someone who thinks she's "all that" and immediately call her a slut, which is one of the most prevalent ways in which girls bully one another. Slut-shaming is designed to crush girls who have begun to express their healthy sexuality. In this context, the sexy Geek is demonstrating that you can be sexy and confidant about the way you look without having to be labeled a slut. Vulnerable young girls often feel as if they are one short skirt away from being plastered all over the Internet with "slut" as the caption. The exaggerated femininity of the Geek Girl cartoon character—a scantily dressed buxom woman—forces people to acknowledge that the Geek in the drawing is a *female* Geek, and then it is her femaleness and not her sexiness that is being emphasized. Many female Geeks proudly label themselves bitches and sluts, all in the name of feminism. It is hard for society to degrade women as Geeks and sluts when they willingly announce themselves as both simultaneously.

Female Geeks, in owning both their sexuality and their assertiveness, can serve as excellent role models for younger girls who are trying to buck gender stereotypes. Lyn Mikel Brown, cocreator of Hardy Girls Healthy Women has seen how these stereotypes harm girls. She explained to me, "Girls are automatically set up in competition with other girls for boys' affections. In my research for my book *Girlfighting* I spoke with middle-school girls and found they fought in three ways: (1) sexuality (who crossed the line from being sexual to slutty); (2) fat talk (commiserating with peers over how fat each girl thinks her body is, but often used as a way to get others to tell her she is *not* fat); and (3) attitude (who crossed the line from nice to bitchy)."[1]

Young girls and women walk a very fine line. If a girl draws the attention of her male peers, simply due to her appearance or personality, she is at elevated risk of having envious female peers denounce her as a slut, regardless of whether or not she engages in any sexual activity. Once this happens, it is very difficult for the girl to recover her reputation. For younger girls, fear of not fitting in makes it extremely difficult to figure out who they really are. They don't want to be nerds. They don't want to be sluts. "Who am I?" becomes a defining question. They feel pressured to look, act, walk, talk, and behave in the "right way," constantly recalibrating who they are to match the current ideals of their peers. Teshara was one of many young women who wrote to us about her identity struggle in school:

> *I was also adopted. I had glasses. Corrective shoes. Freaky curly hair when everyone else I knew had straight hair. I loved geeky stuff when I was a kid. Just like you, I was made fun of. But I wasn't strong. I changed everything about myself. My hair, my shoes, I got contacts, I ate strawberries instead of cherries because "girls ate strawberries and boys ate cherries," I did everything I could to be "normal." I changed the way I walked, the way I talked, and when that didn't work, I started acting less smart than I am because people seemed to like me more.*
>
> *I will never have a bigger regret in my life. I ended up not liking myself. When I got to college and moved out, I didn't know what I liked anymore. I forgot what it was to be me, and I was miserable.*
>
> *It's taken me over fifteen years to remember who I was before I changed myself for people around me, that NEVER cared about me to begin with. I'm back to practical shoes, thick glasses, and being myself. For the first time in a long time, I like myself.*

Good for Teshara for finally being true to herself, but how can we change the culture of our society so that the Tesharas of the world can be spared fifteen years of self-loathing along the winding path to self-acceptance? We start by asking the hard questions and examining how we tend to affirm the importance placed on looks and appearances by valuing some people more than others, even if we do it unintentionally.

The Emphasis Placed on Appearance and Clothing

Kids are concerned about their appearance for understandable reasons. Society bombards them with messages about the importance of creating the right look. Adults are just as guilty as kids of judging children on their appearance. Studies have shown that school teachers respond more positively to children who are attractive and well dressed, which then leads those children to do better in class, creating self-fulfilling prophecies that the favored children are better students.[2]

In defense of all of us, it is human nature to respond positively to physical attractiveness. The basis for this bias is biological; historically, traits that were physically attractive in humans tended to bode well for survival. In the ancient past, a strong, muscular, large man attracted women because he was probably a superior hunter and defender. A healthy, well-endowed woman attracted men because she was more likely to survive childbearing and be able to breastfeed successfully. In today's world, our survival depends far less on our abilities to hunt, gather, and fend off wild animals, and many countries offer advanced medical care that can coax women who might have otherwise perished through the occasionally perilous process of pregnancy and childbirth.

These changes have occurred rather quickly, and our biological instincts have not caught up with the realities of our environment. A slightly built, short man is no longer at a survival disadvantage compared to a tall, muscular man, because most of us do not live in a hunting and gathering society. Sure, there are a few specific professions where large size might mean superiority, such as in football or basketball, but for the majority of jobs, a tall man is no more adept than a small man. Size matters not when it comes to practicing medicine, fixing cars, programming computers, gardening, painting—yet the culture at large still views small men as weaker. Short boys are much more likely to be targets of taunting and bullying.

Likewise, girls who are not slim or traditionally feminine are more likely to be targets of taunting. More than thirty years after the steroids scandal at the 1976 Olympics, people still crack jokes about how women that are unusually strong, large, or unfeminine belong on the East German Olympic team. Lyn Mikel Brown told me, "That's why female athletes have to do sexy poses in *Maxim*— because otherwise they get coded as lesbian. Sexy Geeks need sexy in order to announce their femininity. They say, 'Yes, I'm a smart Geek, but if you are anxious about that, don't worry, I am feminine because I am sexy.' It keeps the status quo in place; it is both brilliant and troubling. The question is . . . what version of femininity do these women own? Are they just appeasing the male ideal or are they truly being feminine in the way they want to be?"[3]

To combat these stereotypes, we can remind ourselves to draw on our humanity. We have the power to rationalize and empathize, and this allows us to challenge the biological instincts that tell us physically attractive people who fit the traditional gender norms are worthier. The bully treats others with contempt and feels entitled to marginalize them. We can do better, and we can welcome and respect others, regardless of appearance. Recall the beautiful words by Emma Lazarus engraved inside the Statue of Liberty—

> Give me your tired, your poor,
> Your huddled masses yearning to breathe free,
> The wretched refuse of your teeming shore.
> Send these, the homeless, tempest-tossed to me,
> I lift my lamp beside the golden door!

Despite these admirable ideals, our society devalues the tired and the poor and prefers to shove the huddled masses out of sight. Aggressive exclusion is a frequent component of bullying, and it is not just the children who participate in excluding others. It is a society-wide problem. Children learn exclusion from the media, what with the superficial importance placed on looks, clothes, accessories, and brands. Sometimes we need to remind our kids that Emma Lazarus did not write, "Give me your tired, your poor, as long as they have the latest Nike shoes and trendy highlights." The immigrants whom the Statue of Liberty beckoned most assuredly did not have the "right look." And in many cases, they were and still are bullied. If you ask targets why they are bullied, they will tell you that they just don't fit in. This is not limited to the United States. We heard from girls all over the world about their struggles to be accepted. "I don't look like everyone else. I wear black leather and black boots and lots of black eyeliner," wrote Heather from England. "I have frizzy hair and I like to read books on the bus," wrote Elsa from Sweden. "I dye my short hair purple, and I wear a nose ring," wrote Carolina from Colombia.

Louise told me, "I was the only 'goth nerd' at my school. I was the classic lanky, skinny little Geek Girl who liked all the alternative things, dark music, fantasy, computer games, science, drama, reading, and, most of all, writing. I liked to wear dark makeup (I still do) and dye my hair bold and vibrant colors (mainly red, and it is another thing I still do). I was a bit of a loner, to be honest, and though I did have a few select friends, they were just outcasts like me who didn't fit in anywhere else. This made me stand out like a sore thumb against the 'normal' and 'popular' girls."[4] Over and over, young girls report being bullied because they have the wrong hair, the wrong clothes, the wrong purse, or in Katie's case, the wrong water bottle and backpack.

Societal Pressure to Choose Gender-Typical Interests

The Geek Girls who reached out to us frequently mentioned their appearance as a reason they were taunted, but that was not the only issue. There were plenty of women and girls who wrote to us about bullying that had nothing to do with their looks. A commonly cited reason why girls were taunted was their interest in "boy toys, boy clothes, and boy games." Lainie, for example, wrote to Katie about her own boy interests, which she learned to accept as a young adult.

> While I never really watched Star Wars (although I might now) I grew up loving Lord of the Rings and Harry Potter. (I even have a Harry Potter Lego collection :)) And I was in upper-level science and math classes all through high school. Now I'm almost 21 and looking back, I realize that there's something really powerful about being one of the only girls. You're brave and special, Katie. And no one can take that away from you. I have a younger sister, and her name is Katie too. She's really smart, and I saw her get teased because she wanted to collect bugs or go to

*museums over playing house. But today she's almost 17
and is growing up to be a fantastic young woman. This is
your life! You can like whatever movies you want! You can
play in the dirt or play with Barbies or even play with
Barbies in the dirt. :) Don't let anyone tell you otherwise.*

One of the things I liked about Lainie's comment was that she emphasized how Katie can like *anything* she wants, even Barbies. Quite frankly, Katie does like playing with dolls. She chose to paint her bedroom in two shades of pink, and she absolutely loves to play dress up in fancy dresses. Just as Katie need not defend her right to love Star Wars, she need not defend her girlie interests. While I do not like the terms "girl toys" or "boy toys" because gender labeling is how we ended up with so many problems, I will use those words here for the ease of communicating general toy categories. From the time Katie has been a toddler, I have cheered on her interests in boy toys. I loved to watch her build tracks for Thomas the Train, and I filled our house with baseballs when my then one-year-old started following the White Sox. The feminist in me jumped up and down when Katie wanted me to make a Harry Potter cake for her fourth birthday party instead of a Cinderella cake like so many of her peers. She even insisted I pipe frosting that said Happy Birthday Hermione (a Harry Potter character) instead of Happy Birthday Katie, and I was glad to see that she wanted to identify with a strong, bright female such as Hermione.

But late in preschool, in the famous words of author Peggy Orenstein, "Cinderella ate my daughter," and Katie was asking for Disney princess costumes. I suppose Cinderella only nibbled Katie, because she did retain her passion for Star Wars, Harry Potter, the White Sox, and playing in the dirt, but I noticed a sharp uptick in Katie's preference for pink clothes and princess toys. One of the reasons Katie initially developed an interest in girlie things was that her preschool girlfriends were obsessed with them, and it is natural for children to emulate one another. Initially, I refused to buy Disney princess dolls, but Katie received them from other people as birthday gifts and holiday gifts, and I quickly saw how much she enjoyed them.

And therein begins the trouble. It is easy to say no to things that are absolutely harmful—for example, I would never let Katie play with gasoline or household bleach!—but most things are not that black and white. It is true that there are harmful stereotypes about body image that come along with Barbie dolls, but the dolls also allowed Katie to engage in fun social interactions with her Barbie-loving girlfriends. And I remember how I used to love playing with Barbies when I was her age, especially braiding their hair, and it has not done permanent damage to me. Worried about eating disorders down the road, I have tried to talk to Katie about how real girls do not look like Barbie dolls (unnaturally thin, impossibly long legs, huge perky boobs, and an unattainably small waist), thus using Barbie as a way to converse with my daughter about the issue of appearance. Is talking about it good enough to prevent problems? Time will tell. Some people won't let their daughters near a Barbie. Others would never consider restricting their daughters from playing with Barbie. Weighing both sides, I decided to subscribe to the theory of everything in moderation, and I support Katie's exploration of girl toys as well as boy toys.

After all, pink is not the enemy; stereotypes are. There is nothing wrong with girls liking pink and princesses, as long as they have equal access—both practical and psychological—to toys that promote scientific skills and critical thinking. If Katie likes princesses because society has told her that girls *must* like princesses, then we have a problem. But if Katie likes princesses as her own genuine choice, and she is not limited in her pick of toys, then we do not have a problem. I have noticed with dismay that there is an increasing faction of girl-empowerment advocates who seem to be pitting girlie girls against rough-and-tumble girls, and we do ourselves a disservice if we start to mock girlie girls.[5] Why respond to stereotypes with more stereotypes? Gender equality does not mean stripping the girliness from frilly girls. A better tactic would be to encourage our girls to do more cross-gender play without putting down their girlie leanings. Unfortunately, parents are not well supported in this effort because toy companies rarely encourage cross-gender play.

I asked Nicole Knepper, author of the fanatically followed blog *Moms Who Drink and Swear*, for her thoughts on gender stereotyping. Knepper is excellent at analyzing both sides of an issue. "In a feminist utopia," Knepper observed, "a few thousand years of history as well as the powerful female biology could be set aside so that each toy our daughters played with would be an empowering, equalizing, and politically correct object. But we don't live in a feminist utopia." Knepper pointed out that so much of who and what we are is rooted in history, and she thinks one of the most important parts of play is that children have the opportunity to incorporate different realities into their fun without adults imposing rules.

"Of course I consider the skank factor as well as the helpless princess mentality when seeing how thrilled my daughter has always been with girlie girl toys," Knepper commented. "She can't get enough of the glitter, fashion, and pinkness that comes with a zillion and twelve accessories. However, she puts her own spin on each character as she creates their world within hers. This world doesn't have to shrink when toys have previously prescribed attributes, names, and roles, especially when the toys incorporate characters, concepts, and themes that have historical significance."

Knepper believes that it's important that girls are empowered to choose just how much they want to incorporate stereotypical roles and expectations for women into their own lives. "Play helps them to do this," she explained. "They can try on just about any type of personality and exercise their power in an environment that satisfies their curiosity until they can experience these things in real-life situations. How exciting!"

"How do you feel about your daughter trying on the story lines of Monster High dolls or Barbies?" I asked.

In classic frank style, Knepper pointed out, "Beauty, power, and position are important. Denying this reality is as dangerous as promoting it as the only way to find happiness and identity. I would probably not be a big fan of crack whore, stripper Barbie, but I just can't find it in me to understand the hostility that some parents have when it comes to allowing their daughters to really explore the ideas of the past so that they can appreciate the options the present and the future hold for them. If they choose them." As always, talking to Knepper opened my mind.

Curious to hear from a mom who is concerned about Barbies and Monster High dolls, I called Peggy Orenstein. We talked about the enormous marketing push to separate products into girl toys and boy toys in the past twenty years. She told me, "The idea of girl products has become so narrow that whole numbers of toys are no longer considered girl products." Orenstein visited a toy fair, and in the Fisher-Price showroom, the toys were divided into Girls and Boys. She was disturbed to see that "the girls section was decorated with a banner that said BEAUTIFUL, PRETTY, COLORFUL, and the boys section had a banner that said ENERGY, HEROES, POWER."

"That really boxes kids in," I said.

"You wouldn't believe how much," Peggy commented. "For example, Tinkertoys marketed to girls pink prepackaged kits that made flowers." Orenstein pointed out how flower-only kits took away all the creativity of building with Tinkertoys, because all the other things a girl might think to build were replaced by the flower. "Over time," she said, "these repeated messages actually change the development of girls' brains, and they become more limited in what they build and draw."[6]

It is no wonder that kids taunt girls with boy interests. They are taught by society that girls should only stick to dainty things like flowers and princesses. Girls who want to play with science kits and solve math equations do not fit into the stereotype and get labeled as "Other." These messages start early and continue through high school. In the 2004 movie *Mean Girls,* based on Rosalind Wiseman's book *Queen Bees and Wannabes,* Lindsay Lohan plays a high school student who is gifted in math. When she considers joining the math team, the popular clique tells her in horror, "No!" Even her outcast friends, a gay boy and an ostracized girl, warn Lindsay Lohan's character that joining the math team would be "social suicide." Apparently, even the marginalized students looked down on Geek Girls.

Despite the forces against them, the Geek Girls are a resilient, loving group. The letters they wrote to Katie are filled with poignant tales of hardship and survival. Human beings are social creatures, and one of our most fundamental needs is companionship. In the original "anti-bullying" post, I wrote that Katie felt alone because she wore glasses, a patch, was adopted, and liked boy toys. What the Geeks responded to above all was the first part. She had them at "alone."

> *Dear Katie,*
>
> *I'm sure by now you know that you are not alone. When I read your story, I teared up a bit. Why? Because it's my story too. Although I'm much older, I was once in first grade too. I loved a lot of the things boys liked. He-Man, GI Joe, Transformers, Thundercats, and especially Star Wars. I tried to get my hands on almost anything involving outer space that I could. Not only did I get made fun of for that, but I wore glasses. When I was in first grade, I had to have surgery on each of my eyes. I had to wear patches over each of them as they healed. Afterward I wore glasses. I was also the only kid I knew who was adopted. I knew my parents loved me, but I still knew that it made me different. It was hard. If I wasn't teased for one thing, it was another. But you know what? I made it through. And I still love all of those fun geeky things that people made fun of me for, especially Star Wars!*
>
> *Love, Amanda*

In Katie's case, it was the boys who gave her a hard time for loving Star Wars, but often, it is not just the little boys who taunt superhero-loving girls. Girls are equally quick to throw out a member of the group who does not conform. In the past twenty years, the stepped-up gender-based toy marketing machine has created very clear demarcation lines between what characters are for girls and what characters are for boys. The Disney princesses, now a cohesive unit, are foisted upon young girls, in effect teaching many of them that a little girl who strays from the pink crowd is no longer welcome. Dara, a mother of three kids, wrote to me about the ongoing trauma that her daughter has experienced at the hands of another little girl:

*My oldest, Sarah, is seven years old and a second grader.
Sarah has loved Star Wars (and all "boys" stuff) since she
was three years old. Her first week of kindergarten, Sarah
got off the bus and told me she needed a new umbrella,
because a girl on the bus said she could not have a "boy"
umbrella (it was a Spiderman umbrella). The girl told
Sarah that if she continued to use the Spiderman
umbrella, Sarah could not be her friend and could never
come to her house to play.*

*Sarah and I discussed how it was not fair of this girl to
tell her to change what she really liked. Sarah continued to
use the umbrella and never became friends with this little
girl. I thought the incident had passed, but I was wrong. It
reared its ugly head two years later.*

*This year in second grade, the same little girl is in her
class again. When Sarah found out she was her classmate,
she was afraid the girl would make fun of her again. Sarah
is now scared to be herself. For example, on Halloween she
wanted to be a Stormtrooper, but on the day of the school
parade, she decided at 7:45 a.m. she did not want to wear
the outfit for fear of being made fun of. I was unable to talk
her out of it.*

I wrote back to Dara and suggested that we introduce Sarah and
Katie, because she had mentioned that they live about forty-five minutes away from us. During the week of Katie's spring break, our entire family met with Dara and two of her daughters for lunch and ice
cream. Katie brought a Star Wars book to show Sarah, and when we
arrived at lunch, we saw that Sarah had brought the exact same book
to show Katie. The two girls sat together and talked nonstop through
lunch. "This is the best lunch ever!" Katie told me, her face shining.
Our two little Geek Girls delighted in the sense of belonging they
found with each other.

Chapter Five

Princess Boys and Nonconforming Guys

It is not easy to be a feminine boy in our society. More androgyny is accepted for girls than boys, a truth that I learned from speaking with numerous parents who wanted to share the stories of their feminine sons. Sarah Buttenwieser, who writes a thoughtful blog called *Standing in the Shadows*, spoke with me at length about her oldest son, now a teenager. "We want to keep him safe [from teasing], but we also want to keep him whole [in his true personality]." Sarah reminisced with me about a time when her son, then aged five, wanted to wear a dress to a family wedding. "We thought a lot about it. We imagined as parents—if he is sitting on a therapist's couch in twenty years—will it be harder for him that we didn't let him do what he wanted or that we did?" Sarah and her husband decided it was best to let their son express himself. She went out and bought a couple of dresses, one that was really plain and one that was very dressy, and he chose the fancier one. "I was hoping he would pick the understated one," she admitted. Sarah prepared family members ahead of time by calling them to talk about the situation, and fortunately for her son, the hosting family members were accepting.

All three of Sarah's sons have chosen to wear their hair long, and in their liberal hometown, very few people seem to mind. "If we are on vacation, you could say we occasionally 'censor' because when strangers assume that my kids are girls, sometimes we say nothing. Other times we correct them. But," Sarah clarified, "if we choose not to correct someone, it's not out of fear but simply to avoid a hassle or a longer discussion than we want to deal with. The boys are very comfortable with themselves and don't mind when people think they are girls."

"Has anyone ever given them a hard time about their hair in your town?" I inquired.

Sarah recalled that when one of her sons was in preschool, he had a teacher who was uncomfortable with his long hair. Sarah took note of it and decided against letting him wear a dress in that classroom, in the interest of wanting him to be well treated by the teacher. "So, yes, I did protect him in that situation," she concurred. "Oh, and my dad is not thrilled with the long hair."[1] Sarah's boys prefer long hair and the occasional dress, but for the most part they wear clothing that is gender-typical of boys.

But what happens when a child pushes gender stereotypes to an extreme? What about a boy who looks like a typical boy but dresses like a princess? Imagine a short-haired little boy all dressed up in a frilly pink dress—should his parents prevent him from going out in public dressed as a princess in order to protect him from taunting and bullying?

One little boy who has found himself at the center of this debate is Dyson Kilodavis, a six-year-old from Seattle. Dyson's mom, Cheryl Kilodavis, has written a children's book called *My Princess Boy*. On the book's Facebook page, the following description is given: '*My Princess Boy* is a nonfiction picture book about acceptance. It is about our son who happily expresses his authentic self by dressing up in dresses and enjoying traditional girl things such as anything pink or sparkly.'

The case of young Dyson is being tried in the court of public opinion, and the jury is most definitely still out. There are thousands of supporters writing to the Kilodavis family, thanking them for allowing their son to be who he wants to be. But alongside the cheerleaders, there is a vocal contingency of naysayers who disagree with Cheryl for "parading her son around in a dress."

Comments range from those who respectfully disagree with Cheryl's decision to those who spew hate at her. Some readers have called Cheryl a brave heroine, and others are calling her an abusive mom. Dyson's story is polarizing in a way that Katie's story was not. Of the thousands of comments, stories, and articles written about Katie, there was not a single one that suggested it was morally wrong for Katie to dress up in Star Wars clothes and play with boy toys. The few negative comments we received were from people who thought that being teased was no big deal and that Katie should toughen up.

It is less acceptable to be a gender-nonconforming boy than it is to be a gender-nonconforming girl in our current society. Dyson wore a princess costume for Halloween, and some people stared with disapproval. But when my four-year-old, Annie Rose, dressed as Abraham Lincoln for Halloween (including a beard and stovepipe hat), everyone smiled at her. Why? Because there is a deep-seated fear of homosexuality in the world, and there is enormous social pressure not to be gay, particularly for boys. Many people interpret Dyson's clothing choices as a sign that he is, or will become, gay. Those same people believe that his parents can discourage him from becoming gay if they force him to wear pants, although many educated people will testify that what a child wears on the outside does not change who he is on the inside, and that if Dyson is gay, he will be gay no matter what his parents do. Furthermore, if Dyson is gay, why change him? We do not try to change heterosexual people, so why would we try to change gay people? It all goes back to the homophobia in our culture. Dyson may grow up to be gay, or he may not. It should not even matter, because whether or not he is gay does not determine his worth.

Still, many of Cheryl's critics pointed out that Dyson might grow up to be gay directly because he is allowed to wear dresses and princess costumes. "People are confused," Cheryl Kilodavis commented. "Dyson choosing to dress as a princess is not about sexuality. It is about gender. They aren't the same thing."[2] All we know now is that he likes to wear pretty clothes, and it makes some people uncomfortable.

As Dyson becomes a school-age child, he is bound to encounter others who taunt him. If you talk to tweens and teens today, they will tell you that one of the most common forms of verbal taunting is to say another boy is gay. Adam, age eleven, told me that "kids torture

other kids by calling them 'princess' and 'sissy boy' and 'faggot.'"
These words are meant to be derogatory in nature.

The first word, "princess," takes on a new twist when applied to the Kilodavis family. Dyson owns the term "princess boy" in a positive way. He willingly claims himself as a princess boy, thus in one fell swoop neutralizing a bully's power to taunt. One of the strategies that bullying expert and author Judy Freedman recommends is to accept a tease or a taunt to remove the power from the bully.[3] Dyson has demonstrated the effectiveness of this. If another child sings to Dyson in a mocking voice, "You are a *princess* boy, *princess, princess*," Dyson answers with, "Yes, I am a princess boy. You're right." There is not much for the other child to say when Dyson does not respond with tears or protests. Dyson's response to those who make fun of him is, "If you don't like me in a dress, then we don't have to be friends," and he is okay with that. Interestingly, at that point, Cheryl said most young children respond with, "I do want to be friends!" and they no longer care that Dyson is wearing a dress. It is often their parents who still care, and Cheryl has received her most vicious opposition from other adults. Dyson exudes confidence in himself, which often translates into acceptance by other children. Dyson is comfortable enough with himself that it radiates outward, and this helps keep him safe.

This brings us back to the question of which is more important—to keep your child safe or to keep your child true? Should Dyson's parents protect him from unrelenting bullies by refusing to allow him to cross-dress? Or should they protect his desire to express himself by allowing him to cross-dress?

Cheryl said, "I don't think if I take Dyson out of a dress that he is no longer susceptible to being bullied. My whole premise is to continue to help him build his internal radar. It's no different than if someone were to try to harm him physically for some other reason—he needs to get to a safe place. He carries the book *My Princess Boy* in his backpack at all times, and if kids comment on his clothes, he pulls it out and says, 'Let me show you this story.' But, as he gets older, he will learn that there are times to walk away and not engage. I want him to know when it is not worth his time to pull out the book and try to talk to people. As bullying is addressed in schools, the responses to Dyson will evolve. Bullying is a part of who we are, but we have to figure out what are we going to allow."

Cheryl Kilodavis is trying to find an external way to make Dyson safe and keep him true by asking the world to be more accepting. But many parents do not want to offer their child up as the public figure to make a political statement about gender norms. Plenty of parents pick safe over true, because they feel it is their job to protect a child from the cruelties of our society. "I would never let my son wear a pink tutu to school," one mom told me, "because I know that he would be teased and called a sissy, and I'd rather he feel bummed out about not wearing the tutu than ashamed and embarrassed by being made fun of." Another mom confided, "My three-year-old son saw a hot pink jacket in a catalogue, and he asked me to order it. I worried and worried about how other kids or grown-ups would treat him if he wore a pink jacket. Finally, I told him a little white lie—I said that the store had sold out of the pink jackets in his size and asked if he wanted another color. I feel a little bad about it, but I also feel like I am protecting him."

I called Lyn Mikel Brown, coauthor of *Packaging Boyhood*, and asked what thoughts she could offer to parents whose boys wanted to wear pink clothes.

"Parents might think that by not letting their boys wear pink, they are protecting their sons from being teased. But in reality, the only thing they are protecting is the stereotype. It perpetuates the fears. There comes a time when you have to choose. Are you going to protect your child's true interests and let him express himself, or are you going to protect the people who are afraid of differences? The best way to truly protect your child is to let him be who he wants to be and help him learn to negotiate the reactions of others. Then he will really be complete."[4]

Using Brown's philosophy, Cheryl Kilodavis has chosen to protect her son Dyson, rather than protect the stereotype that boys cannot be princesses. With his family's support, Dyson has found a way to embrace the words "princess boy," but what about the other phrases used to taunt boys for being effeminate or gay? One term that Adam mentioned—"sissy boy"—opens a host of problems. Whereas the word "princess" can have some positive connotations (beautiful, sparkly clothes, refined manners, Kate Middleton), one is hard-pressed to say the same about "sissy boy." As a female and a mother of daughters, I find the phrase disturbing when used as an insult because it demeans women and girls. Do we want to teach our young daughters that "running like a girl" or "throwing like a girl" is a bad thing? Calling someone a "sissy boy" is mean to *all* of us. It is mean to the boys because the term is being used in a cruel, taunting manner. It is mean to the girls because the term assumes that being a girl is a negative. A child will have trouble owning the term "sissy boy" in an empowering manner. The same goes for hateful words such as "faggot." These words are simply unacceptable, and they are used by girls just as readily as they are used by boys.

The word "sissy" has become so normative that even females use it as an insult without considering the self-insulting nature of the term. I remember noticing this while watching the hilarious film *Forgetting Sarah Marshall*. There is a scene where Jason Segel, who plays the main character, is afraid to jump off a cliff into the ocean. The female character, played by Mila Kunis, has successfully made the jump. She is treading water down below, and she yells up, in a mocking voice, "I can see your vagina from here." Sure, it was funny, but it was a classic example of how the media portray women demeaning themselves as comedic. Our culture claims to celebrate girls, trumpeting girl power and calling out, "You go, girl!" but at the same time we hold up "sissy" as the ultimate insult. Moms would rather buy their boys a jacket in a nonpreferred color than send their boys into the world to be labeled a sissy.

What about older boys, the ones who have more say over their clothing, hairstyles, and activities? One soon-to-be-adoptive mom, Queenie, told me about her nephew, Jake, who is old enough to self-censor some of his feminine interests in order to protect himself from bullies.

He's nine years old, almost ten. He's in the process of being adopted—by me! I'm so excited.

He lives with a family right now, though, that isn't very understanding. He likes to read; they don't see the point. He likes to learn; they tease him. He likes Star Wars and pink. He likes to draw and play piano and wrestle and watch iCarly.

He also has an interest in makeup. I think he likes the fact that you can paint on your face and change your whole appearance with random colors. Anyway, the point is that he has an interest that would get him bullied and he hides it, but he knows he's safe here with me. So we face paint. He knows he'd be called all kinds of names if other kids knew.

Jake has found a way to express himself in a safe place—when he is at home with Queenie—while protecting himself in public, and this compromise feels acceptable to him. But when it comes to his hairstyle, Jake has chosen to publicly embrace his unconventional preference for long hair. Queenie told me, "It's something he stands up for because he's decided that whether the bullies like it or not, he does. And they can just deal with it."

As boys like Jake or Dyson can tell you, long hair, dresses, and makeup are associated with girls. The other thing that is overwhelmingly identified with girls is neither a hairstyle nor an article of clothing. It is a color. The color pink has come to represent femininity from infancy through old age. Pink is more than a color. Pink is a statement, a way of life, a brand. Pink means girl even more than blue means boy. A girl can wear blue pants without anyone thinking twice about it, but a boy in pink draws critical eyes.

It was not always this way. A hundred years ago, there was not a strict gender code. I spoke with historian Jo Paoletti, author of *Pink and Blue: Telling the Boys from the Girls in America*, about the history of the colors pink and blue. "Before the twentieth century, all babies wore white, mostly because white was easy to bleach and keep clean," she began. "But then two forces arose that created the trend toward gendered things—one was the rise of psychology, and the other was the rise of child marketing." Paoletti went on to address the issue of child psychology first, which was a new field at that point. Freud thought that homosexuality was caused by things that happened early in childhood, and parents became convinced that they had to make their boys masculine right away. So, she explained, people began to cut boys' hair earlier, dress them in pants, and so forth. "The second force that simultaneously occurred in the early 1900s and created a desire for gendered clothing was child marketing. Parents began asking kids what they wanted to wear, and if you ask a toddler, he or she will want clearly gendered clothes due to a strong developmental need at that age for gender identification."[5]

So there was a new desire for gender differentiation, but it did not lead to a declaration of pink as the girl color. Quite the opposite. In 1927, *Time* magazine printed a chart showing gender-appropriate colors for boys and girls based on recommendations from top U.S. department stores. Marshall Field's in Chicago recommended that parents dress boys in pink, as did Filene's in Boston and Best & Company in New York City, because pink was a stronger and more noticeable color. Gentle and delicate blue was allocated to the girls.[6]

In the 1940s, the trend was inverted, and pink became associated more and more with girls, although for many years, pink simply meant "baby." Jo Paoletti confirmed, "As recently as the 1950s, pink was the color chosen for most first-birthday cakes, regardless of whether the baby was a boy or a girl." In the 1953 film *Peter Pan*, younger brother, Michael, was clad in pink footie pajamas, while older sister, Wendy Darling, was wearing a light blue dressing gown. And in the movie *Sleeping Beauty*, Princess Aurora wore a blue gown, while Prince Phillip was wrapped in a dark pink cape. Nowadays, the colors would be reversed. Eventually, Disney redesigned Aurora's dress to make it pink, the easier to distinguish the blonde-haired princess from Cinderella, another blue-gown-wearing female.

Along the curving path of pink and blue, there was a time period of tan and taupe. In the 1970s, parents took up a huge movement against gender identification, and it became very popular to dress children in unisex clothing. Mothers refused to dress their girls in pink, which by then was a designated feminine color. Paoletti remembers, "There was a blip of just under twenty years long where we could easily find unisex clothing for girls." I was born in 1974, and there is not a single picture of me in a pink dress, nor are there any photos of my three sisters in pink dresses. When I look back over our infant, toddler, and school-age portraits, we were *always* dressed in reds, yellows, blues, and browns. Primary colors dominated my wardrobe throughout my childhood.

The Free to Be You and Me era ended with a bang in the mid-1980s. Paoletti notes that the change occurred between the births of her daughter in 1982 and her son in 1986. "My daughter had a lot of unisex clothing. Four years later, the red overalls that used to be plain now had a train or a bear holding a football printed on the front to make them more masculine." This was also when companies introduced feminine accessories like elastic headbands with bows for baby girls. Paoletti knew the unisex era was definitely over when his-and-hers diapers hit the market.

Where does that leave us twenty-five years later? J.Crew published a catalogue in the spring of 2011 that featured creative director Jenna Lyons hanging out on a Saturday morning with her five-year-old son, Beckett, in the comfort of their home. Jenna was painting Beckett's toenails neon pink, his color of choice. Some social conservatives, such as Keith Ablow, claimed that J.Crew was pushing a transgender agenda. Defenders swooped in, decrying the charges that painting a little boy's toenails pink had anything to do with transgender issues. Conservatives took issue with the boy's toes being painted at all, and they were particularly outraged that the color used was pink. Ironically, as we learned earlier, pink has only meant "girl" in recent decades, and many of those men who criticized Jenna Lyons probably wore quite a bit of pink as youngsters themselves.

Pink may have been for boys in the past, but our current culture sends a very clear message that pink is now the domain of the girls. Despite this strict gender code, there are men who support pink for boys. In fact, a number of them wrote to Katie, affirming that strictly gendered clothes and toys have affected them personally.

Damian told us:

This blog post hit me pretty hard, as I'm adopted, and strange beyond belief. I've struggled with it all my life, because I've never fit in, anywhere. To this day, I still feel outcast. I'm a twenty-three-year-old guy, and recently I started to love the color pink.

I wear pink Converse shoes, they're my favorite, a pink button-up shirt, another favorite, and I play Star Wars: The Force Unleashed on my Playstation 3 . . . with a pink controller.

For a while, I felt uncomfortable, because I knew people would look at me weird. And trust me, I get made fun of because of it, even by my own friends. My mom thinks something is wrong with me because I like pink, and honestly . . . I can never understand why, it's just a color. I like it, it gives me a little bit of joy, and it's a cool, odd color on a guy, depending on what you mix it with.

I try to follow my own punk code, a sort of "live and let live" mentality. If it suits you, and doesn't hurt me, do it! And, Katie, I think if Star Wars suits you, and you love it, then do it!

And remember that one of those boys making fun of you about Star Wars might just love the color pink.

One of the major differences I have noticed between princess boys and Star Wars girls is adult response. Young kids do not discriminate in their criticism—they give an equally hard time to girls who infringe on boy territory as they do to boys who infringe on girl territory. But this is not at all the case with the adults. Emily Rosenbaum, the mother whose first-grade son was taunted for bringing My Little Pony to school, told me, "Teachers and parents will tell you that it's *cool* for Katie to like Star Wars. It's not cool for Zach to like My Little Pony." Herein lies a stubborn problem, and it is directly related to our cultural message that feminine boys aren't cool. Boys would rather suffer the pain of bullying than the shame of asking for help, and this needs to change. We need to show them that it is okay to say that things are not okay.

William Pollack's groundbreaking book *Real Boys* has taught us that boys feel things just as deeply as girls, but they do not express these feelings, because our society gives negative feedback to boys who are openly sensitive.[7] They get labeled sissies and fags, crybabies and mama's boys. The prevailing stereotypes hurt everyone, but they are particularly cruel to children who directly challenge the norms. The stereotypes teach kids that it is okay to mock a girl who likes to play football and it is okay to taunt a boy who likes to knit. As long as society maintains the view that girls are to be cosseted in pink dresses, waiting to be rescued by strapping young men, we will have bullying.

Chapter Six

Quirky Kids and Kids with Hidden Disabilities

A large-scale study of middle school students recently found that students with disabilities reported significantly higher rates of victimization when compared to their general education peers.[1] But parents of special-needs children do not need a study to tell them what they already know—their kids are bully magnets. Joslyn Gray, author of the funny, insightful blog *Stark Raving Mad Mommy,* said to me, "You can have one quirk and get away with it, but you can't have more than one or you become a target." Joslyn's son, publicly known as Little Dude, has a collection of quirky behaviors. When I was speaking with Joslyn about how communities differ in their acceptance of quirky kids, she shared an interesting observation. "When Little Dude was diagnosed with Asperger's syndrome at age four, it was in a different town than the one he had been raised in. We had recently moved from Philadelphia to Houston, and the disruption to routine and the new environment exacerbated and highlighted Little Dude's quirks." In Philadelphia, Joslyn's family had lived in a community that was extremely accepting, and Little Dude's quirky behaviors were celebrated as assets. In Houston, the same child was labeled as disordered. Joslyn agreed with the diagnosis but found it fascinating that the framing in one town was totally different than in another. Eventually, Joslyn and her family moved back to Philadelphia, yearning for a more accepting community than the one they found in the suburbs of Houston.

Joslyn explained some of the challenges that she and Little Dude face. "Many parents worry about the 'label' of special needs, as though the terminology will somehow taint their child's academic record and cause teachers to view their child differently. He was the same person before the diagnosis as after the diagnosis; the only thing different was the myriad of services that became available to us after the diagnosis." Joslyn did find it a relief to have a specific diagnosis, an answer to the questions about her son's quirks. She told me, "Although our friends and family embrace Little Dude for who he is (which reduces his stress level, thereby engendering fewer "odd" behaviors), strangers are often less understanding. His flapping hands, which express excitement or happiness, sometimes startle adults and older children. He's still young enough at age four that most of his quirks fly under the radar, but the occasional full-blown public meltdown does happen." Strangers tend to comment on the fact that he still wears diapers, still rides in the front of a grocery cart, and often refuses to respond to questions. According to Joslyn, most of these comments start with the phrase "Isn't he getting a little big for . . . ?"

Now that Little Dude has a diagnosis, Joslyn feels more confident explaining his behavior to strangers, many of whom she feels are well meaning. If a stranger comments that he is shy, Joslyn responds with, "He's not shy; he just feels uncomfortable making eye contact with new people. That's a normal part of Asperger's syndrome." Joslyn reveals his diagnosis because she and her husband hope that being matter-of-fact about it is better than seeming to be ashamed of his quirks. And, as Joslyn notes, "He hears these strangers' comments. He may not appear to respond, but that doesn't mean he's oblivious. In fact, if he's *not* making eye contact, you can be sure he's listening intently. If he's looking you in the eyes, he's tuning you out and is probably replaying a scene from *Return of the Jedi* in his mind."

Although Joslyn perceives most questions and comments as innocent or well intentioned, she has observed that they do still inflict damage. She explains, "Contrary to popular myth, autistic people are not emotionless. The hurt, frustration, and shame that my son feels when an adult comments on his diapered status are real, but challenging to express. He also struggles with the speaker's intention: he often cannot decipher whether the remark is helpful or snide." Joslyn believes that these exchanges, and how she responds, set the stage for how Little Dude will respond when he is challenged on his own. Little Dude has started preschool, which exposes him to more interactions with children his own age. At this age, Joslyn has noticed, most kids are a little goofy themselves, so many of her son's quirky behaviors generally go unnoticed by his peers.

Little Dude struggled with some of the normal games and rituals he first encountered in preschool. "Until the game of tag was explicitly explained to him, he found it terrifying," Joslyn remembered. "He could not fathom why other children were gleefully running at him, touching him, and then running away. In his mind, it seemed to be some sort of fearsome punishment. We did two things: explained the game, and also explained that he could simply say 'no chasing!' if he didn't like it." And at the beginning of the school year, Little Dude was repeatedly pushed while standing in line. Each afternoon, he would sadly and confusedly tell his mom that the boy behind him would push him, yelling "Go!" at him. The loud yelling, the close contact, and the pushing were all terribly upsetting.

Joslyn knew immediately what was really happening, because her son has a motor planning deficit. She explained, "The teacher was telling the class to line up, and then walk to the library. Little Dude is only able to process the first piece of information: line up. Then he would stand still, awaiting further instruction. The neurotypical child in line behind him was baffled as to why Little Dude wasn't moving forward, and that child didn't want to be left behind or get in trouble. 'Go!' he would yell. When he got no response, he would give Little Dude a shove and yell louder." Joslyn spoke with the teacher about the situation. She suggested that Little Dude be put in the beginning of the line, where the teacher could give him a physical cue, such as a gentle tap on the shoulder, when it is time to move forward. Joslyn was happy to report that, "This, combined with the teacher's continued enforcement of a 'no pushing' rule, solved the problem."[2] Little Dude was fortunate to have such a supportive, understanding teacher.

Kids with Asperger's have had a long history of being tormented by their peers. Joslyn's son is still very young and cannot easily articulate in an interview how it feels to have Asperger's, so Joslyn does the reporting.

But Candice, now an adult, was clearly able to tell me about the traumatic schooling experiences from her childhood as a girl with Asperger's. "As early as kindergarten, I got in trouble for fighting back when other kids attacked me. In addition to name calling, there was physical violence—rocks thrown at me, having an older girl hold me while another girl punched me. There was destruction of my property—my books ripped up, paint thrown on my new T-shirt and new winter boots (that one was in art class). For a while we had an answering machine (in 1989) because I was getting harassing phone calls from my peers, so we had to tape everything for the police." The worst part of the bullying for Candice was that she is severely phobic of snakes, and in third and fourth grades her classmates constantly shoved toy snakes into her world. "In my desk, in my coat pocket, on my desk, in my pencil box, every time I turned around, there they were. I had panic attacks."

Unfortunately for Candice, the principal at her school took no steps to resolve the problem. "The principal was of the "kids will be kids" school of thought and didn't do ANYTHING to make my life easier. My teachers tried to look out for me as best they could since the principal wasn't going to punish my tormenters." Candice's fourth- and fifth-grade teachers kept an eye out for her, and both used to confiscate all toy snakes they saw. But the damage to Candice has been real and lasting. Just thinking about her childhood causes her to feel very tense and can bring her to the edge of a panic attack. She recalls being suicidally depressed as a teenager. "I was afraid every day when I had to go to school. I dreaded it." When I asked Candice if anyone supported her, she responded, "They started to help me in junior high, but in elementary school I was totally on my own. In junior high when I got bullied, the bullies turned on my friends too. I met my best friend in eighth grade when she moved to town—it was the first day of drama class, and the teacher said you needed partners for class. Nobody wanted to be my partner, and since she was the new girl, nobody wanted to be hers either. Twenty years later, we are still each other's best friend."[3]

Candice's ability to bond with one other girl may well be what saved her. Barbara Coloroso, author of *Kids Are Worth It!*, told me that "having at least one good friend who is there for you through thick and thin" is one of the four most powerful antidotes to bullying. "The other three best antidotes to bullying," she went on, "are having a strong sense of self, being a good friend to others, and being able to successfully get into a group and back out of a group if it does not serve you well."[4] In examining Coloroso's four strongest antidotes to bullying, it does not surprise me that kids with autism, ADHD, behavioral quirks, and other psychiatric diagnoses struggle with bullying, because one of the hallmarks of these conditions is difficulty getting into a social group. Kids who have hidden disabilities often struggle to manage basic conversations, much less the skills required to be a good friend or blend into a group. When social interactions were too taxing, Candice sought solace through reading books. She remembered, "I could shut the world out and live in a different world through the pages of books. I still read many of those books as an adult. It's like a visit to old friends. And I survived because I had a plan when I was a kid. I was going to get really good marks in school and move away from my very small hometown (10,000 people), go to university and start my life fresh."

When Kids with Special Needs Are the Aggressors— A Successful Intervention and a Failed Intervention

Although kids with special needs are often targeted, there are other circumstances in which these kids become the aggressors. Janice's first-grade son, Bradley, is one such example. "When he was three, we needed to change preschools, because his current preschool was unable to manage his behavior. We put him into a special preschool run by the school district. He received occupational therapy and we did a ton of work with him on self-regulating."

When Bradley was old enough to start kindergarten, his parents wanted to put him into the local public school. They met with his kindergarten teacher before the school year started, and they talked with her about his behavioral problems. Bradley is a very bright boy, enthusiastic, and full of energy, and his parents had high hopes for kindergarten.

On the second day of school, Bradley was playing on the playground after classes were dismissed, and Janice noticed that he was about to shove another boy, Cole, off some playground equipment. "I saw him reach out, and I screamed, 'Bradley, NO!' at the top of my lungs, and it caused every parent at the playground to turn and look at my son just in time to see him push this other kid down. And it was so awful, because Cole got a serious bruise on his face. The bruise was still there two months later, and it just killed me to see it."

Starting from the first week of school, Bradley and Cole developed a very antagonistic relationship. Janice explained, "I would say that sixty to seventy percent of the aggression was initiated by Bradley, but Cole occasionally starts it." Janice refers to Cole as Bradley's "nemesis" and said that the two boys are like oil and water. "Bradley likes to test limits and bend rules, and Cole is a rule follower. Whenever Bradley does anything out of line, even if it does not affect other kids, Cole immediately tells the teacher. And then Bradley gets mad at Cole for getting him into trouble, and Bradley retaliates by hurting him."

Janice was tormented by the bruise Bradley inflicted on the other boy. She met with the teacher regularly to keep tabs on the situation, and she spoke frequently with Cole's parents, who were very kind and willing to help. The other parents of children in the class knew about the situation between the two boys, and they assisted in monitoring activity on the playground and at birthday parties. Janice admitted, "I cannot tell you how hard it was to let Bradley play after school on the playground, but I knew the social interaction was good for him. I would stand there with a huge knot in my stomach, praying that he wouldn't do anything, watching his every move."[5] Fortunately for everyone, Bradley's mom was tuned in to his aggressive tendencies, and she was willing to acknowledge and help him be accountable for his behavior. Janice and the other parents have done a great job of uniting and supporting Bradley's efforts to play with other kids, as opposed to excluding him from playdates and games.

The boys' kindergarten teacher also took steps to improve the situation at school. Bradley, Cole, and one other kid were pulled out of the lunchroom once a week to eat together with a school social worker. After several months of weekly lunches, the relationship between Bradley and Cole improved. In mid-February, Janice told me with a shining face, "Cole asked if he could come have a playdate at our house with Bradley yesterday. And it went great! It seemed fitting that it was on Valentine's Day!"[6]

There were many ways in which this relationship could have deteriorated after the first week of school back in September. The other parents of kindergarteners could have labeled Bradley "a bully" and simply excluded him from organized playdates and birthday parties. The other parents could have shunned Janice. These behaviors would have led Bradley to feel isolated and angry, and he would have likely responded with aggression. Additionally, Janice might have felt abandoned and alone in her attempts to provide Bradley with a healthy social environment.

But instead, the deeply caring environment at the school allowed Bradley to continue building relationships under the close eyes of adults. Six months later, Janice was all smiles as she recounted Bradley's most recent parent-teacher conference. "It was phenomenal!" she enthused. "His teacher said he is like a new person! The other kids like him, and he is doing really well academically, and his entire manner in the classroom is different. My husband and I have noticed a real change in Bradley at home, too, right around the time we returned from winter break." Janice credits a number of interventions with helping Bradley. "It helps that he continues to play with other kids and learn social skills, and the weekly lunches help. Also, when Bradley was acting out in the classroom, the feedback he received from other kids was not positive. He began to notice their negative responses to his behavior, and he made a bigger effort to change."

Bradley's case really demonstrates the benefits of creating an empathetic, loving environment, as well as the importance of teaching social emotional skills to kids. Nobody wrote Bradley off as a "bad kid." In fact, Janice shared how she overheard one little girl saying to her dad early in the school year, "That's Bradley. He's a bad boy." And the dad responded with, "No, he is not a bad boy. We're all just learning here, and Bradley is learning too." The dad could have said, "Oh, really? Then stay away from him," which could have fostered feelings of isolation, fear, and hostility. But that is not what happened, and everyone will benefit from Bradley's evolving social skills.

Although Bradley and Cole's relationship improved, everything was not sunshine and roses. They had a few playdates, but the honeymoon period wore off, and problems resumed. The two boys unexpectedly ended up at the same summer camp, and without the benefit of the weekly lunches with the school social worker, their relationship struggled. Despite the up-and-down nature of his interactions with Cole, Bradley is able to function as a contributing member of the summer camp and has developed friendships with other peers. In fact, last year at summer camp, Bradley required a one-on-one counselor assigned especially to him. This year, after the first week of camp, the counselors determined that Bradley was doing so well that an aide was unnecessary. Now halfway through first grade, Bradley is performing extremely well in school and has required no interventions in the classroom.

Let us contrast Bradley's experience with that of another little boy whose mother I interviewed. Francine, the mother, also has a son, Adam, who has aggressive tendencies. Adam initially displayed rough, impulsive behavior in preschool. Francine and her husband, Mike, placed Adam into a small private preschool, and he managed pretty well, especially under the care of a loving and involved teacher. Like Bradley, Adam was on track to start kindergarten at a local public school. Before the school year began, Francine met with the principal and the kindergarten teacher at the school. From the first moment, the meeting was rancorous. "The principal started telling me that Adam sounded spectrumy and needed occupational therapy and speech therapy, and she had never even met him yet. She was throwing out diagnoses and labels prematurely." School started, and the classroom environment aggravated Adam. He had extreme difficulty controlling his impulses, and his sensory issues impeded his ability to function.

One day at nap time, Adam lashed out and injured a girl next to him because her mat was too close to his. Within a few weeks of school, he began wetting his pants every day. Francine lamented, "We repeatedly asked to meet with the teacher, but she wouldn't listen to us; she kept saying that Adam made bad choices and that was the problem. Other kids did not want to be his friend, and they always said they didn't like him. The kindergarten teacher was mean to him in the classroom and would say 'suck it up' when he cried." After six weeks of kindergarten, Adam sobbed to his parents, "I'm stupid. I can't do anything right. I want to go jump off a building." Francine cried every day too, telling me, "None of the parents would have anything to do with me or Adam. And then I pulled him out of that school."[7]

Adam is still struggling with aggression and has been through several elementary schools. His parents enrolled him in private school, and he was asked to leave after his behavior became a distraction in the classroom. That is one of the luxuries that private schools have—they can kick out the children who are too difficult to manage. In public schools, a child cannot be refused an education simply because he has behavior management problems, and this makes it all the more important for public schools to have empathetic, well-trained teachers. Since Adam's local public school was ill-equipped to provide for him, and the private school refused to renew his contract, Francine decided to homeschool Adam for first grade. Some parents do turn to homeschooling as the answer for bullying, particularly for those children who are persistently targets. Homeschooling obviously cuts down on episodes of school-based taunting and bullying, but it does not eliminate social difficulty altogether.

Francine described how she arranged for Adam to join other homeschooled kids at the park for regular playdates. To her dismay, Adam continued to act aggressively when he congregated with homeschooled peers, and within a short time Francine was snubbed by the parents and Adam was rejected by the kids. Francine told me sadly,

"Other people make you feel like you have done something wrong. That judgment is so strong. They make you feel like you made a mistake. But we are trying so hard—we limit screen time; we are going broke paying for psychiatrists and occupational therapy; we are on top of this; we have Adam in social-skills groups. Sometimes I just cry. Other people judging us at the park, at school, everywhere—it hurts. I think about Adam's little sister, who is an easy kid, and I can't imagine how hard it must be for her to be his sister. I try to give her extra attention when I can, because he gets everything from me." Francine is proof that the families of kids who act as bullies need our help and compassion as much as victims.

Adam, who responds to victimization with aggression, is a bully–victim. Children who have behavioral disorders and anger-management problems are particularly at risk for becoming bully victims, and they need multiple interventions.[8] To compound the difficulties faced by these kids, teachers tend to discipline them for their bullying behaviors while blaming them when they are victimized. The children often have trouble advocating clearly for themselves, and life at school becomes fraught with anxiety and tension.

Chapter Seven

Kids with Different Appearances or Physical Disabilities

Shortly before kindergarten, Katie was diagnosed with amblyopia. Her left eye was weaker than her right eye, and in addition to wearing corrective lenses, she needed to wear a patch over her good eye to force the bad eye to strengthen. At age six, Katie was old enough to be aware of looking different. She was at that vulnerable phase where she wanted to be a little kid, but she also wanted to be cool. The patch was distinctively uncool. What surprised and dismayed me was how many adults stared at her and asked questions about her patch. I'd expected it from kids, but not from grown-ups. Katie became increasingly sensitive about it, and I always felt a tug in my heart when she covered her right eye with her hand and ducked her head to stop someone from staring. In the grocery store, at restaurants, always someone asked her, "What happened to your eye?" And Katie simply said, "I need to make my other eye stronger."

When I look back on the water-bottle taunting incident, I see how the patch was another piece of the puzzle that made Katie respond as she did. Perhaps a child who had never known the pain of being different would have looked at the taunting boys and said, "So what? I like this water bottle." But not Katie. She was already familiar with the uncomfortable sensation of being singled out and stared at, and she wanted to avoid it at all costs. She had learned to be afraid of drawing negative attention, and if ditching the Star Wars water bottle would decrease her chances of being targeted, she was ready to drink out of another bottle.

The patch itself is an arbitrary example, interchangeable with any characteristic that makes a child feel different. Another child's "patch" may come as an overweight body, frizzy hair, short stature, a birthmark . . . anything that makes a child vulnerable to taunting. As thousands of parents have experienced, many kids do not have any noteworthy physical or behavioral differences, and they still become targets of taunting and bullying. Some kids have looked different for as long as they can remember, and others can pinpoint the moment when a change occurred and drew the critical eyes of bullies.

Perhaps a child gained a significant amount of weight one summer, and when she returned to school in the fall, she was taunted for being fat. Or maybe a child with previously clear skin developed a bad case of acne that stayed throughout adolescence. Racial differences are particularly prevalent in America, where we have a much less homogenous population than in many other countries. A mom named Susan wrote to me that "my daughter, adopted from Mongolia, was Princess Leia for Halloween. She is dealing with bullies too. She was devastated when a little girl told her she could only be a princess if she was Irish, among other things (she's had other kids and even a teacher give her problems over her race). She decided that she hated being Mongolian, hated being adopted, and wished she had been born here." I remember when an African American friend of mine lamented that her daughter wanted to be Sleeping Beauty for Halloween and asked for her hair to be "smooth and flowing." My friend told me, "There is no way I can make her hair flow!"

Looking different from your peers is hard at any age, but never more so than when you are a socially aware child or teenager. When I spoke with adults who do not fit the idealized image of beauty in our culture, many of them expressed that they have made some peace with it. They have suffered and then found a way to come to terms with their distinguishing characteristics. Likewise, parents of extremely young children with physical differences (age two and under) mostly report that their young children are oblivious to looking different. But something happens as children grow socially aware, and they feel devastating pain when the world judges them, stares at them, ogles them. Even the strongest, most confident of children cannot help but be affected by the critical eye of others. Some physical differences, such as speech impediments, literally take away a child's ability to advocate for himself, because others laugh every time he opens his mouth. People often assume that a child with speech delays or physical disabilities also has cognitive delays, when that is not necessarily the case. Parents of some kids have to fight society's assumptions that their children are mentally impaired.

Paula is one such mother. She met with me to talk about her experiences raising six-year-old Shelley, who is physically disabled but cognitively normal.[1] "When Shelley was three weeks old, she got whooping cough, and as a result she developed spastic diplegia cerebral palsy." Now in kindergarten, Shelley cannot walk or stand independently and walks with a walker. She has undergone weeks of serial casting and wears braces on her legs. It has become apparent that Shelley also has difficulties with her fine motor skills, more so than Paula anticipated.

Paula regularly takes Shelley out in the community to help people feel more comfortable with kids with disabilities, even though she admitted that it would sometimes be easier to just stay home. Wherever they go, people stare at Shelley. "She doesn't like the attention she gets. Kids stare at her blatantly. Adults stare and look away, stare and look away." Some people go beyond staring and say cruel or ignorant things, and Paula described a recent outing. "Not long ago, we were at the ice rink, and a little boy repeatedly made fun of how she moved with her walker. He mimicked her and laughed, mimicked her and laughed again. His older brother stood there and watched him make fun of Shelley but did nothing to intervene." Paula looked around to see who was in charge of the boys. She saw their father on his cell phone and went to get him. When she explained what was happening, he was very embarrassed. "But here was the interesting part," Paula observed. "The dad was more concerned with whether Shelley's feelings were hurt than with teaching his own son that his behavior was wrong. He kept asking if she was okay but never engaged with his son."

Paula and I mused about the fact that a teachable moment was lost for that boy and his dad. To Paula's dismay, there have been multiple times when potential teachable moments pass children by, because their parents do not respond appropriately to cruel situations. One of the most egregious times still causes Paula to cringe as she recalls a day at the pool. They had been swimming at Lifetime Fitness, she remembered, and Shelley was having a great deal of fun. Her confidence was blooming; her body was alive with joy. Paula's face darkened with pain. "After we swam, we took showers; it had been the perfect day, but then in the family locker room, two eight- or nine-year-old boys stood on either side of Shelley's walker, trapping her, and they asked over and over, 'What's wrong with her?' And it was so awful; Shelley's whole glow disappeared. She sort of collapsed into herself, and the light went out of her. The mom of the boys was standing nearby and pretended she didn't hear."

"How do you help Shelley recover from incidents like that?" I asked her, after a moment.

Paula replied, "I asked her if it hurt her feelings, are you okay, what are you thinking? And I try to build up her self-esteem so she is proud of her differences. But she says, 'I still can't walk and run like my friends.' My friend Lynn has a six-year-old with severe cerebral palsy; she has a walker, too, and Shelley adores her. Being with other kids with disabilities is great—they have walker races, and Shelley sees there are people like her. And the truth is, Shelley *can do* things more than she *can't do* things. When she and Lynn's daughter are together, they don't care about their disabilities." Paula took Shelley to a place where they help kids with physical challenges learn how to water-ski. "When I saw teenage girls jump out of their wheelchairs to water-ski, I felt this immense sense of relief and thought, *It's all going to be okay, because Shelley has these great role models who don't let their disabilities stop them*." And now Shelley can water-ski.

We talked about how children are young and malleable; there is much to gain by teaching them empathy and respect. It is much harder to manage this behavior when it comes from adults—very few grown-ups are receptive to those teachable moments that involve others' telling them why their behavior is disrespectful. Paula nodded and recalled an incident with an older woman while they were shopping at Target. Shelley had asked to walk, and "she was having so much fun, acting like a regular little kid, trying to hide and lose me while using her walker. She ran around the aisles, laughing and thumping along. This woman stood right above Shelley and asked over and over, 'What's wrong with her?' as if Shelley couldn't hear. I kept saying, 'Nothing's wrong with her,' and the woman kept insisting, 'Yes, yes, there is something wrong with her. What is it?' Shelley's demeanor changed, and all the fun was gone. Because, of course, she understands everything people say about her."

While talking with Paula, I thought about one of the people who had written to Katie, a man who had been taunted because, like Shelley, he could not walk normally. I sifted through my email until I found his note:

I'm a guy in my thirties, so I'm an old fogey. I now use a wheelchair to get around, but when I was your age, I could walk. But I walked with my knees bent and feet turned inward. I walked "funny" as they used to say. And when I was your age, I was made fun of for that. But I learned something very important when I was being made fun of. First, that the kids making fun of me were just acting out from their own lack of confidence. So do yourself a favor and forgive them and be kind to them. Secondly, I knew then, as I know now, that I was a good person. That I tried to be a good person and thus there was nothing wrong with me. In fact, I learned that if we weren't all different to some degree, we'd be bored to death!

And don't forget that what they see on the outside of you and comment on doesn't matter, because they don't know the inside you, like your family and friends do and will. Remember that when Luke first met Yoda, he laughs at the thought that this creature before him was a great warrior. And Yoda told him not to judge him by his size.

Be Yoda. The bullies don't know what a great warrior you can be. :)
Michael

Shelley is just a child, and she has years ahead of her to test her limitations, accepting some and defying others. Hopefully, as an adult, she will be at peace with herself, the way Michael is. In the meantime, Paula takes an active role in teaching compassion to Shelley's classmates. When Shelley started kindergarten at a public school this year, Paula worked with the school to demystify her daughter. The school did a great job of collaborating with Paula and supported her efforts to communicate with the kindergarten community. Paula wrote a book about Shelley, and she read aloud to the other kindergarten students about how Shelley can still water-ski, ride horses, and swim. "I brought in her walker, her orthotics, her canes, and I let the kids touch them and feel them. I also wrote a letter and put it in every kid's backpack the first day of school. The letter described Shelley's condition, explained that cognitively she's no different from other kids, gave my phone number for questions, and let everyone know that Shelley has a one-on-one aide with her at all times so parents wouldn't be afraid that the teacher's time would be taken up by her." The response was "amazing," Paula enthused, and at this point, kindergarten has been a huge social success for Shelley. The other kids like her so much that they argue about who gets to sit next to her, and the teacher has had to make a rotating schedule.

Shelley has an uncommon physical disability that sets her apart from the other students in her class, but many children are bullied for more common physical traits. Anything that draws attention can become a negative. This is never more prevalent than in middle school, which is why it becomes critically important to many children to be just like everyone else in clothing and appearance. Something as innocent as wearing the "wrong" style of jeans can set a child up for merciless taunting. We saw in the letters to Katie that kids were teased for any and every reason.

Dear Katie,

My name is Michelle. I really love Star Wars, just like you. Hearing this story just broke my heart. I haven't been bullied for liking Star Wars, but something else about me that people see—my zits. It really hurts me. One day I broke out in tears because someone said some really mean things to me. Being bullied isn't fun, and even though we have entirely different cases, I want you to know that changing who you are just won't work. People love you already for who you are, and those are the people whose opinions really matter, right? Just ignore those boys, or, if it gets any worse, talk to a teacher who will take care of it. It's good to be different. It lets you express yourself. While I was bullied, I longed to be just like everyone else, but then I learned that I was much happier being who I am. It's a hard world out there, but there will always be people who love you.
With love,
Michelle

Bullied children often find solace in the company of other bullied children. One man wrote to us about his own physical differences and how he sought companions in his same situation:

I am thirty-six and male, but when I was your age, I had a part of my hip missing, and I was teased all the time, by both boys and girls. I would only play with the other kids that were different, and this was in an age where different was not cool at all like it is now. We were picked on a lot, and we all had stuff in common. One of my friends had ear problems; another had very thick glasses; one had behavior issues, and you know what, Katie? They were the best friends I have ever had. We all liked Star Wars, and in the eighties, I don't remember any girls or guys NOT liking it!

And the same thing happened in high school—I was bullied for my back being different too. It really hurt at the

time, but I look back on it now and realize something.
When people are what they call "normal," I usually hear
the words "boring" or "in denial about being different."

Appearance is the top priority of many kids, because they learn at an early age that the world judges them by the way they look. We can reduce these incidences of taunting and bullying by teaching kids empathy.[2] Once kids understand more about why someone is in a wheelchair or has no hair due to chemotherapy, we remove the fear of those who look different. Then we make room for acceptance.

It is harder to do this for issues like body weight and acne than for physical disabilities, because kids make stereotypical judgments about why a child is heavy or pimpled. The bullying then attacks both the child's appearance and her character, i.e., you are fat because you are lazy; you have acne because you never wash your face.

As many parents can tell you, it is not just the kids who make stereotypical judgments about other kids who are overweight or who look different. Sarah Hoffman, the pen name of the author of a popular blog about raising a boy who is different, began chronicling her son Sam's experiences with bullying at his elementary school in the spring of 2011. Sam, who suffers from celiac disease and several other physical conditions, had put on about twenty pounds during the school year, and his peers were taunting him about being fat. Additionally, Sam wears his hair long, and he was taunted for looking like a girl. Sarah realized that judgmental adults often thwart anti-bullying efforts, as evidenced by a comment she received from a man who thought it was ridiculous for Sarah to try to intervene. Among other things, Mr. H. claimed:

Sometimes people conflict, and there are no institutional poli-
cies that can ever solve this. People who don't like your son for
whatever reason will never like him, regardless of whatever
policies you draft or punishments you dish out. In light of this,
your son has really two options:

1. *He can grow a thicker skin, a quicker tongue, and faster fists, learning to advocate for himself instead of having mommy fight his battles.*

   or

2. *He can stop acting so femininely, lose weight, be less conspicuous about his illnesses, and learn who is actually interested in hearing about his obscure hobbies.*

This is a dog-eat-dog world, where you either learn to blend in or, if you must stand out, stand out on your own two feet, not being propped up by the rudimentary defenses of an overprotective mother.

Mr. H. then tossed out this recommendation:

Have Sam put down the video games and go for a jog, perhaps? I know it doesn't seem that easy, but as someone who has struggled with weight issues, it truly is usually just a lack of willpower that keeps the pounds from flying off. You have to take control at some point, so why not today?

Sarah asked me to help her write a response to Mr. H., and we prepared the following:

Mr. H. asks, "Why is it the duty of the school . . . the taxpayers . . . the parents you've attempted to 'rally,' to devote so much time, effort, energy, money, and resources to such a small proportion of the population . . . (your son)?"

Here's the thing about bullying: the circle of people affected is much larger than the victim. Since we know that Sam is not bullying himself, we can safely assume that there are other children involved.

Where there are victims, there are bullies—and kids who engage in bullying are in need of intervention just as much as the kids they victimize.

According to a 2007 study by A. Sourander et al., bullying behavior is predictive of future substance abuse, depression, and anxiety.[3] Other research shows that simply witnessing bullying creates anxiety and depression.

As Mr. H. is concerned about the economy, he might consider the economic impact of allowing Sam's bullies to continue without intervention. Shall we turn a blind eye as all children—bullies, victims, bystanders—walk the path toward increased risk of health and mental-health disease? The cost to society from these conditions is far higher than the cost of teaching kids empathy and respect.

Beyond misunderstanding the harm that bullies do to themselves and to bystanders, Mr. H. underestimates the harm done to targeted victims. This is a common misperception.

In D. Espelage and S. Swearer's Bullying in North American Schools, *Susan P. Limber writes:*

> *Some adults seriously underestimate bullying's frequency. ("Kids will be kids," "It's a normal part of growing up," "Kids need to learn to deal with bullying on their own.") These adults misjudge the significant social, emotional, and academic costs of bullying for victimized children and overestimate the ability of victimized children to stop bullying without the assistance of adults.[4]*

"Sometimes people conflict," Mr. H.'s comment continues, "and there are no institutional policies that can ever solve this."

The term "conflict" implies the possibility of resolution, a possibility that doesn't exist when one child is simply being mean to another. Disagreements, occasional fights, and social conflicts are all normal parts of childhood. But bullying— repetitive, unwanted attacks in the context of a power imbalance—is not normative, and it cannot be lumped in with typical childhood conflict.

Mr. H. suggests that Sam grow a thicker skin and fight back, or, alternately, change to become "less conspicuous." ("If you must stand out," he advises, "stand out on your own two feet, not being propped up by the rudimentary defenses of an overprotective mother.")

This is a classic case of blaming the victim for the attack. Telling Sam to stop acting so femininely is the same thing as telling a rape victim to wear different clothes. Sam has the right to be who he is and still walk safely through his school.

Mr. H.'s comments about how he, too, struggled with weight issues point to some genuine concern behind his suggestion that Sam "put down the video games and go for a jog," and it is true that a healthy lifestyle is important for all children. However, Mr. H. makes his suggestions based on stereotypical assumptions about Sam. There are more sensitive ways to approach a weight-loss discussion.

Sarah is not asking people to like her son. She is, however, insisting that he be treated with respect. Respect is a basic human right, something we owe to Sam and all children. A child should not have to hide his gender expression and physical characteristics or limitations in order to fit in.

Would Mr. H. tell an African American child to lighten her skin (or a short child to use growth hormone, or a child in a wheelchair to get up and walk) so other kids wouldn't bully her?

As long as there are adults who hold opinions like Mr. H., it will be difficult to teach compassion to children, but change must happen at some point, so why not today?

Chapter Eight

Gay, Lesbian, Transgender, and Bisexual Students

A child who is bisexual, gay, lesbian, or transgendered is an extremely high-risk target for peer victimization. The taunting starts early and persists for years, and children barely old enough to understand their sexuality have been driven to take their own lives in order to escape the bullying. Carl Joseph Walker-Hoover, an eleven-year-old in Massachusetts, hanged himself in April 2009 after enduring daily taunts that he was gay.[1] His mother had repeatedly begged the school to do something to help her son. In the fall of 2010, people across the world were grief stricken after a cluster of young boys in the United States committed suicide after being bullied about their sexual orientation. The gay community, in particular, took the suicides as a call to action. On September 9 in Indiana, a fifteen-year-old named Billy Lucas hanged himself after being taunted for years about being gay.[2] On September 19, thirteen-year-old Seth Walsh hanged himself in Minnesota after his peers mercilessly bullied him for having feminine mannerisms and being gay. His mother found Seth unconscious, and the boy lingered on life support for a week before passing away.[3] And Asher Brown, a thirteen-year-old from Houston, Texas, shot himself in the head on September 23 after enduring antigay bullying at school.[4] These children had suffered more than they could bear, and they sought solace in death when no one was able to help them stay in this life.

The suicides, while horrific and very visible due to ample media coverage, only represent a small percentage of the population of gay, lesbian, bisexual, and transgender students who are bullied. For every gay child who takes his life, countless others are suffering. Most find a way to endure until time passes and conditions eventually improve. That was the experience of Josh, a kind soft-spoken man with whom I met to talk about his childhood.[5] The taunting of Josh began in fifth grade. At that point, the kids did not yet specifically call him gay, but they did say he acted like a girl.

"I didn't know I was different until I was made fun of for being different. And then I didn't know what those differences meant," recalled Josh. "I didn't know that I was gay, but I knew that I was interested in flowers—I loved arranging them—and that was perceived as a girl thing. The worst thing about the bullying was learning about what was different through the bullying." As Josh moved through grade school, he continually gravitated toward things that were perceived as feminine. "In terms of being perceived as gay, I unintentionally gave people a lot of material to work with. My interests included playing the flute, which was perceived as a girl's instrument. I was completely uninterested in sports and had no aptitude for sports. Part of it is that I'm not particularly well coordinated, and part of it is no one taught me how to throw or catch a ball. Kids would tell me, 'You throw like a girl' or 'You run like a girl.' In junior high, the boys would mock how I held my hands as I walked and spoke. They would repeat the gesture back at me. And physically, I was very small. My voice was the last to change, and it didn't happen until ninth grade." Josh discovered that merely being perceived as gay subjected him to intense bullying, long before he knew whether he actually was gay.

Uncertain about how to respond to the taunts, Josh mostly kept his head down and switched into survival mode, particularly in gym class and health class. He was intensely self-conscious about his body, even as a small child. "When I was a little boy, I never took my shirt off and ran around in my shorts. I was and still am uncomfortable in my own body."

There is widespread acknowledgment that overweight children are at increased risk for peer victimization, but many people overlook how difficult it can be to be a short, skinny boy. Our society values strong, macho boys, and the media does not give positive feedback to slight, effeminate boys. Others picked up on Josh's discomfort, including teachers. "It was as if there were no adults around, as if no adults were aware of bullying. I remember a teacher in health class laughing at me along with two boys."

Josh did find relief by engaging with one group of the bullies so they would see him as a person and not an object. He recounted for me how several boys two grades younger constantly teased him about his voice and gestures. Every time they passed him in the hall, they would say "Hi" in an over-the-top feminine way. "I started just saying 'Hi' back to them in a normal way," Josh recalled, "and it helped because they realized I was a human being and they were being ridiculous. It took a few months, but they finally stopped taunting me."

In grade school, the kids mocked Josh for acting like a girl. By middle school, there was a shift in the language of the taunts, and the bullies began calling Josh "gay." Josh did not know what it meant to be gay, and his sense of confusion was compounded by the fact that his parents were the only evangelical Christians in a small town of Catholics and Lutherans. His parents believed everyone else was going to hell, and it took Josh's social isolation to a whole other level. "All the messages I received about homosexuality were from people like James Dobson, people who said gay was a negative thing, and so I thought, well that's not who I am, because I know I'm not a bad person. So I didn't think I was gay. But I had no opportunity to even find out, because my parents discouraged us from dating, parties, movies, and social functions. I wasn't learning about whether or not I might be attracted to a girl or a guy. I had no context to understand what I was feeling."

Josh felt overwhelmingly isolated. He recalled, "There were religious and social barriers in place that made it difficult for me to relate to my peers, and when you put all that alongside being perceived as gay, there was no mechanism to address my feelings." Josh sought relief by pretending to be sick, a not-uncommon tactic used by victims of bullying. Sometimes it wasn't just pretending. The stress and anxiety created psychosomatic symptoms.[6] "As a student, I had headaches all the time. I faked being sick a lot to stay home. I could miss a whole week of school in junior high because I didn't want to deal with the bullying."

When Josh started high school, the pain of being perceived as gay eased, because he found more activities on which to focus his attention. "Junior high was the worst," he told me quietly. "By the time I got to high school, there were more ways for me to be engaged socially with my peers, and it was much easier to seek out people I wanted to be with. The independence of being able to drive made a huge difference—I could drive to a friend's house, and we could study together." Josh found a place for himself and was better able to ignore the people who didn't have a place for him. The bullying didn't hurt as much because he had other more meaningful things to do, and finding a few good friends made it easier to deal with the people who weren't his friends. Although the struggle with bullying became easier, "the struggle with being gay did not."

Josh's parents refused to even entertain the possibility that their son was gay. It would reflect too poorly on them as evangelical Christians. "My parents believed you can teach your boys not to be gay, and so they didn't want to talk about my being gay, because it felt like a failure on their part that they didn't prevent it." The James Dobson mentality has been increasingly nudged aside, as the world's scientific community learns more about homosexuality, and by 1980 homosexuality was no longer included as a behavioral disorder in the *Diagnostic and Statistical Manual* of the American Psychiatric Association. Harvard University faculty member William Pollack, in his bestselling book *Real Boys*, addresses the fact that homosexuality is now regarded as constitutional: "Today, even the most conservative psychoanalysts are beginning to accept that homosexuality is a normal part of human life and that being gay is not something that mental health professionals should attempt to change (or that they *can* change)."[7] Despite the increased understanding of homosexuality, Josh's parents, like many evangelical Christians, do not view homosexuality as a normal variation of human sexuality. While Josh remained in the fold of the Nazarenes, he was psychologically unable to come out as a gay person.

Josh left home after high school to attend a Nazarene college, which was what Nazarene children were expected to do. "In a weird way, my status as a Nazarene protected me from antigay bullying. Everyone socially and religiously was in the same place of denial about homosexuality. My peers would never conceive that another faithful Nazarene student was gay, because being gay was perceived as something horrible and ungodly." By the time Josh was able to acknowledge his sexual orientation, he was in his late twenties. His parents did not easily handle the news that Josh was gay, but with time, they came to accept his partner, Greg. "I don't know how they reconcile their faith with my being gay, but they do admit to their friends that I am gay."

Greg was also bullied for being gay. He worked an outside job all through high school—at least twenty hours a week—to avoid thinking about his bullying. By filling up all his time with school, choir, and work, Greg was able to pass the time during his agonizing adolescence. Greg and Josh met as adults and fell in love. Each man brought his own inner strength to the relationship, and together they were able to heal sufficiently from earlier psychological trauma to build a healthy life together. They adopted a baby boy named Carson, and Josh's parents have come to view Greg as a son-in-law and Carson as a grandson. Josh remarked that he and Greg had a relatively easy time adopting together. "Gay adoption in Illinois is based on court precedent. Because a nonmarried couple can adopt a child in Illinois, the court eventually ruled that this includes nonmarried gay couples, and so we were able to adopt. We went through an adoption agency that intentionally includes gay families."

Josh and Greg have not yet come up with a strategy for how to help Carson manage taunts he might receive about having two gay dads. There have been several incidents where a religious person has harassed them about their unusual family, and Josh and Greg reacted with anger. "We need a plan. The challenge for me will be not being too judgmental of those who perceive our family as different," Josh admitted.

Josh and Greg were able to survive their childhoods as gay boys, and it will never be as difficult again as it was when they were young.

For school boys, the stigma attached with being perceived as gay is so painful that it has spilled over into the way boys navigate their friendships, regardless of whether or not they are actually gay. Niobe Way, author of *Deep Secrets: Boys' Friendships and the Crisis of Connection,* conducted hundreds of interviews with black, Asian, Latino, and white boys from early to late adolescence. She found that younger boys want and successfully build deep, intimate friendships with their male friends, but they gradually lose these close relationships and their trust in male peers as they become older teenagers. Homophobia plays no small role in the deterioration of these friendships. Niobe Way writes:

> *Homophobia, as the boys in all my studies tell us directly, is clearly one of the primary factors explaining the loss of friendships. Homophobic statements (e.g., no homo) are scattered throughout boys' interviews during late adolescence, whereas they are virtually absent in their first two years of interviews. Boys turned our questions about close male friendships by late adolescence into questions about their sexual orientation. "No homo" became a common phrase following statements of how they felt about their closest male friends. According to Urban Dictionary, "no homo" is a "slang phrase used after one inadvertently says something that sounds gay."*[8]

Homophobic bullying inhibits all boys' abilities to connect with one another in deep, meaningful ways, and they suffer terribly as a result. Boys feel as if they can no longer trust their closest friends, and they cease to talk about their feelings and emotions. They become lonely and isolated, not because they lack social and emotional skills, but because society discourages them from accessing and using these skills. Boys are afraid of being labeled "gay" and thus subscribe to extreme gender stereotypes, which is part of their attraction to ultramasculine music and media.

The fact that most boys live in terror of being labeled "homosexual" is deeply damaging to the boys who actually are homosexual. How wrenchingly difficult it must be to acknowledge—much less embrace—your homosexuality when everyone around you considers being perceived as gay as a fate worse than any other. Much of our culture is screaming at these frightened children that they are abhorrent, worthless, godless, and deserving of torment and bullying. This societal view stifles parents' ability to support their homosexual children as they go through the angst-filled process of coming out, which compounds their sense of isolation immeasurably. At a time when children most need the reassurance and affirmation of their parents, they are denied this support because their parents are frequently struggling with their own fears of stigma, shame, and embarrassment about having a homosexual child. It is in this lonely context that some children view suicide as their only option. Dan Savage, coauthor of *It Gets Better: Coming Out, Overcoming Bullying, and Creating a Life Worth Living,* reports: "Nine out of ten LGBT students report experiencing bullying in their schools; LGBT teenagers are four to seven times likelier to attempt suicide. LGBT children who are rejected by their families are eight times likelier to attempt suicide and at much higher risk of winding up homeless and living on the streets."[9]

Parents, and fathers in particular, who have been influenced by the cultural importance placed on masculinity often begin reinforcing the "no homo" mentality when their baby boys are still in diapers. A dad named Jerry told me, "My two-year-old son, Christopher, was playing in the house and asked, 'Where's my purse?' and I immediately corrected him and said, 'You carry a backpack, not a purse.' Christopher has three older sisters and loves to play with their girlie stuff. Every chance I get, I try to teach him that boys don't do that."

It would be easy if we could just write Jerry off as a stereotypical homophobe, but it is not that simple. In observing Jerry playing with Christopher at the park, I could see that Jerry is a loving dad who is very affectionate and doting. He genuinely thinks it is in Christopher's best interest to be a masculine boy. "I don't want other kids picking on him for being girlie. That would just break my heart," Jerry said earnestly. Jerry's attitudes point to the complexity of the problem behind antigay bullying. The cultural nuances run so deep that even people who do not consider themselves antigay make decisions that feed into gender-based stereotypes and homophobia. Another man at the park, Kyle, became interested in our conversation and admitted to me, "I watch my three-year-old grandson, Rashawn, and when he comes crying to me that someone pushed him down, I don't pick him up and baby him. The other boys will think he's a sissy, you know, and so even though I want to hold him, I give him a pat on the back and say, go on, you're a big boy, don't cry."

Jerry and Kyle are promulgating the Boy Code, a cultural message about which William Pollack writes extensively in *Real Boys*. Pollack explains how the Boy Code demands that boys must live according to stereotyped male ideals: Boys should not show weakness by crying in pain, grieving openly or complaining; boys should be daring and risky and attracted to violence; boys should "avoid shame at all costs" and "wear the mask of coolness"; and boys should not display any "sissy stuff," such as emotions and feelings, particularly of empathy and dependence.[10] Boys who break the Boy Code are roundly punished by their peers, and to a lesser extent, by their parents and teachers. A violation of the code immediately opens a boy to taunts about being gay, as does any other action that might be perceived as feminine. As boys enter early adolescence, the Boy Code is more rigidly enforced than ever before, because, as Dan Kindlon and Michael Thompson report in their groundbreaking book *Raising Cain: Protecting the Emotional Life of Boys*,

> *Eleven-, twelve-, and thirteen-year-old boys fear homosexuality, literally, like the plague. They don't understand where it comes from, which makes it all the more frightening, but they do know it's not a 'cool' thing to be. Homosexuals are male, but they aren't manly. The amount of teasing that goes on among early adolescent boys about possible homosexual leanings is staggering. 'Gay' or 'fag' is a constant taunt, whether a boy's 'crime' is his hairstyle, his accent, his clothes, a good grade, or a bad pitch. Repetition does nothing to lessen its power to hurt. The taunt is searing because a boy's fear of homosexuality runs that deep.*[11]

It is understandable that early adolescent boys do not understand where homosexuality comes from, because educated professionals still argue about its genesis, although most people have come to accept the fact that being gay is how someone is born. Knowing why a child is homosexual is the single biggest factor determining a parent's response. Bedford Hope, the pen name of the author of the well-known blog *Accepting Dad,* spoke with me about the two main theories guiding therapists' approaches to gender nonconformity.[12] "There are two different therapeutic models: the fixers and the acceptors. The fixers have these weird psychogenic theories based on Freud about what caused this, and then they devise weird theories about how to fix it, and the acceptors are the supportive professionals who say these kids were born this way, and these kids need support and help because society doesn't accept them and our goal is to advocate for them, keep them safe, but allow them to express themselves. The paradox is keeping them safe and allowing them to express themselves."

Hope commented that it is especially terrible when one parent believes in acceptance and the other believes in fixing. Fixing doesn't really work on the person's inner feelings, he observed, and it is amazing how many people start off trying to use therapy to normalize their kids and then come over to the side of acceptance. Furthermore, Hope added, "the implications for bullying are critical: whatever damage the peers do to these kids with bullying seems to be less than the long-term damage done by having a completely false existence, by pretending to be heterosexual."

Hope's son, Oscar, first began acting in feminine ways when he was a toddler, and the family sought out counseling and therapy to help them with their response to the boy. After joining support groups and doing research, Bedford accepted that Oscar's gender nonconformity was an unchangeable part of who the boy is, and he and his family decided that the best course for all of them was to be accepting. Oscar, who is now twelve, continues to present in an ultra-feminine way. Bedford told me, "The fact is that many—not all, of course—but many of the boys who are very feminine do eventually come out as gay, and so it is better for their families to accept them and accept that possibility when they are young instead of trying to fix them."

It is important to note the difference between children who are bullied because they are *perceived* as gay and children who are bullied because they have *actually come out* as gay. Communities are gradually becoming more accepting, and there are some pockets of the country where gay children can come out and feel supported, but the harsh reality is that many regions of the country still respond with open hostility when children come out. These children are bullied, not just by their peers, but sometimes even by their teachers and families, because our country has come to equate being gay with being weaker. Children taunt one another for acting "gay" when they show emotion, sending the message that a more expressive boy is a weaker boy. Gay children would be bullied less if we could do away with the association between gay and weak. To do so requires a change in the way we label behavior and relationships.

In *Deep Secrets*, Way advises:

> If we were to value a full range of relationships—a biodiversity of sorts—where cognition and emotion were understood to be deeply integrated, as neuroscientists have proven, and where being emotionally literate and invested in relationships were not a "girl thing" or "a childish thing" or a "gay thing" but an inherent and fundamental part of being human; if we could enter into the thick of it instead of staying on the surface, these changes would lead to better psychological and physical health, less bullying, higher rates of graduation, more school engagement, better marriages, better friendships, increased satisfaction at work, longer lives, and a healthier society more generally.[13]

How do we make these changes? It starts in the earliest phases of life. When boys are babies and toddlers, it does not make them weak if they want their mothers. The attachment can be encouraged and nurtured. Preschool boys who cry when they are upset need not be denigrated as "sissies." As children grow older, their interests may diverge from gender-typical areas. School-age boys who love musical theater do not require football practice in order to "cure" them of their "gay" interests. Making these cultural changes will ease the next generation's rigid adherence to the Boy Code. When we as a society address the deep-rooted social norms that contribute to gender stereotypes, we will also see a drop in antigay bullying.

Although gay boys are more often portrayed in the media as victims of homophobic taunting, many lesbians, bisexuals, and transgender students are also brutally victimized. Naomi, who is currently in college, was in seventh grade when she first experienced bullying about her sexual orientation. She remembers how during an out-of-state cheerleading competition, "my roommates fought over who would have to sleep in the bed with me. I ended up sleeping on the floor because one girl remarked 'She is a lesbian; I don't want her touching me in my sleep.'" Naomi didn't know what the word "lesbian" meant, and so she asked her mom when she returned home. "My mom told me it was a sin and that only sick people liked people of the same sex. She said she would disown me if she ever found out that I harbor same-sex tendencies. When I realized that the attraction I had to females was because I was bisexual, I cried for hours. Of course, I didn't feel safe 'coming out.' I fell into a deep depression. I was too scared to ask for help."

Naomi responded to the taunts and bullying by developing anorexia nervosa, an eating disorder characterized by dramatic weight loss, self-starvation, and a terror of gaining weight. In addition to becoming anorexic, Naomi turned to cutting as a release for the pain. "My sister walked in on me cutting one day," she said, "and I broke down and told her everything. After that, I had a few cousins come out to me, and I came out to them. We set up our own support system; we were all afraid to tell our parents. My mom is a severe homophobe, and my father is an alcoholic with a tendency to become very demeaning and verbally abusive." Naomi has managed to survive through the ongoing support of her sister and cousins. Throughout middle and high school, she hid her bisexuality from her parents, and she never reported any bullying to her teachers because she was afraid it would get back to her mom and dad. "As a bisexual, it is easier to hide, but when you hide, you lose a part of yourself," she confided.

One day, Naomi was talking with one of her college professors, and she sarcastically referred to herself as "a big fat dyke," which was a slur kids often called her in high school. "And," she remembered, "I began to cry. I did my best to suppress the memories of being bullied, and it just came out of my mouth. Anyway, I then told her everything from the bullying to my home situation. She then told me she is bisexual and she remembers how hard it was when she was my age. It is nice to know that I'm not alone." Since Naomi is still living at home while she attends college, she continues to hide who she really is from her parents. "But, when I have a house of my own, I will tell my parents everything," she has decided.

Historically, when GLBT students have reported incidents of bullying to schools, little has been done to protect them. But this situation is slowly improving as some schools become more aware of the issues. Olivia, a student who was bullied for being a lesbian, kept asking for help until someone actually listened to her, and it made all the difference in her life. Olivia's bullying began after she confidentially told a friend that she had feelings for other girls, and the girl revealed her secret to the "popular girls," who then spread the news throughout the school. Olivia explained how her physical-education class was particularly painful.[14] "Every day when I walked into the change room, the looks came, and slowly people started calling me things like freak and dyke. I told my teachers, but they didn't do anything." One night, Olivia called Kids Help Phone (which is a place kids can call when they need someone to talk to in Canada, where she lives) and asked them what to do. "All they said was that they had heard worse stories and didn't really give me advice," she said.

The next day, Olivia reached a breaking point and began screaming at the girl who had first outed her. Right after that incident, Olivia again reached out for help by going to the school guidance counselor. "I told her everything, and she was so supportive! I was in complete shock at her response, because up until then, all the teachers I had previously confided in didn't have anything to say." The guidance counselor asked Olivia what she thought would help. "We sat there together through period one discussing options, and I decided that I had to get to the root of the problem: my phys. ed class. That class was in period two, so when we finished talking, she told me to go to the change room and she'd meet me there." Once everyone was in the locker room, the guidance counselor told everyone to listen to Olivia. And Olivia spoke out for the first time. "I spilled my heart out to that class, in hopes they would stop. I was almost in tears when I had finished. And so was the rest of the class. One girl (a girl I actually really liked) was bawling her eyes out because she had been bullied as well for being "overweight" a couple of years before that, and everything I had said was what she was feeling."

The girls in the class hugged Olivia, and her phys. ed teacher offered complete support, promising an open door in case Olivia ever needed to talk. When Olivia subsequently came out to her family, they were not supportive, but the positive outcome at school was enough to carry her through. To other kids in her situation, she advises that "the best thing to do is talk it through with someone you trust. Tell them how you feel, and work together to find solutions to the problem. Keep in mind it doesn't have to be a counselor, or even a friend. It could be a neighbor, or someone else in the community. You always need to remember that if people are criticizing you for being who you are, then they're wrong, no matter what their social status or even if they're your friends."

When working with schools or communities to combat antigay sentiment, it helps to look beyond the surface. There can even be cultural considerations when it comes to homophobia, such as shared historical experiences. Kesha Burch-Sims, a Chicago-based psychologist who treats many victims of bullying, has a large percentage of African American clients in her practice, and she spoke with me about the unique challenges that gay black children face.[15] "Research shows that black parents try to help their kids get along in the mainstream, because they don't want their kids to stick out more. Black parenting is stereotypically harsh about being different, because black parents fear that their kids will become targets for the police. As a result, there has been a behavior of not promoting anything that would further stigmatize an African American child, and being gay, lesbian, or transgender would definitely stigmatize an African American child." As a result, the black community can be less supportive of gay children.

Burch-Sims then explained how this cultural aversion to being different affects outspoken gay and lesbian black people in adulthood. "There is this feeling of love that happens in black churches—GLBT people who are black are loved and included, but when they get so confident that they start speaking publicly about being gay, sometimes people become uncomfortable again." By understanding some of the reasons behind the black community's reluctance to support openly gay members, our society can do a better job of helping African American GLBT people find acceptance. Cheryl Kilodavis, who wrote *My Princess Boy* about her young African American son, is an example of the shift to acceptance among black parents. The fact that her son, Dyson, is celebrated as a tiara-wearing black boy helps break down stereotypes on multiple levels. "I had to travel my own path of acceptance, when Dyson wanted to wear a dress," Kilodavis admitted. "It took time for me to see that this was what made him happy. But now I want to help other parents find acceptance."[16]

Chapter Nine

Victims of Cyberbullying, Sexting, and Sexual Harassment

In today's society, children can be bullied twenty-four hours a day. There is no safe house, because the Internet has created a way for us to be connected at all times. This can be a wonderful thing, but it can also be severely damaging. Fifty years ago, bullied schoolchildren could at least find a quiet place at home to recharge and prepare for the next day. Now, we have kids who may be shoved, pushed, and taunted at school, and then they come home to see vicious messages popping up on their computer and phone screens. The anonymity of online communication makes attackers even meaner. They write things that they would never say to someone's face. As a result, a victim is beaten up in every possible way.

Bullied children often experience a combination of physical, verbal, and cyberbullying. Anne Collier, codirector of www.connectsafely .org, told me, "Cyberbullying and bullying are enmeshed. You almost can't even separate them out. And we have learned that the kids most at risk online are the same ones most at risk offline. The same vulnerabilities lead to cyberbullying as to bullying."[1] To illustrate how bullying often progresses into cyberbullying, let us examine what happened with Meg, a young woman who is now in her twenties. Beginning in seventh grade, Meg suffered from the whole gamut of bullying behaviors.

When I asked Meg how it all started, she began speaking in a soft, earnest voice.[2] "I had been teased and taunted as a younger child, but it turned into harsh physical bullying in seventh grade. I had bruises from being slammed into lockers, and my favorite notebook was thrown in the toilet. The leader of the bullying was this boy named Jack." Meg and Jack had gone to school together since third grade, and he had a history of being nice and charming one minute and mean the next. He brought people presents, she reported, and he was very manipulative. He was not her boyfriend, but he singled her out. "In middle school, I was friends with a group of kids, and Jack was in the group." Meg paused and reconsidered. "Well, I thought they were my friends, but then they dropped me. And, honestly, I would have done anything Jack asked me to do to be back in the group. Whenever the other kids actually spoke to me, they told me I was worthless and I deserved what I was getting. And I believed them. I kept hearing whispers about a website about me, but I was afraid to look into it."

Meg was quiet for a moment, remembering. She took a deep breath and continued, speaking in a rush: "Then one day, a transformer at the school blew, and we had no power, so we were all sent outside. A group of us went behind some trees, and while I was back there, six kids grabbed me and held me down while Jack broke a large stick off a tree branch and stuck it into my arm. That incident was my breaking point. I got an awful cut and I realized how dangerous things had become, how badly I could have been hurt. I was like, I'm done. I'm done being bullied."

Meg had tried to manage the bullying on her own, often pretending to ignore it, but that did not help. "I had a social-studies teacher who, looking back on it now, I think he knew something was wrong. He saw me grow quiet, withdrawn." On the day that Jack cut her arm open with the stick, Meg went to her social studies teacher and told him what had just happened. Uncertain what to do, he sent her to the guidance counselor. "But because we had no electricity in the school," Meg explained, "the guidance counselor took me to a hallway in the middle of the eighth-grade wing, and that's where she asked me to tell her what had happened. All the eighth graders were able to hear me, and that's when my older brother found out what was going on. He was shocked because I had been totally hiding it."

"Meg," I wondered, "did anyone else see the six kids hold you down? Did anyone try to help you or go get a grown-up?"

"Yes, that incident was the turning point for a lot of people, not just for me. There were a bunch of kids standing around watching, and some of them got uncomfortable and said, 'Jack, let her go,' but he didn't." Many of those kids were very shaken up by what they saw, and the school received sixteen calls that night from parents whose kids went home and confided in them about what had happened to Meg. The parents were horrified. Even so, Meg said, the school had no anti-bullying policy at that time, and the principal had no idea what to do about the behavior. The school called Meg's parents and Jack's parents in for a meeting and merely told him to stop bullying her.

Meg's experience demonstrates how bullying harms more than just the targeted victim. The children who witnessed Meg's being attacked were also traumatized and sought help from their parents. It is common for bystanders to suffer anxiety as they wonder if they, too, will be targeted. As reported by Tracy Villaincourt et al. in *Bullying in North American Schools,* the need for humans to belong is so ingrained that a human's "ostracism detection system"[3] becomes activated even when a person witnesses another person being ostracized.[4] Nobody feels safe in the presence of exclusion and victimization.

For several weeks leading up to the incident with the stick, Meg had been hearing rumors about a mysterious website. At the meeting with Jack and his parents, her worst fears were confirmed. "Jack admitted that he had created a website he called *I Hate Meg.* He had gotten 150 kids to sign up, basically my entire seventh-grade class, and they would write terrible things about me. It was devastating. On Facebook, you can make any kind of group. Sometimes I still Google *I Hate Meg* to make sure there is nothing there. It will follow me for the rest of my life."

Meg's mom cried when she learned the full extent of her daughter's suffering. She could not believe how bad it had gotten, and Meg had done a thorough job of hiding what was happening at school. "As I got older, I have come to understand why I didn't tell my parents—I felt ashamed. I was embarrassed and didn't know how to tell my parents that 150 kids hated me. I don't even know what my parents could have done anyway. I think schools should have policies and procedures in place about bullying, because my school didn't know what to do—they only made Jack take down the website, but they never punished him. Not even lunch detention. I was angry that the teachers didn't do more," Meg confided. Meg was focused on the fact that Jack received no punitive response, but I also noted that the school took no restorative measures. They never had a social worker sit down with the kids who were involved to talk with them about the bullying. There was never a safe place where the kids could address their feelings, their fears, and Meg's pain. As a result, even after the website was removed, Meg was treated like a pariah. She was very lonely throughout seventh grade. In eighth grade, she became close to a group of seventh graders, and they are her dear friends today, even though she is now in college.

When Meg and her classmates moved on to the local high school, she continually encountered Jack. She spoke about how difficult it was to face her bully day in and day out. "None of the high school teachers knew about the bullying because it happened at middle school, and since no one was ever punished, it never ended up on a record." Jack and Meg were put in the same class in high school and had to sit together, which was very awkward for her. Once Meg was assigned to collaborate on an English project with Jack, and when she got up the courage to tell the teacher why she could not work with him, the teacher asked in disbelief, "Are you sure you have the right kid?" That was exactly why the bullying went on for so long in middle school, Meg observed, because Jack hid it well from the teachers. "He put up a great front," she said wistfully. "He volunteered; he was a good student; he worked hard. And then my English teacher asked, 'Why don't I already know about this? Why haven't the teachers at the high school been briefed about this?' That was a big issue in my middle school—there was no communication."

Meg's description of Jack did not surprise me. Some kids who act as bullies look the part, but there are plenty of others who have learned how to stay in the good graces of teachers and administrators. Strong athletes and accomplished students operate from a position of power, and they often look like angels to authority figures. Sometimes, teachers and coaches are even complicit in known bullying, because they don't want to get their star athlete suspended before a big game. This leaves the targeted victims feeling helpless and vulnerable because they know that the adults who are supposed to protect them will sell them out if it serves their own self-interest.

Interestingly new research by UC Davis sociology professors Robert Faris and Diane Felmlee shows that the kids at the very top of the popularity hierarchy are less likely to engage in bullying than the kids one notch down. The professors studied about four thousand middle and high school students in three North Carolina counties, requesting that the students each name their five closest friends, as well as five students they bullied and five students who bullied them. After mapping each student's popularity and comparing it to aggressive behavior, the researchers found that the kids in the second tier were the ones who had the most to gain from bullying. They wanted to be on top with the Queen Bees and Top Dogs, so they often resorted to malicious rumors, gossip, and aggression to climb their way up the social ladder. The kids at the very top and the very bottom were less aggressive.[5]

In Meg's case, Jack was a student who worked to amass power among his peers. Meg remembered how her situation improved when she entered high school, and a number of students apologized to her and told her that Jack had threatened them into signing up as members of the *I Hate Meg* website. "They told me that Jack had blackmailed them, and they went along with the website to keep him from turning on them. But I still felt like it was my fault, like I did something wrong to get 150 kids to hate me and talk about me online. One time I tried to talk to Jack about it. He brushed it off and said,

'I was just a kid' like it was no big deal. I don't talk to him about it anymore. Nobody deserves to go through that."

Meg fits into the profile of a student at high risk for bullying, which means, as Anne Collier mentioned, that she was also at high risk for cyberbullying. Meg acknowledged, "I'm different. I'm a heavy girl; I'm overweight. My dad's a professional magician, which other kids thought was weird. I never really had a group I could get into, and when I met Jack, I found a group for the first time. Jack did this to two more girls after me." Bravely, Meg risked Jack's anger and warned the other girls about his past. The other girls upon whom he preyed also fell into high-risk target categories. "There was one girl who was new in town. Like me, she was also a heavy girl, an awkward girl. Jack started to give her his attention, and she was thrilled. I told her right away to be careful when I saw what was happening. I told her that he would start calling her obsessively, which he did, and she got out while she still could."

Clearly, Jack had psychological problems, which needed to be addressed if he was ever to treat other people, especially women, with respect. Meg is now a college student, and she has found new self-confidence in her life on campus. She advocates widely for bullying prevention, alongside her father, who is very vocal about his daughter's experiences. Meg is moving forward, but the middle school years have not left her unscarred. "I find that I have problems connecting with kids my own age," she admitted to me, "and I still struggle with feeling that I somehow brought this on myself."

Anne Collier, who founded netfamilynews.org, wants to make sure that parents understand that cyberbullying is a continuation of existing aggressive adolescent behavior. She pointed out to me that the context for cyberbullying is school—not Facebook, not the Internet.[6] "The drama starts at school, and the kids bring it to the computer. Cyberbullying adds another layer of intensity because of the instant mass distribution and the unknown audiences. When you add these components to the inhibition, it can compound the pain and hurt of cyberbullying. But it's not accurate to say that cyberbullying as a concept is an epidemic or new. It is a factor that affects the bullying equation, but the equation itself is unchanged."

Although the behaviors behind cyberbullying are ancient, the technical act of cyberbullying is a relatively new phenomenon, and, therefore, the field of research around it is quite recent. Sheri Bauman, associate professor and director of the school-counseling master's-degree program at the University of Arizona, spoke with me about the complicating factors surrounding cyberbullying research.[7] Bauman, who authored *Cyberbullying: What Counselors Need to Know*, explained,

> *There are three aspects of cyberbullying that affect what we know:*
>
> 1. *There is not a universally agreed definition of cyberbullying. Different studies and different outcomes may reflect a difference in definitions.*
> 2. *There is not a standard definition of measures for cyberbullying. Some surveys say, 'Have you been cyberbullied?' which relies on the respondent's understanding of terms. Other surveys provide an inventory that relies on behaviors, and the sum of your responses classifies you as a bully or a victim.*
> 3. *There is not consistent methodology. We use questionnaires, self-report, and so forth. Self-report data are very useful, but then we are relying on only one source and his or her bias.*
>
> *So, what this means is that we base a lot of theories and recommendations on imperfect measures.*

When I recounted Meg's story to Bauman, she was not surprised that the school did not take any decisive actions other than having Jack take down the website. She commented, "It gets very tricky with cyberbullying. It frequently happens or originates off campus, and then schools like to wash their hands of it. Some principals do not want to know if cyberbullying is happening at their schools, because then they have to deal with it, and they don't know how."

There are some simple questions that school administrators can ask to ascertain if they need to get involved in off-campus bullying situations. Justin Patchin, coeditor of *Cyberbullying Prevention and Response: Expert Perspectives,* shared his thoughts with me.[8] "Schools do have the ability to intervene with behavior away from school if that behavior disrupts the learning environment at school. Does what's happening interfere with the ability of students to learn? And if so, you must do something." This is the standard that Eric Witherspoon, superintendent of District 202, successfully applied when confronted with a mass cyberbullying situation at Evanston Township High School in 2010. I met with Witherspoon to learn more about the situation and the school's response.[9]

"On a Monday morning," he explained, "a number of girls came into school very upset about a Facebook page called the Evanston Rats that had been created over the weekend. This was a resurrection of something that had happened in the school a long time ago. Back in those days, it was a Xeroxed piece of paper that would be handed out underground and was called Evanston Rats because it was about ratting on girls who were promiscuous." For many years, the Evanston Rats had disappeared.

Now the list was back, but this time the distribution channel was digital. During the course of the weekend in which the page had been launched, over one hundred students had already posted mean, cruel comments about other students, and hundreds more had visited the site just for the purpose of reading the comments. Some of the targeted girls came into school crying and traumatized that Monday morning, and they reported what was happening to the school safety officers.

"It was brought to my attention almost immediately," Witherspoon recalled, "and we recognized the seriousness of the problem. The first thing we did was launch our own investigation. We had people gain access to Facebook [the school blocks Facebook] in order to check it out and see what was going on."

It only took minutes for school officials to verify that there was indeed a cyberbullying Facebook page called Evanston Rats. "I could see it was clearly disrupting the learning environment at school, as we had students in tears and other students threatening one another over things that had been written, and I knew that it was due to this disruption that I had the authority to intervene and take action," Witherspoon told me seriously. The webpage was already going viral among the students, no small incident at a school with several thousand attendees. Within an hour or two of learning about the problem, Witherspoon called the Evanston police to report the situation and ask for their assistance. It is remarkable to note how quickly he mobilized the school and the community, rather than letting the situation fester for days or weeks as he deliberated about whether or not to take action.

As the police began investigating the case, the school also contacted Facebook to report the situation, although Facebook ultimately refused to reveal the identification of the student who had originated the page. Witherspoon, who is well known and connected with the students at school, decided to capitalize on his relationship with the kids and make a direct appeal to them. He rarely uses the public-address system, but on that Monday, he prepared a statement to read to the student body during the midmorning announcements. In part, his remarks included the following text:[10]

> *Good morning. This is Dr. Witherspoon. I must talk with you this morning about a very, very serious matter. A Facebook site called Evanston Rats is causing embarrassment, humiliation, and harm to many people. Sadly, many of our students have already signed on as fans to contribute to the site or to read the malicious things being said.*
>
> *Today I am urging you to immediately stop any and all participation in the site or any similar sites. Your actions are hurting other people. Bullying at ETHS, including cyberbullying, is a serious violation of school rules and can result in serious consequences; students can be suspended for up to ten days and/or expelled and removed from extracurricular activities, including prom and graduation.*
>
> *Moreover, cyberbullying can be against the law. Evanston Rats is now a police matter, and the police can subpoena the IP*

*address of the accounts of those who have visited the site.
People could be prosecuted.*

*But most important, every student at ETHS needs to reflect
today, right now, on the kind of human you will be. We need
to be here to build a safe and respectful community to protect
one another. Strive to do good things. Strive to be kind and caring. Strive to never do harm to other human beings. Your character defines you. Your life will be what you make of it.*

*If you feel you are a victim of this cyberbullying, counsel-
ors and social workers are available right now to assist you. If
you have any illegal activity to report, deans are available right
now to take down information. Let's make sure nobody else is
hurt.*

Witherspoon admitted that it was a risk to openly address the
situation, knowing that curiosity might spur even more kids to visit
the site. "But it had already snowballed; it was already going viral,
and I believed that there was nothing to lose," he decided. By the late
afternoon, posts had been taken down from the site, and by that
evening, the site was taken down. It is unclear whether the person
who created the site is the one who took it down or if Facebook's
administrators removed it. But one thing was certain—the message
about how serious the situation was reached the right ears. Fear of
accountability put an end to the Evanston Rats.

And then something amazing happened, something that Witherspoon and the school officials could never have predicted. Two senior
boys, Paul Pint and Joey Fisher, created a new Facebook page called
the Evanston Mice, and the whole purpose of the page was to go and
write something nice about other students. Fisher, who is now a college student, told me, "We wanted to make everyone feel better and
do something positive for the school." With pride and warmth, the
student body participated in an unprecedented act of restoration.
Witherspoon marveled, "There were over four hundred posts in a matter of days. Like the Evanston Rats, it was not done on school time
or school computers. It was something the students did organically.
Students stepped forward to say, this is not who we are, and this does

not represent what our school is about. We saw student leadership, students rising to the occasion to turn a negative situation into a positive one. They turned it into a teachable moment. It was an incredible thing to witness."

Most important, the school intervened before any of the victims of the attack became overwhelmingly depressed. Rather than the case's resulting in tragedy, it was ultimately affirming for the girls involved, because their classmates responded so positively to the intervention. School administrators set the right tone, and students rose to the challenge, yielding a happy outcome in an ugly situation. Two years later, the Evanston Mice page is still active.

When cyberbullying spills over into the school environment, it is extremely difficult for targeted students to learn. If the school does not take sufficient action, students often ask to switch schools or to be homeschooled. This was what happened after the famous YouTube video release of thirteen-year-old Rebecca Black singing her debut song, "Friday." The music video, which went viral in March 2011, inspired an outpouring of overwhelmingly negative comments about Black. Viewers attacked her voice, her body, her appearance, and her talent level. "The meanest thing I read was, 'I hope you cut yourself and I hope you get an eating disorder so you'll look pretty,'" Black said in an interview with ABC News's Andrea Canning.[11] The comments on the YouTube video were disabled in May 2011. By June 2011, the video had received over 167 million views, and Black had it removed from YouTube due to copyright claims. In August 2011, Black told ABC's *Nightline* that she had dropped out of school because the cyberbullying had turned into merciless taunting in the halls at schools.[12] Her mom is now homeschooling her. According to the standards set out by Patchin, Black's school was responsible for protecting her learning environment at school, but that did not happen.

Sexting and Sexual Cyberbullying

For numerous victims of cyberbullying, the attacks take on a blatantly sexual nature. There is a fuzzy line between sexual harassment and many types of bullying, which makes it difficult to know how best to respond. For children who have been the targets of sexting or sexually based attacks, it is increasingly difficult to regain control over cyberbullying situations, and due to the sexual aspect, the repercussions can continue long after the initial wave of bullying activity has passed. Carla, the teenage victim of a sexual online attack, talked with me about what happened to her.[13]

"When I was still seeing my ex-girlfriend, Stephanie, I texted her pictures of me in my underwear, and she also took pictures of me undressed." Six months later, Stephanie's younger sister, Jill, who is actually the same age as Carla, found the pictures. By that time, Stephanie was twenty and no longer in high school, and she was dating someone else. Carla explained that "Jill was upset to find out her sister was a lesbian, and she took it out on me." Jill and Carla were both sixteen and attended the same high school. Jill uploaded the pictures of Carla to MySpace and wrote slanderous things about her. Carla said ruefully, "She got her gay stereotypes mixed up and wrote how much I liked anal sex. It was monumentally unfair."

It took only a few days before Carla's life fell apart. Jill alerted people to look at the photos, and word spread rapidly. Kids began calling Carla names like "dyke" and "slut" and "fag lover." Someone slashed her car tires. A group of boys in Carla's weight-lifting class harassed her, repeatedly saying how "hot" they thought it was that she liked anal sex. She soon became too uncomfortable to wear her workout clothes in class. "I was afraid to take off my hoodie sweatshirt around the guys," she admitted. Carla called Stephanie to tell her what was going on, and Stephanie ended up coming out to her family about the fact that she was a lesbian. Jill did take the pictures down after about a week, but the damage was done. Carla did not feel able to talk to her family about what had really happened, so she lied about why she was no longer spending time with other kids. The repercussions of the incident spread far beyond Carla's social life.

Previously a star player who had started during every game on her high school softball team, Carla was suddenly and inexplicably benched for the rest of the season, after the coach heard about the pictures. She confronted the coach, and he pretended not to know what she was talking about, so she quit the team, taped her own ankle before going home, and told her parents she had stopped playing because she was injured. Carla turned to alcohol to deal with her pain. "After my parents went to bed, I would drink," she admitted. "My dad is a pretty heavy drinker, so he keeps a large stash. I was able to dip into it without his noticing."

Eventually, Carla's AP chemistry teacher, who was very religious and conservative, learned that Carla was a lesbian. The teacher (who had a daughter in the same grade) wrote a lengthy letter to the district, accusing Carla of being a serious disruption to the learning environment of the class. The teacher claimed that Carla committed "lewd and lascivious acts" and called for her immediate expulsion. "The principal received the letter," Carla remembered, "and he was sympathetic toward me. He didn't even touch the issue of the discrimination because he was uncomfortable about the issues, but he was a decent person who was trying to help me figure out how to graduate and get out of there. He told me that if I could just take the SATs and the California exit exam, I could basically graduate as a sophomore. So that's what I did." Carla forged her parents' signatures on the documents and told them the school was letting her graduate early because she was so advanced. What started as a few sexual photos on MySpace ultimately ended her high school career at the age of sixteen.

Despite it all, Carla is a resilient person. She never made plans to take her own life, even when her whole life was crumbling. "I told myself that the other kids were being juvenile and didn't want to face their own problems, and I became an easy target," she explained. Carla's ability to cognitively redefine the situation was critical to keeping her from sinking into suicidal despair. She was able to recognize that the problem was with other people, not with her, and this is one of the most important things to teach bullying victims. "Also, even though my parents never acknowledged outright what was happening, I think they knew on some level. My mom told me that she was aware I was having a rough time, that I would get through it, and that one day I would go far away and start over. I felt a sense of support from my parents, and it really helped," Carla told me. This demonstrates that even parents who are unable to explicitly talk about uncomfortable issues with their kids can still help them by continuing to show love and support as much as possible during tough times. Carla's parents did not specifically endorse her lifestyle, but they did not reject her, either. Carla is currently making plans to attend college in a different city.

Carla managed to look ahead to a time when things would get better. For some people, the rapid-fire contagion of a juicy YouTube video or sexual text message can obliterate the target's sense of hope at ever regaining normalcy, which is when the risk of suicide is greatest. This was the agonizing case in September 2010, when Rutgers University freshman Tyler Clementi committed suicide after his roommate posted a video online of Tyler engaging in a gay sexual encounter.[14] As a result of this highly publicized tragedy, New Jersey Senator Frank Lautenberg introduced new legislation to require colleges to adopt a code of conduct that prohibits bullying and harassment. On September 1, 2011, New Jersey's Anti-Bullying Bill of Rights took effect, the toughest law against bullying in the nation. It requires every school to designate an anti-bullying specialist to investigate complaints; each district must, in turn, have an anti-bullying coordinator; and the State Education Department will evaluate every effort, posting grades on its website. Superintendents said that educators who failed to comply could lose their licenses.

For further recommendations on what to do if your child is the victim of a cyberbullying attack, see chapter 12.

Cyberbullying Is Often a Two-Way Attack

Anne Collier, who served as cochair of the Obama administration's Online Safety and Technology Working Group, told me how most parents immediately think of dangerous predators when they imagine someone looking at naked pictures of their children on the Internet. "But the reality is," she explained, "that kids are far more likely to be harmed by their peers or by the consequences of their own online behavior than by adult criminals. And we have also seen that what goes around comes around, at least when it comes to being mean online. We found that kids who engage in aggressive behavior online are more than twice as likely to be on the receiving end of online victimization."[15] This means that many of our children are not just innocent sitting ducks, waiting to be cyberbullied.

The roles of bully and victim are never more fluid than in an online environment, where vicious comments, barbs, and embarrassing information can trade hands at the click of a mouse, often hidden behind a cloak of anonymity. Collier advised, "When a child reports that she has been attacked online, that is one snapshot of information. Before parents get up in arms and demand consequences, it is important to look at the bigger picture and the history of the online situation, because often we see kids who have been engaging in online attacks prior to reporting their own victimization." The real takeaway here is that our kids can protect themselves by being good digital citizens. It's the old "do unto others as you would have them do unto you."

When the Bullying Is Actually Sexual Harassment

Many of the behaviors that comprise sexual bullying are actually sexual harassment, which is illegal in the United States. The federal law that prohibits sexual harassment in schools is Title IX of the Education Amendments of 1972, which prohibits any person, on the basis of sex, to be subjected to discrimination in an educational program or activity receiving federal financial assistance. Under Title IX, a school is required to have and distribute a policy against sex discrimination, particularly one that addresses sexual harassment. According to the Equal Rights Advocates, sexual harassment is defined as[16]

> *Requests for sexual favors or unwelcome sexual behavior that is bad enough or happens often enough to make you feel uncomfortable, scared or confused and that interferes with your school-*

work or your ability to participate in extracurricular activities or attend classes. Sexual harassment can be verbal (comments about your body, spreading sexual rumors, sexual remarks or accusations, dirty jokes or stories), physical (grabbing, rubbing, flashing or mooning, touching, pinching in a sexual way, sexual assault) or visual (display of naked pictures or sex-related objects, obscene gestures). Sexual harassment can happen to girls and boys. Sexual harassers can be fellow students, teachers, principals, janitors, coaches, and other school officials.

We can easily find concrete examples of sexual harassment in some of our aforementioned case studies. Eric Witherspoon described the Evanston Rats situation as cyberbullying and also as sexual harassment, because people were using the webpage to spread sexual rumors and make sexual accusations about specific girls. Knowing the school had a duty to protect its students under Title IX factored into Witherspoon's decision to take immediate action when he learned about the webpage. Another example of sexual harassment is what happened to Carla in her weight-lifting class, when the boys heckled her about anal sex and created an environment in which she felt unsafe. Had Carla made a formal complaint to the school, the principal would have been required to address the situation under Title IX.

If your child has been sexually harassed, there are steps he or she can take:

1. It is important to reassure your child that he or she is not to blame, even if there was initially mutual flirting. The person who is doing the harassing is responsible for the inappropriate actions.
2. Encourage your child to clearly refuse the harassment with a firm no. If the unwanted behavior persists, have your child record each occurrence, writing down the date, time, and description of the event. If, at any point, your child needs medical care or counseling as a result of the harassment, seek immediate professional assistance.

3. Then you and your child *must report the harassment to a
   school official,* because the law only requires that schools take
   action to end harassment if a school official knows what has
   been happening. The school's Title IX officer should help you
   obtain relief under the school's Title IX Grievances Policy.
4. If the school is unsuccessful at stopping the harassment, you
   can file a complaint against the school with the U.S. Department of Education's Office of Civil Rights (OCR). Their toll-
   free hotline is 800-421-3481. In most states, you must file a
   complaint with the OCR within 180 days of an act of discrimination.
5. If the harassment still persists, you can file a lawsuit against
   the school, and keep in mind that it is illegal for others to retaliate against a person who has taken action under Title IX.
   Should a person or a group of people try to take revenge on
   your child for reporting sexual harassment—sadly, a not unlikely outcome—you can contact the police.

When your child comments that he or she is being bullied, it is
important to examine the situation to see if it includes sexual harassment. "Bullied" is a popular catchphrase, and it covers a vast array of
behaviors. The more specific your child can be, the better chance you
have of helping him or her find sufficient relief and protection. Please
see appendix C for sample surveys that researchers have used to assess how much sexual aggression is taking place in a school. These
surveys can help your child assess if he or she is acting as an aggressor or is being victimized.

Chapter Ten

The Harmful Effects of Bullying on the Brain

Bullying that takes place in school can impact a child for life. Humans are social beings, and we are hardwired to belong to a group.[1] When children are bullied, some tend to internalize these experiences, blaming themselves for the victimization and expecting the poor treatment to continue.[2] Because of the psychological effects reported by victims, Barbara Coloroso, anti-bullying author and expert, has actually expanded her definition of bullying to include a fourth element: terror. In severe and persistent bullying, she writes, "Terror is created, and the bully can act without fear or recrimination of retaliation. The bullied child is rendered so powerless that he is unlikely to fight back or tell anyone about the bullying. The bully counts on bystanders becoming involved in participating or supporting the bullying or at least doing nothing to stop it. Thus the cycle of violence begins."[3]

As we have already seen, there are children who choose to take their own lives in the face of severe bullying, and their parents are taking legal action against schools and bullies as a result. Neil Marr and Tim Field introduced the term "bullycide" in their book *Bullycide: Death at Playtime*. Here are a few tragic deaths that have been attributed to bullycide:

- **Amanda Cummings**, 15, *died in January 2012*
  Cummings, a sophomore at New Dorp High School, killed herself by stepping in front of a bus after years of being bullied by classmates. During the six days that the teen lingered before dying, bullies continued to post hateful comments to her Facebook page (such as "LMFAO* she stepped in front of a bus"), and after her death, users posted vicious, mocking comments on multiple Facebook pages about her.[4] *

- **Ashlynn Connor**, 10, *died in November 2011*
  Connor, a student at Ridge Farm Elementary School, killed herself after being taunted for three years by kids at school and in the neighborhood. Kids would call her "fat, ugly, and a slut," and the little girl asked her mom on a Thursday if she could be homeschooled to escape the torment. Her mom promised they would talk to the principal the following Monday, but on Friday night, the child took her own life.[5]

- **Jamey Rodemeyer**, 14, *died in September 2011*
  Rodemeyer, a student at Williamsville North High School, killed himself after being taunted for twelve months by cyberbullies who made cruel comments with antigay slurs on his Formspring account, a website that allows anonymous posts. Rodemeyer had uploaded a supportive message to other gay kids on the It Gets Better Project website not long before he was overcome with despair.[6]

- **Eric Mohat**, 17, *died in March 2007*
  Mohat, a student at Ohio's Mentor High School, killed himself after being taunted for years about his unusual physique (at six foot one and 112 pounds, he was nicknamed "Twiggy")

---

* *For those of you not up-to-date on urban slang, LMFAO means laughing my f*ing ass off.*

and his preference for wearing pink. A classmate reportedly told him: "Why don't you go home and shoot yourself? It's not like anybody would care."[7]

- **Phoebe Prince,** 15, *died in January 2010*
  Prince, who had recently moved from Ireland to South Hadley, Massachusetts, with her family, killed herself after being viciously taunted and cyberbullied by peers at her school. The case brought international attention to the problem of bullying in U.S. schools.[8]

- **Alexis Skye Pilkington,** 17, *died in March 2010*
  Pilkington, who lived on Long Island, New York, killed herself after being repeatedly attacked on the social networking site Formspring. Alexis is *still* being cyberbullied after her death by anonymous posts on a memorial Facebook page set up in her honor.[9]

Bullycides occur when victims can no longer endure the psychological effects of being bullied. Although the torture ceases for the sufferers, it continues for their devastated families and loved ones, who must live with the ramifications of unimaginable loss. But what happens to the victims of severe peer victimization who do not take their own lives? Many of them survive the hellish school years but remain scarred for life. One girl, Andrea, told me of her years as a victim, "It tore me down. I began to believe what was said. I was ugly. I was a freak. I was unwanted, unloved, unneeded. I'm still struggling with those today."

Scott is another victim who shared with me his own traumatic history and current ramifications from being bullied:[10] "I'm personally affected every single day by bullying that took place starting more than twenty years ago. I'm thirty-two now, and the field of neuroscience is finally blossoming enough to show us just how our repeated experiences shape our behavior. It has really opened my eyes to a lot of who I am—and it all goes back to the bullying."

Scott was a gifted kid who attended private schools through fifth grade, but at that point his parents could no longer afford private education. Starting in sixth grade, he attended the local public middle school. "My first day began with being thrown in a dumpster by the two class bullies. That was the beginning. It didn't stop. I was physically and verbally abused from sixth grade through the end of my high school career. I had a few friends, but at one point the bullying got so bad that even my friends turned on me—avoiding association with me and even joining in on the bullying." Scott was a small, skinny boy who did not break five feet tall until he was fourteen years old, and the bullies saw him as an easy target.

He remembered how "every school day I was shoved into lockers. I was punched. I was kicked. I was taunted by dozens of kids any time I walked the halls. I had my books thrown across the halls. I had kids writing fake notes 'from me' to other kids, trying to get them to fight me. I had kids following me home from school, bullying me to the point that I took different routes home every day. I had thoughts of suicide throughout my childhood. I lived in a perpetual state of fight or flight. My brain was always on the alert—scanning everywhere for the next threat."

Fight or flight refers to the body's autonomic nervous system and our response to acute stress. When animals and people perceive danger, their autonomous nervous system prepares to either fight off an attacker or flee the scene of danger. Symptoms of fight or flight mode include an elevated heart rate, shortness of breath, shaky legs, dilated pupils, constipation, and loss of appetite. When someone is in a constant state of fight or flight, as Scott was, it can be indicative of a generalized anxiety disorder or a panic disorder, and bullying is highly correlated with anxiety-related conditions.[11]

Scott suffered profoundly as a result of the bullying. "It ruined my academics. I went from being a gifted kid who was speaking in full sentences before age one to being an average student just coasting by." Although Scott was taking honors and AP classes, his As turned to Bs and Cs. *Who cares about school,* he thought, *when you have to spend all of your time there worrying about getting beaten up?* Scott's experience speaks to one of the warning signs of a child who is being bullied—a drop in grades. Many parents worry that poor grades indicate problems with drugs or alcohol or simply a lack of caring about school. But another possibility is that their child's performance at school is taking a back seat to basic survival concerns. Scott found relief when he finished high school. "Finally, sweet release—I went away to college and got to start mostly fresh. It was hard to adjust, but I was fortunate enough to make some good friends. I was still occasionally ostracized for being different, but it wasn't anywhere near the same." Scott had a honeymoon period where he thought that his troubles were over, and he felt like he had successfully survived the bullying.

As the years went by, Scott reevaluated his opinion of his survival. "Here's the thing—and I've only started to realize it over the past few years—I thought I'd moved past it all. I thought I was 'over' it . . . and I am, in a sense . . . but it also sits with me permanently in how my brain is wired. In the workplace, I have extreme difficulty dealing with aggressive people. I can have all the work done, all the right answers, all prepared in my head—but an aggressive or rude tone from someone freezes me in my tracks. I lock up. I don't get upset or view it as the same thing as bullying, but I can feel my brain freeze up. It seizes and goes into protection mode. I'm frozen. I can't answer a question I have the answer to. It's awful."

Scott's experience is not uncommon among victims of school bullying, say researchers who have found that childhood victimization can have effects that last into adulthood. A study by Deborah A. Roth, Meredith E. Coles, and Richard G. Heimberg in 2002 discovered that adults who reported victimization during childhood had higher levels of trait anxiety, social anxiety, worry, and anxiety sensitivity.[12] The constant stress on children like Scott changes their danger perception radar, and the slightest threat triggers disproportionate anxiety. It is a terrible way to live.

Scott faces additional repercussions from the bullying. He reports having trust issues and is unable to accept a compliment or any positive feedback, "because I was told for eight to ten years by hundreds of classmates that I was a loser, a freak, a nobody, a nothing . . . and it was reinforced with beatings. Nobody cared when I was in school. 'Kids tease other kids . . . get over it' was the mantra." Scott has a hard time believing that even his closest friends or significant others truly like him, let alone love him. His immediate reaction to praise from a coworker, friend, or loved one, he admits, is dismissal and self-deprecation. "I can't help it. I can sit here and tell you that it's irrational—but it's hardwired in my brain now." Scott will be suffering from the effects of being bullied for the rest of his life. With time, therapy, and possibly medication, he should be able to find relief, but he will always be shaped by the bullying. Scott is a real person telling a real story, not just another statistic in a research report. Fortunately, Scott is able to be a productive member of society, in that he holds a job and maintains relationships, but he is still symptomatic from anxiety.

Some people are so damaged by the psychological effects of peer victimization that they are far less functional than Scott when they reach adulthood. Raya, who was bullied at school by her peers for years, has not been able to move forward. She told me about some of the ways in which she was tormented.[13] "Girls bullied me with teasing, mind games, shunning, and elaborate plots to cause shame. One particular memory of mine involved a 'friend' tricking me into thinking she gave me the password to a girl's clubhouse in the playground, only to be embarrassed in front of everyone when the password was completely wrong." Raya recalled the boys being even more aggressive. One boy in her third-grade class threatened to poke her eye out with a stick from the game KerPlunk. "I'm afraid of KerPlunk to this day," she said. "Another boy in my grade-five class told me bald-faced that he despised me, the first time I'd learned that word. I was quite fat by the time I was a young teen, and the boys behind me in grade eight would make pig noises in class when the teacher was occupied." Throughout high school, boys sitting behind her on the bleachers at assemblies and school games would pinch the fat rolls on her back tightly and then deny it. Raya escaped from her horrifying reality by reading and writing. Books became her solace, her greatest comfort.

Most recommendations from adults did nothing to bring Raya relief. She recalled, "My parents would say, 'Just ignore her or him; they're trying to get to you,' and it did NOTHING for me! In fact, I found it amazingly off-putting. Bullies definitely want reactions, but telling a scared, sad, lonely little girl to not show a reaction when she's being bullied is like telling a leaf not to shake in the wind! 'Stand up for yourself and tell them what's for, bullies are just as scared as you!' was another one that did nothing. I actually tried, often—I alternated between shyness and being a loudmouth—but they always laughed in my face. They found my attempts to tell them off funny. And I heard a lot of 'Just remember, words can't hurt you,' which always just made me feel weak for letting the words hurt me."

Today, Raya is unable to hold down a job or relate to peers. "The bullying has completely crippled my life. I am a barely functional twenty-six-year-old; I have a government disability pension and suffer from social anxiety and agoraphobia. I'm constantly terrified of acting "wrong" with someone, being thought stupid or inadequate, being rejected, being judged. The particular incident with being embarrassed by a friend on the playground crippled my ability to trust, and I find it very hard to get close to people and constantly worry my friends will betray me. I find it difficult to be around even one other person for longer than an hour at a time." Raya's mental health diagnoses fit in with research by Gemma L. Gladstone et al. in 2006 that found that adults were more likely to suffer from social phobia and agoraphobia if they were victims of childhood bullying.[14] Although things feel bleak for Raya right now, there is always hope for improvement with therapy and medicine.

Victims of bullying often do reach out to clinical psychologists when they realize their symptoms are interfering with their lives. Kesha Burch-Sims has treated so many victims of bullying in her Chicago-based clinical psychology practice that she now speaks at schools about the topic and also runs several workshops on bullying. She told me, "I have seen long-lasting effects of bullying. Victims have prolonged difficulty with their own identities and how to fit in and socialize appropriately. They learn behaviors to compensate for their experience of being victims, and these behaviors in adulthood give them trouble. Their adjustment to life is painful."[15] Burch-Sims has observed that bullying victims feel intense anxiety about initiating conversations with other students. Group projects are very frightening to victims, and their grades can suffer because they fear asking to join study groups.

I remembered one girl, Maddie, who told me, "I was afraid to go to school, honestly. I was an emotional wreck." Maddie would rather fail her classes than face her bullies. Burch-Sims said, "College requires a lot of group work, which is terrifying for childhood bullying victims, because bullying is a traumatic experience. It is systematic and repetitive trauma, and it affects brain chemistry. Students become afraid of every social interaction." The good news is, she adds, that people are resilient. And this includes victims of bullying. They do respond to therapy. But it is an up-and-down struggle, especially for those with other mental health problems such as Asperger's or depression.

When people think of the harmful effects of bullying on the brain, they immediately assume we are talking about the victim's brain. But, as briefly mentioned earlier in the response to Sarah Hoffman's commenter, bullying is also unhealthy for bullies and the bystanders. In a longitudinal study that followed 2,540 boys born in 1981, researchers found that being classified as a bully was predictive of future substance abuse, depression, and anxiety. Boys classified as victims were more likely to be diagnosed with anxiety disorders, and boys classified as bully victims (kids who are bullied but also act as bullies themselves) were at risk for antisocial personality disorder, depression, and anxiety disorders.[16] Bully victims were the most at-risk for depression.[17]

Furthermore, according to Laura Hanish, an expert on gender-based bullying in preschool, "children who bully are also at an elevated risk for later diversifying their aggressive behaviors to more extreme forms of violence as well as to sexual harassment and dating aggression in early adolescence."[18] The sooner we identify bullying behavior in children, the sooner we can help them obtain necessary treatment and hopefully avoid these types of problems down the road. Left unchecked, bullying is not just a problem that causes children and teenagers to suffer. Michele Borba, whose proposal "Ending School Violence and Student Bullying" (SB1667) was signed into California law in 2002, told me, "A repeat bully by age eight has a one-in-four chance of having a criminal record by age twenty-six. By

age eight, behaviors became entrenched habits. The best prevention
is early intervention."[19]

Those who bully can carry their aggression into adulthood, and
those who have been victimized can continue to suffer from gripping
social anxiety. According to the Workplace Bullying Institute, 35 percent of working Americans, more than 50 million people, reported
that they had been bullied at work in 2010.[20] In its severe forms, bullying at work triggers stress-related conditions such as hypertension
and anxiety disorders. Businesses are recognizing the seriousness of
the problem, and at least seventeen states are considering introducing antibullying laws in the workplace. If we can teach today's children how to interact socially without bullying one another, we might
reduce incidences of bullying among the next generation of workers.

Part Three: Where Do We Go from Here? Prevention, Intervention, and Reconciliation

Chapter Eleven

Create a Home Environment That Produces Neither Bullies nor Victims

Parents hear horror stories about bullying, and their first thought is, *How do I protect my child from being bullied?* Our initial response is to worry that some other kid will be the perpetrator. But the reality is, many of our own children are doing the bullying, and we need to acknowledge this. It starts with examining our behavior as parents and role models. We can have a huge impact on how our children act, simply by being aware of the subtle messages we send through our conversations and body language, through our parenting styles and home environments, because children learn about social relationships at home and bring this knowledge into school.

David Shriberg, an associate professor at Loyola University Chicago, who has published extensively on social justice in schools, has identified the following ways in which family collaboration is important in addressing bullying:[1]

Risk Factors—Bullies Are More Likely to Experience:
- Frequent punishment that is inconsistent and ineffective
- Parental harshness, rejection, or neglect
- Maltreatment and witnessing domestic abuse

- Low parental warmth, low family cohesion, low involvement of parents in school

Protective Factors—Parents of Well-Adjusted Students Tend to:
- Use effective monitoring
- Get actively involved in children's school activities
- Set consistent boundaries and expectations
- Communicate frequently with their children's teachers

As Shriberg has seen, kids do not usually wake up one morning and simply start bullying others out of the blue. Their behaviors, worldviews, and personalities are molded and shaped by life at home. Healthy social relationships are not a one-time interaction; they are a lifestyle. Parents and caregivers have a huge impact on watchful kids.

Annie Fox, author of the award-winning Middle School Confidential series, shared some of her thoughts with me about how we influence our kids.[2] "If parents speak disrespectfully to each other, then what are they teaching their kids? To be disrespectful. When we enforce cruelty by benign neglect, it's never a surprise to see kids being mean. If a daughter is mean, the mom should ask herself, 'what am I either modeling or permitting?' Mom is a critical influence on girls. If her five-year-old is behind her while she stands in front of a mirror and makes comments about her fat butt, then the child learns that dissatisfaction with her body is what it means to be a woman."

Children absorb verbal and nonverbal messages from their parents. If a mom is out running errands with her kids and she makes a disgusted expression when she sees an obese person, the kids will pick up on this, even if the mom does not blatantly say, "Look at that fat woman." Every time we judge others, our kids are watching and learning from us.

Fox has also seen how parents can inadvertently put pressure on their kids to be well liked, which makes it harder for kids to confide in them if bullying occurs. Fox advises, "Don't ask your child: 'Who did you play with? Who did you sit by? Did you get invited to that party?' because then kids feel as if they must be popular to be valuable to Mom and Dad. The children are afraid to tell their parents that they aren't popular. If those kids get bullied, they assume it means something is wrong with them, they blame themselves, and they believe they are losers. What parents need to do is change the framing of their questions. Try saying, 'Tell me about the field trip.' If you are a parent who is concerned because the phone never rings, you should first talk to the teachers and find out what's going on before you project your concerns onto your kid. If you know your kid is not doing fine, you make yourself available or you investigate a bit."

The Needs of Younger Children as They Face Social Pain

I thought of Annie Fox's advice during a subsequent interview with Darla, who has been the leader of her daughter's Daisy/Brownie troop for the past three years. Darla ran into a situation where one mother was more concerned with popularity than with her child's pain. Darla explained what happened:[3] "We have a second-grade Brownie troop of twenty-seven girls, twenty-one of whom have been with us for three years, so I know the girls and their mothers well. We are starting to see cliques form in our troop, and lately there has been some bullying, such as hateful comments before meetings, eyes rolling if someone gets paired with someone she doesn't like, and several girls whispering to one another and excluding another child. For example, one girl in our troop is Indian, and a blonde girl was making fun of the Indian girl for being dark-skinned and for having hairy arms, and the mom of the Indian girl brought it to my attention. So we decided to have a meeting about bullying with the girls."

Darla invited the school social worker to come to the meeting to facilitate the discussion. They gave the girls two little surveys that asked questions about bullying, such as: "Do you make fun of other kids? Are you telling secrets? Are you being bullied?" The social worker talked with the girls before they took the test. During the meeting, they also told the girls that the surveys were anonymous. The girls could rip them up when they were done, or they could choose to put the completed surveys in their take-home folders so they could talk about them later with their parents.

Darla recalled that one little girl, Kellie, became very upset. She was being bullied and realized how bad it had become when she filled out the survey. Kellie started to cry, and she told Darla she wanted to take the survey home so she could talk about it with her mom. "When Kellie's dad picked her up, I pulled him to the side and explained what happened at the meeting and told him his daughter was very upset. I made a point of telling him that Kellie told me she really wanted to talk about it with her mom at home. He is a very involved dad and said he would be sure to tell his wife."

A week later, Darla was at a school function with Kellie's mom. "I asked her if she had a chance to talk to her daughter about the bullying questionnaire. The mom said, 'Oh, no, you probably think I'm like the worst mom, but we were busy.' I replied with, 'You should really talk with her because she was very upset,' and the mom changed the subject." And the sad thing was, Darla mentioned, that she already suspected the mom had blown the whole thing off, which was why Darla made a point of asking. "The mom is very social and is always on Facebook herself and places a lot of importance on being thin and popular," Darla observed. "To be honest, we live in an upper-middle-class area, and many of the mothers are quite concerned themselves with carrying the best brands and wearing the right clothes and working out."

I thought about second-grade Kellie, reaching out for help and being shunted aside, a little girl whose own mother pretends everything is okay rather than admit her daughter is having social problems. Kellie could go either way. Currently, her home is producing a victim, but it could switch on a dime, and she could later be a girl who bullies others. She does not have the connectedness with her mom that is needed to produce a strong, empathic individual. It is difficult, because many parents bring their own histories of insecurities and social discomfort into their parenting styles, often teaching unhealthy patterns to the next generation.

It is a delicate balance, the desire not to interfere with your child's social interactions unnecessarily and the simultaneous urge to advocate for your child. The *Atlantic* published an article by psychotherapist Lori Gottlieb ("How to Land Your Kid in Therapy") about the phenomenon of well-intentioned parents who often damage their children by protecting them from negative emotions. Gottlieb has treated many people who, as they became adults, were left feeling lost and adrift because they never learned resiliency, reality-testing, and perseverance. These are qualities that are good predictors of life fulfillment and success, according to Jean Twenge, coauthor of *The Narcissism Epidemic*.[4] Gottlieb interviewed many people for her article, including a preschool teacher "Jane."[5]

> *Let's say, Jane explained, that a mother is over by the sign-in sheet, and her son has raced off to play. Suddenly the mother sees her kid fighting over a toy with a classmate. Her child has the dump truck, and the other kid grabs it. Her child yells, "No! That's mine!" The two argue while the other kid continues to play with the truck, until finally the other kid says, "This one is yours!" and tosses her child a crappy one. Realizing the other kid won't budge, her child says, "Okay," and plays with the crappy toy.*
>
> *"Her kid is fine," Jane said. "But the mother will come running over and say, 'But that's not fair! Little Johnnie had the big truck, and you can't just grab it away. It was his turn.' Well, the kids were fine with it. Little Johnnie was resilient! We do teach the kids not to grab, but it's going to happen sometimes, and kids need to learn how to work things out themselves. The kid can cope with adversity, but the parent is reeling, and I end up spending my time calming down the parent while her kid is off happily playing."*

I read Gottlieb's article, which talked about the narcissism involved in helicopter parenting, and I recognized bits of my husband and me in the hovering, overinvolved parents, eager to be seen as good parents by the world at large. Being aware of the problem has already been helpful for me. Now, when I am at the beach or the park with my girls, I try to hang back when they fight with other kids over sand toys or playground equipment. If an altercation arises, I literally bite my tongue and curl my toes to remind myself not to rescue my kids. A fight over a toy is not bullying, nor is an occasional shove at the swings. How do we as parents learn to differentiate between normal social conflict, where we should hang back and let our kids feel pain, and bullying situations, where adult intervention is often needed? We remind ourselves of the characteristics of bullying: a repetitive, unwanted attack in the context of a power imbalance. Take a look at the following two hypothetical scenarios to help you distinguish between normal fighting and bullying:

Scenario 1

Rachel takes her son, Gabriel, to the park by their house several afternoons a week. They know several other parents and kids who frequently play at this park. Sometimes Gabriel joins a group of kids on the jungle gym; other times he finds a few friends from school kicking a ball around and plays with them. Gabriel is a little on the quieter side, and although he is rarely the leader in a group, he is accepted as a participant. One day, Gabriel sees an empty swing and starts running toward it. Gabriel's friend Lucas notices that Gabriel is eyeing the swing, and he races over to get there first. Gabriel starts to scream and cry. He grabs Lucas by the legs and tries to pull him off the swing. Lucas kicks Gabriel away, shouting, "I got here first! You're being a crybaby!" Rachel and Lucas's mother rush over to mediate, as they always do, trying to make sure each boy feels happy and satisfied. Gabriel and Lucas get into these types of arguments often, each boy competing with the other over toys and territory. In between fights, they have a grand time playing chase and acting out their favorite games. More often than not, Lucas dominates, but not always.

Scenario 2

Liana takes her son, Joey, to the park by their house several afternoons a week. She knows several other parents and kids who frequently play at this park, but Joey has not become close friends with any of them. Joey is in speech therapy for speech delays and speech impediments, and other kids have trouble understanding him when he talks. Joey often keeps quiet, and he has trouble getting into a group, whether at school or at the park. One day Joey is happily swinging when another boy, Damon, shoves him off the swing, claiming it is his turn. Damon often comes to this park, and he follows Joey around from station to station, demanding Joey surrender his space. Sometimes Damon hits and shoves Joey and then calls him a crybaby when he bursts into tears. Joey tries to avoid Damon and is frightened of the boy, even though they are the same age. Damon recruits other kids to play games of tag but leaves Joey out. Sometimes the group runs from Joey. On this particular afternoon, after Damon pushes Joey out of the swing, Joey sits on the ground crying. Damon's mom sits on a bench nearby, talking on her cell phone. She glances up when she hears Joey crying but then resumes her conversation. Liana quickly heads over to the swings to intervene. She keeps a close eye on Joey whenever Damon is nearby, and she often helps Joey navigate the playground.

In Scenario 1, Gabriel and Lucas are two boys engaging in typical childhood behavior. Neither one consistently dominates the other. Neither boy is frightened of the other. Their mothers, Rachel and Francesca, probably monitor them a little too closely when they play. This is a situation where the parents' desire for happy, satisfied children with equal and fair playing time can lend itself to hovering. When Lucas "stole" the swing from Gabriel, this led to Gabriel's feeling angry. It felt unfair. But there was nothing abnormal about the interaction. Sometimes the boys should be allowed to experience the disappointment or frustration of not having equal toys and time. The fact is that young kids do not share well, and they will only get better at it with time and practice. Yes, Lucas called Gabriel a crybaby, which was name-calling, but it was in the context of normal fighting. Long after Lucas and Gabriel are cheerfully playing again, their mothers are likely still examining them for signs of social pain. We parents are so sensitive to slights on behalf of our children! I remember reading with a sense of relief the following passage by Michael Thompson in his excellent book *Best Friends, Worst Enemies: Understanding the Social Lives of Children,* coauthored by Catherine O'Neill Grace:

All children are teased and called names. That's the bad news. The good news is that most children are resilient and find a way to deal with the insults that rain down in school. They enjoy enough social acceptance so that the insults do not really hurt. They are protected. The great majority of children, even if they are not popular, are accepted in a group. Though their highest social ambitions may not be realized, and despite the occasional social pain they experience at the hands of kids who tease them, they find acceptance. They get hurt and they bounce back. They have the cognitive ability and sociability to stay afloat, even when social seas are stormy.[6]

As parents, we do not want to mollycoddle our kids every time someone hurts their feelings, lest our kids view themselves as victims. Most of our kids, while occasionally victimized, are not destined to be victims. If Gabriel's mom is truly worried, she could reassure herself by observing that her son is able to successfully enter groups of children who are playing. He does not need to be the most popular boy in the group, but he does need to be accepted.

Our true concern should focus, according to Michael Thompson, on a small minority of about 10 to 12 percent of children who are "rejected children, either rejected-submissive or rejected-aggressive. These are the children highest at risk socially."[7] In Scenario 2, Joey is a child who is potentially at risk. His speech impediments make him a target for bullying, as does his difficulty getting into a social group. Damon's interactions with Joey have all the characteristics of a bullying relationship:

- Damon *repeatedly* torments Joey.
- Damon engages in *unwanted teasing, taunting, and physical and relational aggression* directed at Joey.
- Damon is *more powerful* than Joey.
- Joey is *frightened* of Damon.

Given these dynamics, Joey's mom, Liana, is correct to closely monitor Joey on the playground. This is not helicopter parenting; it is a parent accurately assessing that her child is in danger. Since Joey does have trouble getting into a group, he may benefit from some careful interventions to help him socially, like a social skills group. Perhaps Liana could arrange to bring a friend with him to the park, so that he has an ally to play with. If Joey is not alone, Damon may be less likely to pick on him. Or Liana could help Joey identify a child at the park that he would like to invite over for a playdate, and the other child could get to know Joey in a less hostile environment. Liana could also approach Damon's mom to discuss the situation, although the mom's demeanor on the playground indicates that she might simply be dismissive. It is important for Joey to know that his mother is aware of the situation and ready to help, particularly since Joey cannot speak clearly. She does not need to be his rescuer, but she does need to be his advocate and his supporter.

Most parents can develop a pretty keen sense for whether their child is at risk or not. Although Katie experienced some gender-based taunting and relational aggression, I do not think she is at risk socially, and I try to hang back a little if she is being excluded or teased (easier said than done). How do I reassure myself she is doing okay? She gets invited to a reasonable number of birthday parties; she can make friends with kids she doesn't know at the park or the beach; she is usually able to get into a group easily. We periodically run into periods of time where Katie laments that she is being left out—sometimes a friend prefers the company of someone else, or she is not invited to a particular birthday party, or she doesn't get asked to join a game during recess—but these painful events happen to all kids. As Michael Thompson told me, "There is an irreducible minimum of social cruelty in children's lives, because this is not heaven on earth." Every time we have an incident like this, I agonize inside. I anxiously await the end of each school day, so I can see Katie's demeanor and assess how she seems. My own anxiety makes me want to ask her, "Was it better today?" "Were you included today?"

But Thompson advised, "With normal social pain, parents should not ask about it every day, because then you are doing what I call *interviewing for pain*. You think you are being caring and helpful, but it makes the child feel like more of a victim. The nature of your questions frames her responses. Don't ask every day, 'Did the other kids include you?' or 'Were the other kids mean?' because then a child has to relive the mean things to report them. What you want to do is evoke the child's strengths by the kinds of questions you ask. You want the child not to hear a story of victimhood coming out of her own mouth but a strategy of resilience."[8] Nine times out of ten, Katie's social troubles sort themselves out on their own, reminding me that any interventions on my part would be unnecessary and even unhelpful. The more practice our children can get in managing normal social pain, the better they will cope as adults when they are on the receiving end of social slights. But it sure is hard to tell yourself to back off when all you want to hear from your child is, "Yes, Mom and Dad, my attachments feel secure, I know I am loved, and I'll have a good future as a productive member of society!"

The Needs of Older Children as They Face Social Pain and "Drama"

Older kids have a catchphrase that covers all manners of social struggle: *drama*. It is a code word that can refer to crises big and small, from the petty to the catastrophic. Drama can mean your child is having romantic relationship troubles; it can also be used to describe problems with friends. I remember one of our teenage babysitters being unavailable to sit one night this year, telling us that she was "dealing with some drama." By referring to social pain as drama, kids are able to avoid highly charged words such as "bullying," "fighting," or even "problems." Saying "drama" can save face and even serves to keep parents from realizing the extent of the issues. "Oh, she is just having some drama with her friends," says one mother to another, thus avoiding the need to admit that her daughter is experiencing exclusion or cruelty. If your child reports that he or she is dealing with some drama, be aware that something more may be going on. The word "drama" invites dismissiveness from parents, which is not what your child needs. Ask further questions, let your child talk, and listen carefully to the answers without providing criticism. Then you can work together to find a mutually acceptable solution.

Social pain changes as kids grow older, and the reasons for bullying become more complex. Tweens and middle schoolers can find themselves perfectly accepted one day and ostracized the next, leaving them bewildered as to how things fell apart. This is what happened with Deanna, who told me that her problems began in sixth grade.[9] "I had never had trouble making friends before, but now that I was in middle school, the girls did not like me because I wore short hair and weird clothes." Deanna's family was barely making ends meet, and her school was located in a wealthy neighborhood. By the middle of the year, the ostracism was overwhelming. "I asked one of the girls why she didn't like me, and she just said, 'because you're weird.' I held out my hand and said, 'I think we got off on the wrong foot; let's start over. Hi, I'm Deanna.' She looked at me and said, 'Start over? We're not going out! What are you, some kind of lesbian?' and then spread the rumor around the school that I was, in fact, a lesbian, and that if any female talked to me, I would rape them."

It got to the point where Deanna was accused of sexual harassment for asking a female student to move out of her seat in class. It lasted throughout middle school. During seventh and eighth grade, if Deanna ever used the girls' restroom, most of the girls would freak out, curl up their noses, or harass her, and she recalled how "they ALL left because they didn't want to get raped. I only used the bathroom in the library hall because I escaped to the library every chance I got, and nobody cool went there anyway."

The bullying extended beyond verbal taunts and exclusion. Deanna was physically attacked each day when she got off the bus. She explained how "the girls would gang up on me and pull my hair, push me around, kick me, and I did nothing, usually." Deanna tried telling her parents about getting attacked at the bus stop after one particularly rough day, but when they found out the main attacker was a girl younger and smaller than Deanna, they told her she should have fought back. "It took me two years to work up the courage to tell them," she marveled, "and then they just blamed me for not standing up for myself. So one time, in eighth grade, I fought back and was suspended because it was the word of seven other girls against me that I started the fight." Given the dismissive response

Deanna had received when she reached out to her parents, she decided not to open up again. Her parents never assumed there were ongoing problems, because at home, she said, "I was as bubbly and talkative as I ever was, but at school, I was silent, speaking up only when I had to, or to ask to go to the library." Deanna's experience with her parents has set the path for her to continue to struggle and suffer, because she did not receive empathy and support. The isolation at school was compounded by emotional isolation at home.

In many circumstances, older children are reluctant to ask for help, because they feel embarrassed or ashamed. If kids experience "drama" and we are unaware of the extent of their pain, they can turn to unhealthy coping mechanisms. Knowing that older kids tend to keep their private lives private, it is critical for parents and educators to be aware of warning signs that a child is suffering. Sometimes parents notice the warning signs but choose not to say anything, because they figure it is a phase that will pass or because they assume their child will bring it up if it is a real problem. It is better for parents to address concerns right away. If you see a child exhibiting any of the following, seek professional help immediately and closely monitor the child.

Warning Signs of Emotional Distress or Possible Suicidal Tendencies

- Changes in eating habits (large amounts of food disappearing indicates bingeing; bingeing followed by frequent bathroom trips indicates bulimia; extreme food restrictions and/or exercising obsessively indicates anorexia)
- Insomnia, restlessness, daytime sleeping, or other changes in sleeping habits
- Long-sleeved shirts and long pants or skirts at all times (to hide marks from cutting); or frequent bandages on arms and legs (cutting or other self-injury)
- Missing supplies of alcohol from the liquor cabinet or drugs from the prescription drug cabinets
- Loss of enthusiasm or interest in usual activities (stops playing sports, musical instruments, and so forth)
- Pessimism and hopelessness; unrelenting depression

- Withdrawal from family and friends; social isolation
- Giving away valued possessions or expressing a desire to die

The Prevalence of Self-Harm

One of the most common red flags in kids today is cutting, as we saw in the chapter on gay and lesbian bullying. High school senior Cassandra told me how she began responding to peer victimization in eighth grade by cutting.[10] "I knew about other friends who were cutting, and I decided to see if it would help release my pain. I first cut my wrist, but I didn't want people to see it, because it would make me seem weak, so I switched to cutting my calves and thighs. I would cut about three times a week, depending on how bad I felt." Someone at Cassandra's school noticed her cuts one day and told a counselor. The counselor gave her one day to tell her parents on her own, or else the school would notify them. Cassandra told her dad, who was supportive of her, and the school also insisted that she begin therapy.

The fact that Cassandra began cutting after she learned other kids were cutting is significant. Self-harming behaviors can happen in clusters, with one kid "triggering" another. This type of triggering can happen with eating disorders, drug and alcohol use, reckless sexual activity, and other unhealthy coping mechanisms. As parents, we can learn a great deal by staying aware of what is happening with our children's friends. If your daughter's best friend becomes anorexic, file that knowledge into the back of your mind. Should your daughter encounter social drama, it would not be unusual for her to respond by restricting food too. Eating disorders become more difficult to treat as the behaviors grow more entrenched, so it is best to approach your child as soon as possible. Your child has turned to these harmful behaviors as a way to manage her out-of-control feelings.

These problems are not just the realm of girls. Boys also turn to eating disorders and cutting as dysfunctional coping mechanisms, much to the surprise of some parents. In *Packaging Boyhood,* authors Lyn Mikel Brown, Sharon Lamb, and Mark Tappan illustrate how boys can turn to harmful actions:

Painful emotion in adolescence feels so much more painful because of teens' inability to emotionally self-regulate. They're given very few models in the media of men coping with their strong emotions through reaching out to others, through conversation. The lucky boys will pick up a guitar or a pen and write poetry. The less fortunate will punch a wall, swear at their parents, or pick up a knife and cut.[11]

Fourteen-year-old Jonah Mowry, a victim of antigay bullying, turned to cutting after kids at his school tormented him repeatedly. In 2011, shortly before entering eighth grade, Mowry uploaded a video to YouTube in which he cried and showed his scars, holding up note cards that read "I've cut . . . a lot. I have scars. Suicide was an option . . . many times."[12] My husband and I watched Mowry's video together, and we were both deeply impacted by his pain.

As much as kids can learn self-harming from one another, they can also influence one another to become healthier. I asked Cassandra what helped her reduce the cutting, and she replied, "At the end of eighth grade, I stopped hating on myself. I was pretending to be someone I wasn't in order to fit in. But I realized this wasn't me, and I started wearing band T-shirts and jeans instead of skirts. It took a few people to show me that it was better to be myself. I had this one friend who was cutting a ton, and she decided to just be herself. She became happier and cut way less, and I slowly decide to be who I want to be. I'm happier now, too." Cassandra has learned to find healthier outlets for her emotions, telling me, "I take the bad feelings and go on a walk with my dog. Walking is a huge coping mechanism for me. I write poems almost every night. It works better than the cutting."

Communicating "I Am on Your Side" to Your Child

Even kids who do not engage in self-harm may still be carrying emotional wounds that they try to hide. When parents are heavily concerned with social status, it has a chilling effect on a child's willingness to report peer victimization. Both boys and girls are sensitive to parental approval, and if you place a high value on popularity, your child will be reluctant to talk with you about social problems. Kyra, who was severely bullied in seventh grade, told me, "Many of the girls in my class were not getting the values right at home. They picked up that it's really important to the mothers to project a certain image, and then they saw me, a vulnerable kid who doesn't care about her image, and they bullied me." Kyra used to wish she had just one friend, even if the mythical friend lived in another town. To compound her loneliness, her parents did not know what was going on, partly because her mom had started a law career at the same time that the bullying began, and Kyra did not feel as if she could approach her mom with the bullying problem.

Kyra remembered, "My mom once asked why I never had kids come over, and she made me feel as if there were something wrong with me for not having friends. She judged me, and when your mom tells you there is something wrong with you, you believe it."[13] If you notice that your child seems lonely or never has friends over, suggests Annie Fox, try to address your concerns without taking a judgmental tone.[14] You might say, "It sounds like you are excited about the playoffs. Would it be fun for you if we invited a friend or even a couple of your friends over to watch the first game? We could order in some good food." If your child declines, take the opportunity to gently check in and see what types of activities he or she enjoys doing with a friend. This might be when you find out that "everyone hates me!" or "there is nobody I want to hang out with!" If that happens, work together with your child to find a solution. "Is there anyone in another class who seems nice that you want to get to know better?" you could ask, in order to help your child cultivate a new friendship.

Sometimes, the answer is to help your child find a completely new social outlet where a fresh identity is possible.[15] Help him to join a nonschool-affiliated athletic team, theater group, music class, or other organization or club. Encourage her to try a dance class or a karate class or a pottery class. Even if your child does not make friends in these pursuits, she may draw comfort from the activity itself. British teenager Shahala told me, "My healthiest way of getting through was by picking up my saxophone and improvising until I felt better. If I were to talk to another person in my situation, I would tell them NOT to self-harm or drink, because it really doesn't solve the problem."[16]

These same tactics can be helpful for kids who act as aggressors. If parents approach aggressive kids with a collaborative approach rather than a punitive or dismissive approach, the kids are more likely to develop positive connections with peers. Sometimes, an aggressive kid needs to find the right outlet for his or her anger, learning how to experience negative emotions without acting on them inappropriately. It can help to bang on the drums or pound the stuffing out of a baseball. Go ahead and smash a tennis ball with a racket. For a kid who needs centering, it can help to practice yoga or martial arts.

"It's okay to feel pissed off," you want to communicate to your aggressive child, "but it's not okay to beat someone up. You can feel mad or sad or angry or scared. Feel whatever you want. But you can't *do* whatever you want." Older kids can learn that they are still accountable for their actions, even when they feel really upset.

A child's social troubles can trigger disproportionate pain in parents who have personally struggled with social acceptance. If you find yourself unduly anxious and distraught upon learning that your child is having a hard time, going to therapy can help you recover from your own wounds and decrease the chance that you will project your personal issues onto your children. It is particularly difficult for parents who have a history of being bullied to gauge whether or not their child is in need of outside assistance. "I am extremely sensitive, probably overly so, to any little situation where my daughter is excluded or treated meanly," said Victoria Stilwell, the previously bullied star of Animal Planet's hit television show *It's Me or the Dog*. "So I talk with her about it when I see it happen, and if she doesn't seem to care too much, I let it go. I don't want to create an issue if there isn't one or make her see herself as a victim."[17]

Chapter Twelve

Set Out Family Guidelines for Responsible Uses of Technology, Media, and Music

We read news reports about how kids are cyberbullying each other day and night. Everyone is asking, "How do we get them to stop?" Perhaps we should be asking, "Did they learn it from us? How do we get ourselves to stop?" Every single day, adults engage in cyberbullying, without even realizing it, and the kids are always watching.

How does this happen, you may wonder? Let's examine two hypothetical scenarios.

Scenario 1

John, a devoted and loving father of two sons, spends a few minutes every morning scanning his favorite online sports blogs. After reading the posts, he likes to scroll down through the comments section, occasionally contributing his thoughts. The commenters can get pretty riled up and often start attacking each other over differing viewpoints. One morning, John glances at his watch, jumps up, and heads into the kitchen to grab some coffee before leaving for work. His thirteen-year-old son, David, wanders into the office to use the computer. The browser is still open on the sports site, and David starts reading the screen. He sees that his father has just written a comment, referring to a basketball player who missed an important shot as a "fucking faggot." Two weeks later, David writes on a fellow middle schooler's Facebook page that he is a "fucking faggot."

Scenario 2

Vicky is a full-time mom of a daughter and a son, and she spends hours taking her children to and from lessons and classes. While she waits for her daughter's ballet class to end, she uses her iPhone. Vicky and her best friend, Michele, have been texting back and forth about an unfriendly mom at the elementary school who blew them off at a recent PTA function. The ballet class ends, and Vicky's ten-year-old daughter, Amy, comes bouncing out. Amy asks for the iPhone so she can play a game in the car. While they are driving home, a text comes in from Michele. Amy clicks on it and sees the whole conversation, including the part where Vicky wrote that the unfriendly mom has a "fat ass and dresses like a slut." The next day, Amy sends an email to her best friend and comments that a girl in their class was "dressed like a slut."

And this is how it happens. With every mean, gossipy text that parents send, with every derogatory comment parents write, we lower the standards for the digital community. People are less inhibited online, frequently writing with a level of self-righteousness and sarcasm that they wouldn't express to another person's face. They hit the "send" button and fire off words as weapons. It is not just on sports websites or in private conversations that adults cyberbully each other—I have seen many well-intentioned parents launch personal attacks at each other over disagreements on parenting websites. Some of the hot parenting topics that can lead to personal attacks? Circumcision, breastfeeding, gender-nonconforming children, childhood beauty pageants, and homeschooling, just to name a few.

What start as passionate and civil discussions often deteriorate into mud-slinging, inflammatory tirades that viciously promote stereotypes. Justin Patchin of the Cyberbullying Research Center told me, "I get more emails and phone calls about adults being cyberbullied than I do about adolescents. But my focus is on the kids, because adults have additional skills to help them cope, and adults can pursue civil action with attorneys. Even short of cyberbullying, you see politicians bullying each other on the news, and you see it on reality television shows like *Teen Mom* and *Jersey Shore*. It's a catch-22—it's so simple to see from our perspective that the culture is harmful, but it's hard to get that to translate to behaviors."[1]

Remember Cheryl Kilodavis, author of the children's picture book *My Princess Boy*? We spoke about the phenomenon of adult cyberbullies, plenty of whom Cheryl has encountered on the *My Princess Boy* Facebook page. The page is intended as a place for healthy discussion about children who challenge gender norms, and opposing viewpoints are welcomed, as long as they are civil. Cheryl told me, "Our rule on the Facebook page is this: if there are personal attacks on us or other commenters, then those comments will be removed. Constructive dialogue is fine. We can disagree. We can even disagree passionately and vehemently, but when it comes to personal attacks, it is no longer constructive."

Cheryl and I talked about how discouraging it is when someone with an excellent argument sabotages his or her own conversation by getting too angry and throwing in slurs or personal attacks. "And, sometimes," she lamented, "a supportive bystander would verbally attack a bully right back, and we would have to remove that very person who sympathized with us. We anticipated that people would have disagreements, but we did not anticipate the intensity of the personal attacks. Some people would even create fake names to come back on to the page after we banned them, and they began cyberstalking other people. The Facebook legal team has had to help us a lot."[2]

Some websites have a moderator who will remove abusive comments and block the authors. But for many websites, the comments section is unmoderated, and the insults fly. I recalled Anne Collier's advice, "Since aggressive behavior increases a person's risk for being victimized, then civil behavior reduces risk. Adults need to model good digital citizenship for kids. Digital citizenship happens when people see themselves as community stakeholders, even if that community is an online community. The citizens care about the well-being of the community and the behaviors that affect it. Then, what psychologists call 'social norming' begins to happen—community members model good behaviors for each other, which is usually much more persuasive than imposing rules from the top down."[3] This does not mean that all children who engage in cyberbullying directly learned it from their parents. There are plenty of aggressive kids online whose parents do not even know how to send emails, much less surf the web or send text messages. But for those parents who are technologically savvy, it helps to be aware of the fact that the kids notice everything.

According to the idea of digital citizenship, we can all influence each other to be more respectful, and this will trickle down to our children. One of the biggest problems with the digital community is that things happen very quickly, and people often respond to each other before taking time to cool off. As Cheryl Kilodavis observed to me, "Some people are moving so fast in their status updates and on Twitter that they don't stop to think of the impact of their words. We see that with celebrities who make an antigay slur and fifteen tweets later, they get called out on that earlier tweet. They think they have already moved on, but the mean words start catching up with them."[4]

The digital media are a constant presence in all of our lives, and many parents spend screen time with their children. But what may appear as quality together time may actually be a chance for parents to reinforce messages of mean behavior. Annie Fox explained how cruelty can sneak into a home. "Too many girls and moms bond by ripping apart other women—for example, they watch the Academy Awards together and rip apart what others are wearing and use it as a bonding experience. They sit at the computer or the television or the iPhone and point out people's flaws."[5]

In the nation's worst example of a parent modeling cruel online behavior, we recall the tragic suicide of Missouri teenager Megan

Meier in October 2006. Shortly before her fourteenth birthday, Meier hanged herself after "Josh Evans," a fictitious boy she was dating online via MySpace and IM, viciously broke up with her. Lori Drew, the mother of one of Megan's friends, had actually created "Josh" to retaliate against Megan for slighting her daughter. Drew, along with her eighteen-year-old employee, Ashley Grills, first hooked Megan by impersonating the charming "Josh" and then abruptly changed tactics. "Josh" wrote to Megan, "I don't like the way you treat your friends, and I don't know if I want to be friends with you." He also said she was "fat" and "a slut," and then other girls who had linked to "Josh's" website added abusive messages to Megan. He wrote a final IM message to the traumatized girl that said, "You are a bad person and everybody hates you. Have a shitty rest of your life. The world would be a better place without you." Megan was so devastated that she took her own life. Drew said she only intended to "mess with Megan" and tried to hide her involvement.[6]

While almost all parents exercise far better judgment than Lori Drew, we do need to protect our children from their own worst judgment about hurting their peers. A child is considered a participant in cyberbullying simply by forwarding along a gossipy text or a revealing photo. Make no doubt about it—passing along the information, even if your child was not the original author of the text—creates culpability.

Help Kids Protect Themselves Against Cyberbullying

Net Cetera, a publication of www.onguardonline.gov, offers the following tips to help your kids protect themselves online:[7]

- Remind your kids that online actions have consequences offline.
- Remind your kids that information they post online can never be taken back.
- When available, enable strong privacy settings on social networking sites.

- Check your child's "friends list" to make sure they are friends with real people they actually know.
- Advise your children not to talk about sex with strangers online.
- Encourage your kids to report suspicious users.
- Instruct your kids not to impersonate someone else online.
- Have your kids create a safe screen name, and make sure their IM names are not the same as their email addresses.

It is increasingly common for young couples in love to share their passwords with each other. DO NOT DO THIS. Sharing passwords may feel like a statement of "I trust you and love you and have nothing to hide." But in reality, it can be a disaster, especially when the relationship ends. There is nothing sneaky about keeping your password private; it is a good and healthy way to protect yourself and others.

Anyone can create an online profile by faking his or her name or age. What kids need to remember, Patchin warned,[8] is that people can also fake emotions, comments, and reactions online. Remind your child that someone can fake romantic interest online, knowing it can create very genuine feelings in the recipient. Teach your child to question the validity of comments that others write online. What others write about you may *feel* true, but it does not mean it *is* true, and this is vital to consider when someone is being cruel. Additionally, if your child receives a comment or a text that seems odd or off from someone he or she knows, it might be that another person is impersonating his or her acquaintance. Teenagers frequently hack into each other's accounts to send emails and texts or write online comments. If it feels weird, it might be that it is coming from someone other than the named author.

When parents learn that their child is being cyberbullied, one knee-jerk reaction is to take the technology permanently away. Justin Patchin told me, "Taking away the technology makes things worse. Parents need to teach kids to take breaks from the technology, not to take it away. The number one goal is for the parents to convey to the child they are on the child's side." Patchin emphasized that kids do not have the same perspective as parents. He commented, "A kid may have two thousand friends and two bullies, and the kid will focus on the bullies. In a parent's mind, cyberbullying may not seem like a big deal, but if it gets to the point that a child is telling a parent about an episode of cyberbullying, it is a very big deal in the child's eyes." When situations escalate, Patchin advises parents to work cooperatively with the school to help their child. And, he added, when parents are confronted about their child being involved, they need to accept culpability and not deny.[9]

Kids today have grown up with technology in a way that previous generations have not. As a result, some parents feel intimidated talking about cyberbullying, because they are uncertain how it happens. Michele Ybarra, president and research director of Internet Solutions for Kids, recommends that parents play around with the technology themselves before trying to tell kids how to use it. "Start texting. Join a social networking site. Get a good understanding of it, and then have natural conversations with your kids about safely using technology. It does not have to be handled in one big talk. Just make it a regular part of connecting with your kids."[10]

One option for parents whose children have engaged in inappropriate online activity is to put a technology contract in place. Rosalind Wiseman advises that putting a family contract in place eliminates vagueness and miscommunication around what is or is not appropriate, and it indicates to children how seriously you regard issues surrounding technology misuse. Here is a sample technology contract from Wiseman's book *Queen Bees and Wannabes,* reprinted with permission:[11]

We, the Edwards family, believe our family values include integrity and compassion. Every member of the family understands that our use of technology must reflect our values. Therefore, we recognize that the following are in direct contradiction to our values:

- Using someone's password and identity without his/her consent
- Spreading gossip
- Making or forwarding sexually suggestive photographs
- Sending viruses
- Participating in Internet polling
- Creating or participating in insulting websites and blogs
- Using Facebook, MySpace, Xanga, LiveJournal, YouTube, or any other website with the purpose of creating, viewing, or participating in the humiliation of others

If any family member is found acting in violation of this contract, the following will occur:

- First violation: Computer or cell phone privileges ended for _____ (amount of time).
- Second violation: Computer and cell phone privileges ended for _____ (amount of time).
- Third violation: One of the person's most valued privileges is taken away. (Remember, an iPod is a privilege and so is participating in team sports—no matter how good your child is.)

While we understand that any of us can make a mistake, we believe that living according to these values is critically important.

Signed on the day _____ of this year _____.

Child _____ Parent(s) _____.

If you are interested in creating a contract for your family, visit one of the following websites to download one that fits your needs:[12]

- *Family Online Internet Safety Contract* (www.fosi.org/resources.html)

- *Family Internet Use Contract and Cell Phone Use Contract* (www.cyberbullying.us/cyberbullying_internet_use_contract .pdf *and* www.cyberbullying.us/cyberbullying_cell_phone_con tract.pdf)

In our discussion about the risks of media use, Rosalind Wiseman mentioned how widespread the problem is of parents modeling inappropriate Internet behavior. She told me emphatically, "Parents think it is funny that their kids can sing along to Ke$ha's 'TiK ToK' or Beyoncé's 'Single Ladies.' It is not. It is not cute to take a video of your young daughter singing along to Ke$ha and posting it on YouTube. It is not cute for your kids to know the lyrics. I will not even allow Ke$ha songs in my car; I turn them off because she sings about how great it is to drink Jack Daniels early in the morning, and I don't want my kids hearing that."[13] After our conversation, I rewatched the movie *Mean Girls* and noticed the Queen Bee's younger sister in the background during several scenes, gyrating wildly to inappropriate music videos. Parents who post videos on YouTube of their young children doing sexual dances are buying into our cultural messages that force children to grow up too soon.

This does not mean that parents and older teenagers cannot enjoy listening to these songs, because the older kids are able to engage in appropriate discussions about the issues involved. I frequently put Ke$ha and Rihanna on my headphones while I am exercising. At thirty-eight, I am old enough to listen to their music without trying to emulate the lifestyle of the singers. I can watch Rihanna's music video "Man Down" and understand that she is making a social statement (albeit extreme) about being an abused woman who has reached her limit and shoots her assaulter. But my young daughter cannot make these distinctions, at least not without a carefully guided discussion, and it is not a discussion I am ready to have with a child her age.

Young girls view singers such as Katy Perry, Beyoncé, Britney Spears, Rihanna, JLo, and Ke$ha as godlike beings and want to be exactly like them. In 2010, the *Journal of Children and Media* reported that preteen girls age nine to eleven are particularly influenced by female pop singers and that these singers directly impact how these girls build their own feminine identities. When these girls spend time in the privacy of their bedrooms or hang out with friends on the school playground, they act as "apprentice" girls to the pop stars. Preteens watch young female pop stars dressed in extremely revealing clothing, dancing in sexually charged music videos, and they are convinced that this is what it means to be female.[14] Knowing how seriously young girls take pop stars, parents need to maintain a close connection with their daughters so they can discuss issues of sexuality and femininity as they arise.

Hip-Hop Music

Hip-hop music is an integral part of American culture, and chances are your kids will listen to it. Keith Robinson, an administrator at a large suburban high school, told me, "We have one of the most diverse schools in the country, with over ninety different languages spoken by our students, and the most popular form of music at our school is hip-hop. When I see kids listening to rap music, I see them doing it as a way of trying to fit in to American culture, because kids want to make connections with the whole. I think a lot of kids are more into the sound and the beat of the music than into the message."[15]

There is undeniably a rough edge to some hip-hop music, particularly the genre known as gangsta rap, because this music is rooted in stories about life in the ghetto. For parents who are unfamiliar with the culture of gangsta rap, the lyrics can be shocking. I spoke with Will Crawford, who teaches courses on African American literature and popular culture, about hip-hop music and its role in our culture.[16] Crawford explained, "People who aren't well versed in rap assume all rap is about drugs, killing, violence, and homophobia. But that kind of content can be found in any music." Informed parents need to know what their kids come into contact with on a daily basis, he continued, and parents who say no to rap music may not realize their kids are still exposed to homophobia, misogyny, and stereotypes about gender in other places, such as in advertising. It is just more subtle. Crawford said ruefully, "Gangsta rap can be a scapegoat for society's ills." We mused over how many of the songs playing on the pop-music stations are just as inappropriate for children and families, yet there is mainstream acceptance of these songs.

Jerry Pope, a national college consultant for two large public metropolitan high schools, spoke with me about how important hip-hop music is to his students.[17] "It brings the kids together," he affirmed. "And, to be honest, there is an element of racism in the scrutiny given to rap lyrics as compared to pop lyrics. Consider the words to Katy Perry's widely played song 'Last Friday Night.' She sings about getting drunk, having sex with a stranger, engaging in a ménage à trois, posting scandalous pictures online, getting kicked out of bars, breaking the law and evading arrest, and planning to do it all again. The lyrics are extremely destructive." Yet parents sing along to this song on the radio with their preteen girls, focusing more on the catchy tune than the message. Many of these same parents would never sing along to hip-hop music with their young girls. There is a double standard.

Pope observed that people are afraid of what they don't know, and this translates into rap music. In the 1970s, older generations would look at young people with long hair and assume they were druggies. He remembered how Elvis Presley appeared on the *Ed Sullivan Show,* and they had to show him only from the waist up, because parents thought if kids saw him swiveling his hips, teens would run out and have sex. Eventually, people stopped fearing Presley and embraced him. "Now," Pope pointed out, "people fear hip-hop because of how it has been portrayed, and they think it will make kids act violently. In the early days, rap evolved from block parties in New York City; it was electronic music that DJs put together. People experimented with scratching, beat mixing, there was a Jamaican influence, some reggae influence, and slowly but surely, MC and rap evolved. The one form that people fear the most is what evolved into gangsta rap with lyrics that are violent, sexist, and homophobic. But those performers would say, 'This is the world we live in, and we are singing about what we know.'" Pope echoed Robinson's sentiment that while a lot of parents are upset by the lyrics, many kids do not even pay attention to the words; they are more interested in the beat.

Whether kids listen to hip-hop, pop, country, rhythm and blues, alternative—parents can use music as an opportunity to connect. Music is a personal preference, and kids will find a way to listen to the songs that speak to them, so outright forbidding music with older kids is bound to fail. If your kid is listening to 2Pac, recommends Crawford, take the time to learn about 2Pac so that you can talk together about the social significance of the song "Changes." If your kid is watching the Katy Perry music video "Last Friday Night," use it as a chance to talk about the stereotypes promoted in the video. But then you can gain even more credibility with your child by pointing out that Katy Perry has conversely created music videos that actually break down stereotypes and empower people. Perry's music video "Firework," for example, features a self-conscious overweight girl, a gay couple, and a pediatric cancer patient all finding their inner joy and beauty. The truth is, most musical artists are complex and multidimensional, and parents can find both positives and negatives in their songs. If you are having a discussion about stereotypes, you may want to ask your child what he or she thinks of Lady Gaga's music. Lady Gaga, who was bullied as a student, has spoken very publicly about being supportive of anti-bullying movements, and you could use her song "Born This Way" to help launch a conversation about bullying issues with your child.[18]

Try to give and take in these discussions, both sharing your thoughts and soliciting your child's opinions. Crawford admitted, "As an older hip-hop head, I can't relate to these new rappers coming up; they are too young for me, but as a parent, it's my responsibility to be familiar with what my kids are listening to. When I drive with my son, we alternate who picks the music. I give him some exposure to my music and he plays his favorite rap for me, and then we talk about it." If your child is listening to Jay-Z, talk with him or her about the derogatory way that Jay-Z refers to women as "bitches," and ask how it makes your child feel. If you have a daughter, now is an opportunity to inquire if she has ever been called a "bitch." If you have a son, ask him if he calls girls "bitches." Some kids may report that they don't really think about it when they hear the word "bitch," because they have become desensitized to it. They listen to the songs, but they don't analyze them. To show your child that you see more than one dimension to Jay Z, you might talk about how Jay Z spoke out in defense of gay marriage, because he doesn't believe in discrimination.

Merely listening to music is a very different experience from watching music videos. A kid can zone out and enjoy the beat of a song without explicitly thinking about the lyrics. But everything changes when he or she pulls up the video on YouTube and sees highly sexualized and violent images that now become associated with the song. It is naive to think that our kids won't find a way to view these videos, so forbidding them is likely to backfire. Lyn Mikel Brown advises that parents talk, talk, talk with their kids about the issues raised in music videos. Ask them what they notice, and do not negate or argue with them about their observations. Instead, listen carefully, and then share your concerns and point out stereotypes. "Help your child be an educated consumer of the media," Brown reiterates.[19]

The ability to connect with kids through their music is valuable for anyone who can serve as a mentor. As a college guidance counselor, Jerry Pope has used rap music as a way to create a bond with students who would otherwise view him as too different from them. He laughed as he told me, "I went to a Lil Wayne and T.I. concert, and the kids were shocked that I listen to that. Then the kids started talking to me about music; they brought me their CDs, and it helps me relate." I commented that research has shown that kids who feel connected at school are less likely to engage in bullying,[20] and Pope added, "The research by College Board shows that the kids most at risk of not going to college are minorities—Hispanic, African American, first-generation kids—and the number one reason those kids do go on to college is that there was a significant person in their lives who promoted college. For many of these kids, it is a teacher or a counselor at school who promotes college, because they aren't getting it at home. I have kids who say to themselves, 'If Mr. Pope promotes college, and he went to a Lil Wayne T.I. concert, maybe I can talk to him, and he can help me.' Music is the one thing that brings everyone together." Pope thought for a minute and then added, "I mean, look at me—I'm a blond-haired, blue-eyed, gay, white man, and I love hip-hop music, and I can bond with African American, Hispanic, and Muslim students over rap."[21]

Sports Blogs

The übermasculine culture that is promoted in much of contemporary music is also rampant in the world of professional male sports, an arena that has a massive online following. Sports-related blogs, websites, and communities foster constant discussions online, particularly among boys and men. In a heartening sign, some high-profile bloggers are taking it upon themselves to raise the standards of their blogs in order to create a more accepting, inclusive environment, which is a great way to model good digital citizenship. I spoke with Jim Margalus, who writes the popular White Sox blog called *South Side Sox,* about the changes he made when he took over the blog in 2010.[22]

South Side Sox gets thousands of hits a day during the baseball season, and Margalus is determined that discussions will be open to everyone. He explained, "Asian, black, white, Jewish, and Latino people all read the blog, and sometimes slurs were made, which would keep people away. A lot of times, those slurs would be written as inside jokes between people who were actually friends, but outsiders reading the blog didn't know that, and they would take offense. I wanted to get rid of the clubby, inside-joke feeling on the blog, so that we would not exclude anyone who could be valuable to the Sox discussion by having them feel unwelcome." With the goal of good, smart, on-topic discussions guiding him, Margalus wrote and published a new set of standards, and the following are a few items listed under Not Allowed:

Personal attacks: threatening, attempting to intimidate, or otherwise lashing out at another poster is prohibited.

Pornography/graphic posts: this pertains to photos of scantily
clad women (or men), gratuitous, disgusting posts, or anything of that ilk—if you wouldn't want your boss's boss to see
it, you shouldn't post it.

Pissing matches: if you don't like another poster, say your piece
and let it die.

Trolling: posts that are intended to annoy the citizens of this
blog, or serve no general use otherwise, won't be tolerated.

There was an adjustment period after Margalus established the
new standards. "Early on," he said, "we had a few people who didn't
want to put up with the rules. They figured everyone was an adult
and everyone could handle all types of content, but it reflects back on
me, since my name is on the blog. I do allow profanity, and we see a
good amount of it when the team is playing badly, but I do not allow
slurs."

Margalus informed me that Al Yellon, who writes the popular
Chicago Cubs blog, *Bleed Cubbie Blue,* is even stricter about standards. I called Yellon, and he explained that "profanity is very limited. Sometimes we see it during a game thread in the heat of a
moment, but other than that, not much." Yellon's blog receives about
eight thousand hits a day during the season, and he has children as
young as fourteen years old who participate in the comments, "making intelligent points and holding their own with people twenty years
older than they are." Yellon wants to create a safe environment for
his youngest readers. He said, "People have the idea of the Internet as
the Wild West—anything goes. Up until recent times, people could
post anonymously on almost any site, and they thought they could
do anything they wanted without repercussions. Some sites recommend changing to Facebook commenting or another platform where
you have to use your real name, which is where I think the future is
headed."[23]

Yellon's written standards include the following examples:

Personal attacks on community members, directly or through sarcasm/belittling, e.g., "You're an idiot," "My Chihuahua knows more about baseball than you do," or posts designed for the sole purpose of mocking any member of the community, are forbidden.

Comments that are intolerant or prejudiced (sexist, racist, homophobic, and so forth) in nature, e.g., "Why don't you go play with your dolls?," "The Cubs shouldn't sign black players," "Doesn't Damon look like a fag?," and so forth are not permitted.

Overall, the responses to both Chicago baseball blogs have been very positive. In May 2011, the South Side Sox hosted its third annual tailgating barbecue specifically for readers of the blog, and Margalus enthused, "I was able to meet a lot of readers, and everyone had great things to say about the blog. People got to know one another, even the people they argue with on the blog, and they were very respectful. It was great." Whenever possible, it is an excellent idea to hold an actual event to allow members of an online community to meet one another in person. After talking face-to-face, readers are more likely to have civil disagreements online, because they no longer view each other as objects.

Both Margalus and Yellon send a warning to commenters who violate the standards, and if the behavior continues, the user is banned. Yellon believes that people are not careful enough with their computers. "I have seen kids write something under the dad's name because the dad leaves his browser open on the computer," he told me, "and that really shows that you want to watch what you're writing, because your kids will see it."

Social Networking Sites, Online Games, and Internet Browsing

Parents can limit opportunities for their children to misuse the Internet by putting the family computer in a public place, such as in the kitchen or family room. If the computer is located in a room where there is regular traffic, children who are looking at inappropriate material will have less warning time to minimize the screen and switch to another one. However, as technology becomes cheaper and more widely available, the family computer may become a thing of the past. It is not uncommon for each child in a family to have his or her own web-browsing cell phone, laptop, and/or iPad, which admittedly makes it more difficult to monitor your children's movements, but not impossible. Parents whose children seek out inappropriate sites can use the highest level of parental controls available on the computer (and the television), and they can check the history on their children's browsers to monitor online activity. If you are unfamiliar with how to use blockers and filters, take the time to learn about how to use them appropriately. Experts Justin Patchin and Sameer Hinduja recommend the following two websites for parent education:[24]

- *Getnetwise* (www.getnetwise.org/videotutorials). The website claims to contain the largest online repository of instructional how-to video tutorials that show parents and users how to keep their family's online experiences safe and secure."
- *GetParentalControls.org* (getparentalcontrols.org)

Online Safety Education for Older Children

Although the required age to join Facebook is thirteen, many children lie about their ages in order to open accounts. Parents who are unfamiliar with Facebook can download "A Parent's Guide to Facebook" (www.connectsafely.org/Safety-Advice-Articles/facebook-for-parents.html) to learn more about how the massive social networking site works.[25] Many parents make it a condition that their younger teens on Facebook "friend" them so they can monitor activity. At what age does a child no longer need to be "friends" with his or her parents on Facebook? What about sites like AIM, Myspace, or Photo-bucket?

Do kids have the right to online privacy at thirteen? At fifteen? There is no magic age, no definite answer to this question. It depends on how connected you are to your children (and their friends), how much trust they have earned, and whether you feel that your children are at risk. Some parents have told me that they think sixteen is an acceptable age, since this is when their children will earn a driver's license and more subsequent independence. Other parents never feel a need to "friend" their children. But if your child protests that he or she needs "online privacy," use that moment to start a conversation about how there is no such thing as online privacy. Anything a child puts on his profile—a photo, a comment, a link—is now public. It can be copied, pasted, forwarded, shared, photographed, even printed out and passed around. If your child has truly private thoughts, feelings, or photos, they do not belong on a social networking page.[26]

Since teenagers are often more willing to listen to each other than to their parents, you may want to direct your older children toward youth-driven cyberbullying-prevention initiatives and activities. Two of the most appealing and effective sites recommended by Justin Patchin and Sammer Hinduja are:[27]

- *Cyberbullying 411* (www.cyberbully411.com). This attractive site is engaging for teenagers and provides excellent information about online harassment.
- *Cyber Mentors* (cybermentors.org.uk). This UK website features young people who are trained to take calls from other young people who are being bullied and cyberbullied. The young mentors are supervised as they respond to requests for help from bullying victims.

One social networking site that author Rachel Simmons regards as a hotbed of bullying is Formspring, and she recommends that kids stay away from it altogether. "Formspring has mostly been under the radar," she told me, "and parents don't even know about it. The site is an anonymous way for kids to say basically anything, and girls in particular are likely to use Formspring because girls have a burning desire to know what people think about them." Simmons has seen girls become addicted to Formspring, believing that it is the best way to find out what other kids really think of them. "It makes them even more paranoid," explained Simmons, who advises parents to check and see if their child has a webpage on the site.[28]

Online Safety Education for Younger Kids

Elementary school children, eager to spend time on the computer, have also entered the world of digital games and communities. Sheri Bauman has studied sites targeted to young kids, and she told me, "Lots of parents love Webkins. But parents should be aware that once you have interactive sites, there is the possibility for dangerous interactions. If parents stay as familiar as possible with these sites themselves and stay connected with their kids about using these sites, then it is okay. An excellent resource for parents of younger kids is www.commonsensemedia.org. If your kid wants to do Club Penguin or Webkins, check out Commonsense and read all about it, and if you think the benefits outweigh risks, go ahead and do it. And teach kids that if someone hurts them online, they should tell their parents. If too much aggression is happening in a game, maybe a kid should pick a different game."[29]

Bauman, along with other cyberbullying experts, does not tell parents to prohibit their children from participating in online games. Doing so would be unrealistic, given the world in which we live. The question is not whether to let kids go online but how to let them do so safely. There are websites designed specifically to teach young children how to be safe online, and two of the most highly recommended are:[30]

- *Hector's World* (www.hectorsworld.com). For children age nine and younger, this is one of the best interactive sites available about how to use technology safely. It is produced in New Zealand.
- *Superclubs Plus* (www.superclubsplus.com). For children age six to twelve and their teachers, this is a protected social networking site. Schools from forty-five countries participate in building their own community websites and in learning how to stay safe online.

Considerations for Educators and Schools

If you are a school administrator, there are steps you can take to create a safer school environment as it relates to online activity. Experts recommend that schools set up a cyberbullying "task force." An effective task force includes teachers, social workers and counselors, students, parents, and members of the community. The task force can then appoint cyberbully "experts" and clearly communicate to the students, parents, and teachers that these experts are the go-to people for prevention and reporting. Furthermore, schools can write a specific policy that defines and prohibits cyberbullying, and they can put protocols into place for intervening when incidents occur.[31] School personnel who are interested in high-quality curriculum materials can visit the following sites:[32]

- *Commonsense Media Digital Citizenship Curriculum* (www .commonsensemedia.org/educators). Curriculum for kindergarten through fifth grade and for sixth through eighth grades.
- *CyberSmart* (cybersmartcurriculum.org). Materials for Kindergarten through twelfth grade.

Setting Limits on Technology Use at Home

Parents who are connected to their children should not be relegated to talking to their children around handheld digital devices. If your child is using an iTouch, iPad, cell phone, or a video game during most of your conversations—occasionally glancing up at you to make eye contact—he or she is more connected to the digital world than to your conversation. When I began speaking with cyberbullying experts, I realized that Andrew and I were guilty of being addicted to our iPhones, and we took up Rosalind Wiseman's suggestion of placing our cell phones in a basket upon entering our house. There was nothing so urgent as to demand our constant attention during family time. For both children and adults, addiction to email and text messages is a real condition. The ping of an incoming message is a hot stimulus that provides instant gratification, and humans are primed to constantly seek out the potential reward contained in the message, such as an invitation to have lunch with a friend or an anxiously anticipated test result.

Interestingly, humans are also driven to check for negative messages. A child who is being cyberbullied has difficulty resisting the temptation to see what new terrible things others have written about her. As Rachel Simmons noted earlier in her remarks about Formspring, there is a horrible fascination that draws a bullied child in and compels her to read the cruel remarks, even when she knows it is against her best interest. Girls are particularly at risk for involvement in cyberbullying, because girls blog and IM more than boys.[33] This is partly due to the premium girls place on being constantly connected to other people.

For several weeks, Andrew and I were diligent about separating from our phones, but then they started to creep back into our pockets as we walked around the house. We both have to actively remind each other to leave the phones in a central location. Andrew's desire to check sports updates and my desire to check my messages have taught us not to underestimate the addictive pull of the phones. "Are you scheduled to perform neurosurgery in fifteen minutes?" Andrew asks when he sees me typing madly as my eggs burn on the stove. Yes! I want to say to him, even though I am probably texting with my mom or my sisters. And it must be a thousand times harder for kids to resist, because their entire world revolves around their social circles. Try to empathize with your children about this situation, even while striving to put limits on digital interaction. As Andrew and I have to remind each other, a face-to-face conversation between siblings or parents is always healthier than two people sitting side-by-side on the couch, fiddling on their phones.

Have your kids unplug before you talk with them. During family meals, consider placing cell phones in a designated spot away from the table, preventing a situation where everyone is busy texting and surfing the Internet instead of having connected conversations.

Sometimes kids are so addicted to their phones that they lose much-needed sleep by texting late into the night. For kids who are already anxious about being excluded, the fear of logging off and missing a possible discussion or an inside joke is enough to keep them awake. Sonya, an eighth grader, told me, "I won't leave the lunch table to go to the bathroom in case people start talking about me when I leave." That same sentiment keeps kids at the "Facebook table" around the clock. Parents can set up a rule that cell phones and computers charge overnight outside of children's bedrooms. If you are suspicious that your child is texting at all hours of the night, review your phone and Internet charges to see the times and frequency of usage. If your child is unable to keep away from the phone, sleep with it in your room. The separation may feel terrifying at first, but most kids will eventually appreciate the uninterrupted sleep, which will also boost their ability to cope with social stress and the barrage of cyber messages.

What to Do in the Event of a Cyberbullying Attack

Despite your child's best efforts to be a good digital citizen, he or she may still become the target of cyberbullying. Sheri Bauman told me, "We have learned how vulnerable some kids are—athletes, top scholars, honors students, and officers in student government—simply because their prominence makes them become higher likely targets. If you miss a basket, you'll be taunted online." If your child is suffering from cyberbullying attacks, there are steps you can take to regain control of the situation:[34]

- Print out the evidence, such as mean comments, videos, or photos, so that you can take the proof to the school and, if necessary, the police. Take a screen shot of the Facebook page or other page if necessary.
- Have your child block or delete the bullies. Use the "Block/ Delete This Person" link if one is available.
- Remind your child not to react online by writing mean or hurtful retaliatory comments. Bullies want a reaction; they feed off it.

- Report bullying to the site or network where it is happening. Some sites will deactivate the bully's account. Use the "Report Abuse" link if the site has one. If not, look in the "Contact Us" area and send an email about the abuse.
- Monitor your child for signs of overwhelming depression or anxiety after using the computer.
- Have your child join a support group for kids who are being cyberbullied, so he or she will not feel so isolated.
- Provide comfort and support at home, and help your child keep the perspective that things will settle down eventually. This too shall pass. It may feel to your child like his or her life is over, but time and distraction will help.

If you discover your child has been involved in sexting, even as a passive recipient of a photo, it is important to have a conversation about the very serious legal consequences of these activities. A lot of kids do not realize that sexting is illegal and that they could be charged with producing or distributing child pornography simply by passing along a nude photo of a fellow student. If the photo is emailed or texted to someone in another state, it becomes a federal felony, and if your children are keeping nude photos of other students on their phones or computers, it is grounds for a charge of possession. Children who are aware of the serious legal ramifications of sexting may think twice before forwarding inappropriate images.

Speaking with Young Kids About Sexting and Sexual Cyberbullying

Many parents of younger children read about cases such as that of Tyler Clementi and assume that sexting or sexual cyberbullying is something they can deal with in the future. But as with all ills, early prevention is more effective. There are ways in which we can even discuss the building blocks of sexting with very young children. *How can I possibly broach this subject with an elementary school child*, a parent may wonder. The key is to start with a natural, age-appropriate discussion of acceptable electronic media use.

Our first foray into a talk with Katie and Annie Rose about inappropriate sexual photos took place in March 2011. We were lounging in the house, enjoying the start to our weekend. Katie and Annie Rose had a banner day that Saturday. First, Andrew discovered them in the basement bathroom with the door locked. "Girls, let me in," Andrew said firmly. He found Katie, Annie Rose, and a giant Star Wars Wampa rug crammed into the bathroom. Katie was huddled in a corner, hiding something behind her back. It was a bag of cookies.

"I accidentally brought the cookies downstairs," Katie explained. "By mistake, I ate six of them."

"I had eight," Annie Rose confessed.

About an hour later, we found the two of them on the couch, giggling over a *People* magazine. "These people are naked," they cried gleefully and held up a picture of an ad that showed a couple locked in a passionate embrace. Although the ad only shows faces, arms, and torsos, it was very clear that the models were indeed naked. Andrew shot me a look and said, "Do NOT leave your *People* magazine out."

I forgot about it until later that night, when Andrew showed me an article he was reading in the *New York Times* by Jan Hoffman: "A Girl's Nude Photo, and Altered Lives." It was the heartbreaking story of a middle school girl who made the poor decision to snap a full frontal photo of herself and text it to her boyfriend. When they broke up, he forwarded the picture to another girl. The recipient was a mean-spirited girl who had had a falling out with the girl in the photo, and she seized the opportunity to engage in cyberbullying.

The mean girl typed "Ho Alert! If you think this girl is a whore, text this to all your friends."[35] And so began a drama that has caused irreparable harm to the lives of several of those involved. Andrew and I talked late into the night about the sadness of the situation. We talked about how frightening sexting is. "The problem is how easy it is to hit the send button," Andrew said, "and once it is done, you can't undo it. And with the hypersexualization of children, they don't think about the long-term ramifications of snapping a nude picture of themselves."

Girls are far more likely to be the subject of forwarded nude photos, because whereas boys and girls will both openly keep nude photos of girls on their phones, far fewer boys will keep nude photos of other boys on their phones. This means the potential audience for pictures of a naked-girl picture is much larger. As a mother of three daughters, I want to protect my girls from their own worst judgment and that of their peers. The best way to do that, beyond limiting use and access to technology, is to talk about it. So, that Sunday morning, we held our first conversation about sexting with our first grader and our preschooler.

Katie had recently received a digital camera, and she liked to snap photos of anything and everything—her toys, her sisters, the carpet in the hall, the cracks in the ceiling. We decided to use her camera as the entry point for our conversation.

"Katie, you can take pictures of people when they are dressed. Or even in bathing suits. But not in their underwear, and no pictures of private parts."

She thought about this and asked, "Can I take a picture of Daddy without a shirt on?"

"Yes," we responded, "because you can go out in public and see men at the beach or at the pool without a shirt on. But you cannot take a picture of Mommy without her shirt on."

"Well, I don't have boobs yet. Can I take a picture of me without a shirt on?" she inquired.

"No, because your chest is still private. In some countries, girls and women do not wear bathing-suit tops at the beach, and it is okay, but where we live, females cover their chests. So, I do not want you taking pictures of yourself without a top on," I explained. "And if you are playing with friends who want to take those kinds of pictures, you can tell them that it is not a safe idea."

Since Katie and Annie Rose do not have cell phones, email accounts, etc., we ended the conversation at that point. Children today acquire technical skills that outpace their cognitive skills, and we need to help narrow the gap between what they know how to do and what they should do. This was a conversation we will have in various forms many many times over the years. Our goal with that first conversation was just to try to introduce them to the concept that they should not be snapping photos of their bodies unclothed.

Chapter Thirteen

Changing Our Cultural Attitudes Toward Aggression and Cruelty

Actress Chase Masterson told me, "I think it's 'in' on some horrific level for people to be mean. Talk shows and comedy shows say it's okay to laugh at other people. But it's not okay. It's certainly not a 'do unto others as they would do unto you' attitude. We don't want to feel belittled, so why inflict it on someone else? Our culture sends a message that you have to be perfect to be accepted. I see it as an actress, with women having to weigh 105 pounds to get a role. It is very sad. My character on *Star Trek*, Leeda, married the guy who was the ugly outcast underdog, but he was pretty on the inside." Masterson mentioned that even today, she thinks she has a thick skin, but when she reads a harsh criticism, "It cuts to the core. It leads to those memories of being bullied when you were young."[1]

Star Trek is not the only show with a valuable social message. One of today's most popular television shows, the megahit *Glee,* deals heavily with issues of bullying. *Glee* has brought bullying of geeky kids and gay kids to the forefront of our country's consciousness, building a meaningful plotline around the social tiers of high school and the plight of those at the bottom of the heap. *Glee* promotes numerous stereotypes (about football players and cheerleaders, smart kids and dumb blondes), but it does so in order to then decon-struct these stereotypes. Interestingly, a number of the main charac-ters in *Glee* simultaneously find themselves affiliated with groups that are both on top socially and at the bottom, such as Finn, the quarterback of the football team, who is also one of the lead singers in the geeky glee club. This creates a unique opportunity for Finn's character to develop empathy and bring his message of acceptance back to the bullying members of the football team. Because the show itself is considered "cool" in our culture, it elevates the social accept-ability of the *Glee* kids. The show has been able to leverage its popu-larity to spread an anti-bullying message, a phenomenon that is translating offscreen too.

Glee has a lot of work to do to combat the messages that our tweens and teens receive from shows like *Jersey Shore,* which basi-cally pushes a steady diet of shallow, appearance-driven entitlement. Stan Davis, author of *Schools Where Everyone Belongs,* bluntly told me, "*Jersey Shore* is the worst thing that has ever been done in the media."[2]

Davis is not the only one concerned about the effects of reality television on kids. According to new research conducted by the Girl Scout Research Institute, girls who regularly watch reality television accept and expect a higher level of drama, aggression, and bullying in their own lives; they are more likely to believe that being mean and lying will earn them success. Furthermore, they place higher value on their physical appearance than nonviewers.

The research, titled *Real to Me: Girls and Reality TV,* states that 47 percent of girls ages eleven to seventeen watch reality television regularly, and they believe it to be an accurate depiction of real life. Consider some of the findings, which indicate how reality television has distorted girls' perceptions:[3]

In Areas of Relationship Drama
- 78% of regular reality TV viewers think "gossiping is a nor-mal part of a relationship between girls" versus 54% of non-viewers.

- 68% of regular reality TV viewers believe "it is in girls' nature to be catty and competitive with each other" versus 50% of nonviewers.

In Areas of Self-Image
- 72% of girls who regularly watch reality TV say they spend a lot of time on their appearance versus 42% of nonviewers.
- 38% of girls who regularly view reality TV programs think that a girl's value is based on how she looks, compared to 28% of nonviewers.

In Perceptions of How to Gain Success
- 37% of regular reality TV viewers believe that "you have to lie to get what you want" versus 24% of nonviewers.
- 37% of girls who regularly watch reality TV say that "being mean earns you more respect than being nice" versus 25% of nonviewers.

I spoke with Maria Wynne, CEO of Girl Scouts of Greater Chicago and Northwest Indiana, about why the Girl Scouts decided to conduct this research.[4] "As a council," Wynne explained, "we had great curiosity and impetus to understand the world through the eyes of the girls. We learned that 'mean girl syndrome' is something they are seeing and learning on reality television. It is very damaging. It is not okay to make your way through the world at someone else's disadvantage."

Fortunately, given the vast numbers of girls who watch reality television, there were also some positive findings. Regular reality television viewers reported higher levels of self-confidence than nonviewers, and they also feel that the reality shows expose them to people with different backgrounds, beliefs, ideas, and perspectives.

Specifically, in Terms of Uplifting Results
- 62% of girls say that reality TV has increased their awareness of social issues and causes.
- 46% of regular reality TV viewers aspire to leadership versus 27% of nonviewers.

- 75% of regular viewers see themselves as role models for other girls versus 61% of nonviewers.

The Girl Scouts plan to capitalize on the positive findings and use them as a way to connect with girls while trying to mitigate the negative findings. Wynne believes that "the point of intervention is now" and advises parents to "ask the girls what they think. Remind them that the footage on reality television shows is heavily edited. What do they think went on behind the scenes? Is it *really* real?" To help parents with discussions, the Girl Scouts published a guide called "Tips for Parents—Real to Me." You can find it at www .girlscouts.org/research/pdf/real_to_me_tip_sheet_for_parents.pdf.

Even the younger children, those who do not watch programs like *Jersey Shore,* are now inundated with television shows and movies that value sex and aggression. This has been an evolving process. Twenty years ago, girls were largely idealized as nice and sweet, and popular television shows emphasized the idea that girls don't rock the boat. That was the heyday of shows like *My Little Pony, Care Bears,* and *Strawberry Shortcake.* As some girls began to rebel against the rigid stereotype of the unassertive female, a revised category of girl characters emerged, but now the pendulum has swung too far in the other direction. Sugar and spice gave way to sassy and saucy.

Mimicking the trend in television shows, the toy industry introduced edgier dolls. Companies produced affordable brands like *Bratz* (made by MGA Entertainment) and *Monster High* (made by Mattel), a slew of backstabbing, fast-talking girls who often exude sexiness instead of sweetness and nastiness instead of niceness. Although these dolls have proven to be a gold mine for MGA Entertainment and Mattel, consumers are starting to speak up about the image the popular toys portray. Hypersexualized and sometimes mean, the dolls and their associated websites are sucking ever-younger children into a world of short skirts, heavy makeup, high heels, and caustic comebacks.

Knowing that counselor Nicole Knepper, author of the blog *Moms Who Drink and Swear,* has enjoyed playing with the Monster High dolls with her young daughter prompted me to ask her: "How do you recommend that parents help their children play with these dolls in a positive way?"

"I realized that these dolls were created using some fantastic literary characters and long-standing mythical creatures," Knepper replied, "and through them, I would have an amazing opportunity to broaden my daughter's knowledge of history and literature through imaginative play. We looked up the myths and stories so that she could have more background information in order to create adventures for her dolls. Her fear of monsters decreased as we discussed history and storytelling."

Knepper's daughter was fascinated to know that millions of children for thousands of years had also struggled with a fear of monstrous creatures hiding in their closets or backyards. "We laughed about some of the more silly concepts and talked about why it's perfectly okay that the possibilities are endless when it comes to imagination," she told me.

But not every parent is going to take the time to play *with* his or her daughter in the way that Knepper does, and some children are only exposed to Monster High through watching the webisodes, which are more shallowly focused.

In an interesting development, Mattel has recognized that the *Monster High* characters often act too aggressively, and they have joined forces with an anti-bullying movement called the Kind Campaign. Founded by two young women, Lauren Parsekian and Molly Stroud, the Kind Campaign is focused on reducing girl-against-girl "crime." Two years ago, as new college graduates, Lauren and Molly piled into the back of a minivan with their moms and a cameraman and drove across the country, filming a critically acclaimed documentary called *Finding Kind*. When the partnership between Mattel and the Kind Campaign was first announced, there was a backlash among anti-bullying advocates who were worried that Mattel was using it as an opportunity to market their dolls during the Kind Campaign's in-school assemblies. Lauren explained to me, "When the initial press release came out, there was a lot of misunderstanding. People thought that *Monster High* was coming into schools and we'd be selling dolls. Not at all. They are not part of our assembly, and their brand is not being slapped onto ours. Instead, Molly and I are being animated into monster versions of ourselves and going into *Monster High* to hold a Kind Campaign assembly, teaching the monster girls—Frankie Stein, Draculaura, Cleo De Nile, and the rest of the *Monster High* students—how important it is for them to be kind to one another."[5]

I expressed concerns about Lauren and Molly being turned into sexually dressed monsters, and Lauren reassured me, "We consulted on our clothes. We know that a lot of elementary school girls watch the show. We wear pants and shirts with collars up to our necks, and we go as ourselves trying to bring a social change to a *Monster High* webisode. It gives us a chance to reach a much broader audience with our Kind message." Since Lauren and Molly acknowledged that elementary girls watch *Monster High,* one can assume that Mattel is also aware that young girls comprise much of the audience, although the corporation claims that the show is marketed to tweens and early teens.

If *Monster High* is truly dedicated to reforming its image, Mattel will need to make meaningful age-appropriate changes that last much longer than one webisode. It would be interesting for Lauren and Molly to show the monsters *why* they should be kind to each other, not just *how* to be kind. This opens the door for discussions of tolerance and acceptance of those who are different. By teaching the monsters about prejudices and stereotypes, the Kind Campaign can uncover the roots of cruelty. The roadblock is that this type of content change would require *Monster High*'s writers to overhaul the general direction of each storyline. "Conflict is what spurs episodes, but we have been able to talk about this with Mattel. We are in there having the conversations with Mattel that so many moms want to have with them. They are listening to us, and we are listening to the moms. In the end, people will just have to wait and see, but we wouldn't have joined with Mattel if we didn't think change was possible."[6]

Ultimately, it is encouraging that Mattel has made the decision to partner with the Kind Campaign, and for the naysayers, I offer up this thought: if none of the nonprofits are willing to work with Mattel for fear of being labeled as corporate sellouts, how will things ever improve? It is better to have Lauren and Molly advocating for our young girls than to throw our arms up in the air, complain about the problem, but refuse to work with the source. Lauren and Molly understand the dynamics behind the bullying, which is apparent to anyone who sees their work. Molly told me, "My personal experience with severe bullying happened junior year of high school. On the last day of school, the mean girl who had orchestrated most of it saw me in the hall and called out my name. I was terrified, but then, to my astonishment, she said, 'I am so sorry for what I have done, and I don't know why I did it.' The apology was so powerful and helped me get past what I dealt with, all the pain. We do something called the 'Kind Apology' when we go into the schools. We pass these apology cards out, and it's amazing to watch the girls fill out these cards and walk across the room and hand it to another girl and see that girl accept the apology. Often, the original conflict point was lost, but they were still mad at each other."

Girl-on-girl cruelty is not a new problem, and the Kind Campaign is one of many efforts to expose and reduce female bullying. In Rachel Simmons's bestselling book *Odd Girl Out: The Hidden Culture of Aggression in Girls*, Simmons writes:

> *Our culture refuses girls access to open conflict, and it forces their aggression into nonphysical, indirect, and covert forms. Girls use backbiting, exclusion, rumors, name-calling, and manipulation to inflict psychological pain. Unlike boys, who tend to bully acquaintances or strangers, girls frequently attack within tightly knit networks of friends, making aggression harder to identify and intensifying the damage to victims.*[7]

Kyra, an outgoing girl with a warm smile, still shudders when she describes the bullying she endured at the hands of girls in middle school. "It was subtle," she says, shaking her head with a rueful laugh. "That was part of the problem. Girls do stuff behind the scenes. Some of it was blatantly aggressive, like not picking me to be on their team and being very outspoken about not wanting me, but other times it was just a feeling, a sense of being excluded. They could smell a vulnerability in me, even though I looked like everyone else. I was very naive, and the girls picked up on it."[8]

Simmons advises that we show our daughters that no relationship is conflict free; relationships cannot survive without conflict, and girls need not be controlled by fear of conflict. The proliferation of online communication exacerbates hidden aggression, because girls can take conflict to the Internet and anonymously attack each other, a phenomenon that did not exist a generation ago.[9] Simmons encourages girls to acknowledge conflicts in face-to-face confrontations, the better to reduce acts of hidden aggression. There is much less social pain involved in directly confronting an issue than in waging a campaign of retaliation, but many girls simply have not learned any other way to address their grievances with one another. The first step is to make kids aware of the dynamics at play, and the second step is to teach them new ways of interacting that call upon their social and emotional skills.

There is a debate among bullying experts about whether children who bully others do so because they *don't know* how much it hurts or they *don't care* how much it hurts. I think it can be either one or sometimes both. In the case of very young children who are learning how to navigate social situations, I want to give them the benefit of the doubt and assume they don't necessarily know how their words and actions affect others. If a bullying child continues to mistreat others after being informed how victimization feels, then we can attribute the continued bad behavior in part to a lack of empathy. This is where cultural messages about cruelty really play a role. It is hard to convince small children that it is unacceptable to be persistently and deliberately cruel when they receive the opposite message from the media.

Annie Fox advises, "Teach kids that they don't have to laugh along with the popular leaders to gain approval. Kids think they will feel better about themselves if they are elevated in the eyes of the leader, even if they have to drag other people down while they do it. I tell kids, 'You are starting to drag yourself down. You are at war with yourself, jettisoning friends and lying to your parents, all to keep a lifestyle in place that isn't you anyway. Cruel is not cool.' "[10]

It makes sense for parents to listen to anti-bullying messages from people like Annie Fox and Rachel Simmons, experts in the field, but what do we do when corporations jump on the popular anti-bullying bandwagon? I mentioned the partnership between Mattel and the Kind Campaign, the results of which have not been determined. A collaboration that has raised a far bigger brouhaha is the highly publicized partnership of World Wrestling Entertainment (WWE), the National Education Association (NEA), and the Creative Coalition to create the Be a STAR anti-bullying program. The WWE is a marketing behemoth, and it has recruited a number of celebrities to endorse the Be a STAR program. The opportunity to spread an anti-bullying message to millions of people is a powerful incentive to join forces with the Be a STAR campaign.

But it is a complicated union. The WWE has produced hours upon hours of entertainment that promotes social interactions based on degradation. The shows are cleaner than they used to be, but they still rely heavily on negative stereotypes. Since the action is all scripted, argues Rosalind Wiseman, the writers have full control over the messages they send, and they still choose to send messages of humiliation and sexualization.[11] WWE produces programs like *Smackdown* and *Raw*, in which we see bikini-clad women mock attacking each other over who is deemed sexiest by the men, and we see men using intimidation and force to prove their masculinity.

Boys who watch these shows are encouraged to be "real men"— loud, aggressive, heavily muscled, sexually attractive to women, vengeful, and skilled with weapons and fighting techniques. There is no room in this picture for quiet, sensitive, intellectual, emotionally expressive boys. If boys have to be macho to fit the image of a real man, then the conclusion society draws is that boys who are not macho must not be real men. They get labeled homos, fags, sissies, pussies, and queers. The scripts promoted by WWE play into the stereotypical identity story packaged to boys, a story that appears over and over again in books, magazines, video games, music, movies, and shows marketed to boys. The authors of *Packaging Boyhood* describe the typical Boy Power story as follows:

It's a story in which those with the most power too often have the wrong kind of power—they are bullies, narcissistic athletes, "dogs," or "players"—the ones who call the shots and get the scantily clad, booty-jiggling, music video girls. It's a story that teaches boys that they need to avoid humiliation at all costs, seek revenge if wronged, dress to impress and intimidate, be tech savvy, show wealth, and take risks, all the while pretending they don't care about any of it.[12]

This identity story simply does not jive with an anti-bullying message. I spoke with Josh Golan, associate director at Campaign for a Commercial-Free Childhood, about the WWE's new anti-bullying partnership. "Be a STAR is a curriculum that goes along with a film called *That's What I Am*," Golan told me. "The film is made by the WWE, and it stars Ed Harris. In the copy I received, before the film began, there was an ad for a WWE videogame." Golan is very concerned about the partnership, describing the WWE as a "celebration of humiliation."

Still, it is hard to turn away a company that wants to spread an anti-bullying message, especially when that company has the ability to reach millions of people. The WWE could become credible participants at the table of kindness, critics say, if they make serious script changes going forward. Given that the WWE has built an empire on depictions of bullying disguised as athletic competitions, it may be impossible to satisfy the goals of an anti-bullying platform while keeping the brand intact. The existing brand is wildly successful, so the WWE may not have an incentive to make fundamental changes merely to appease a proportionately small number of outspoken critics.

Just one week after WWE made a "No Homophobia" pact with the Gay and Lesbian Alliance Against Defamation (GLAAD), a WWE commentator sent a tweet to a colleague calling him a "faggot." When the commentator was called out on his language, he sent a tweet to his followers that stated in part: "I apologize to any and all who were offended by my tweet. It was obviously not meant the way it was taken."[13] Although it may be the case that the two men were

engaging in the type of insider joking that often includes homophobic comments, this does not change the fact that outsiders found it
offensive, and it reinforces the pressure on boys not to be considered
a "homo" by their peers. The tweet incident aside, the WWE has millions of devoted fans who are outspoken in their defense of WWE's
Be a STAR campaign. The corporation clearly employs marketing
geniuses; now it is time to hire scriptwriting geniuses.

In the end, the WWE and Mattel are just two companies, but they
represent the vast power that corporations hold to influence cultural
messages. Ever the optimist and slightly the skeptic, I curiously await
the future to see if these companies can inculcate the ideals of the
anti-bullying campaigns they profess to support. Slick marketing
campaigns, or instruments of change? We shall see.

Chapter Fourteen

Calling on Toy Retailers to Eliminate Gender-Based Marketing

Pink means girl. Blue means boy. At times it feels impossible to change this overwhelming cultural message. Has there ever been a time in history with such strong significance attached to a color, and was it possible to reverse the association? Yes and yes. Jo Paoletti, the historian who authored *Pink and Blue: Telling the Boys from the Girls in America,* observed to me, "The interesting thing about pink is that it is like wearing black in the nineteenth century. At that time, wearing black meant you were in mourning. Any woman in a black dress was a widow. It was a very strong symbolic color. But clearly, black has changed and now it doesn't mean that. Black is a fashion statement." Pink is clearly the new black. Pink has stepped in as the most symbolic color in our twenty-first-century culture. Pink means female, and woe to the girl who rejects pink or the boy who embraces pink. Paoletti commented, "What marketing does is create symbols that people can use to bully people. It's almost like having a recipe and saying these are the ingredients for masculinity and femininity, and if you vary from the recipe, you can get bullied."[1]

Ashley Eckstein, the actress who voices Ahsoka Tano in *The Clone Wars,* is trying to change the recipe. When Eckstein began her role as Ahsoka, she was dismayed to find that there was little to no merchandise for female Star Wars fans. She did some research and discovered that close to 50 percent of Star Wars fans are female. "I asked why we didn't have more female merchandise and was told that women would not buy the products and I should just be happy with a men's size small. This answer was not acceptable to me. Star Wars is for everyone and there SHOULD be Star Wars products in the girls' section too!" So Eckstein started Her Universe, a merchandise line for female Star Wars fans. She explained, "Her Universe is more than a clothing company. It is a community. It's a place where female sci-fi fans can come out of hiding and step into the spotlight. Girls on our site share stories about how they were scared to truly be themselves for fear of being bullied." In 2010, Her Universe announced a partnership with Syfy to do its merchandise because half of the viewers on the Syfy network are women. Eckstein emphasized, "The numbers are there, but the stereotype still exists. How do we break down that barrier? We speak up."[2]

Erin, a reader of my original anti-bullying article, snapped a photo of the toy section in Walmart and sent me the photo, commenting, "No wonder the six-year-old boys are confused! Look how stores are set up! There is no 'Toys'; just 'Girls' toys and 'Boys' toys. This has annoyed me for a few years, but in light of Katie's story, it just fired me up!" Another reader, Milton, emailed Walmart and copied me on the reply from a senior vice president, who wrote, "Thank you for your note regarding perceived 'gender bias' at Walmart in the toy department. We will consider your concerns and see if we can change the words on the signing to be more gender neutral. We want kids playing with ALL toys, without lines being drawn by gender. Thanks again, your comments are valued, and will be treated with concern and attention." Milton has made further attempts to contact the senior vice president at Walmart without success.

IN MARCH 2011, I stopped at Target with my girls to pick up a birthday gift for a friend of Annie Rose's. We zipped past the enticing toys, easily picking out a game for a four-year-old girl, and headed toward the checkout. But then I wheeled my cart back around. I had just read in *Packaging Girlhood* by Sharon Lamb and Lyn Mikel Brown that it is important to talk with children and teens about the way stereotypes are promulgated, particularly as we encounter them in real life, and I decided to experiment with one of these "teaching opportunities."

"Katie, Annie Rose, look at the background behind the shelves of toys. What do you notice?"

The background behind the Star Wars figures, Legos, construction toys, and cars was blue and black. The background behind the Barbies, kitchen toys, dolls, Disney princesses, and dress-up clothes was pink. "Girls," I explained, "The store has grouped toys that are traditionally for girls in the pink section and toys that are traditionally for boys in the blue section. So, if you are a girl who wants to buy a Star Wars Lego set, you are made to feel as if you are crossing into the 'boys' section' to get your toy. Katie, this is one of the reasons why the boys taunted you for carrying a Star Wars water bottle—you stepped outside of the box." Then we walked over to an aisle that happened to be neutral. It was the aisle that contained gift wrap for all occasions. "What color is the background behind these shelves?" I asked. "Yellow," they answered, and we talked about how yellow is for everyone. In that first discussion, I felt like I was doing too much of the talking, as I introduced words and concepts. By the time I got around to soliciting their thoughts, they were more interested in buying a hot pretzel. There's always a next time!

Parents can have these same types of conversations with their sons, because there are numerous stereotypes aimed specifically at boys. In *Packaging Boyhood,* also written by Lamb and Brown, along with Mark Tappan, the authors recommend:

As soon as he's old enough to be sorting out gender and asking what makes a boy a boy and a girl a girl—ages three, four, and five, you can introduce the S word: Stereotype. Maybe not even the word at this young age, but the idea. He'll be getting messages everywhere in the media that as a boy he should love all those other S words like superheroes, speed, and sports. He'll get the message that boys are hyper, tough, and over-the-top,

that emotions (other than aggression and anger) are for girls,
and that he should enjoy grossing people out with farts and
burps. Because these expectations are so pervasive in media,
you can begin this conversation pretty much anytime and
anywhere. We recommend you start with the next trip to the
toy store. Thanks to all those pesky marketers, all you'll need
for a lively conversation has been carefully planned and laid
out for you in pink and blue/black aisles of Toys"R"Us or
Walmart.[3]

The reason why stores segregate by gender is mostly due to money. Imagine you are a toy manufacturer trying to sell a set of red toy blocks. If you slather blue paint on one set and pink paint on the other, you can sell two sets to a mother who is shopping with her son and daughter—his-and-hers blocks. You have reached your goal of selling more, but there are some unpleasant social consequences: (1) the brother and sister no longer need to share the blocks, eliminating an opportunity to develop their social skills; and (2) the pink and blue blocks reinforce gender stereotypes.

I posted a discussion about this topic on my blog. One reader, Kaidlen, said, "The Kmart here where I live groups toys according to type, instead of gender. They have the Toy Story toys on the action figure aisle, which actually include the Toy Story Barbie dolls, instead of the dolls being with the other Barbie dolls on the doll aisle. Kmart here also uses white as their color for behind the toys." Joslyn Grey, author of the blog *Stark Raving Mad Mommy,* told me how her daughters get frustrated with the pervasiveness of gender-based marketing. "At McDonald's, they ask if you want a boy toy or a girl toy with the happy meal. It annoys my girls. They make little comments about it."

Even our beloved Star Wars toys are a classic example of gender-based toy marketing. Star Wars toys are placed front and center in the boy aisles, and it is difficult to even find female characters in action figures. An inside source at Lucasfilm explained to me: "The toy companies surveyed children to see what types of action figures they wanted, but the research was skewed. They interviewed 80 percent boys and 20 percent girls, instead of a fifty-fifty split, and they phrased questions in a manipulative way." Ashley Eckstein, one of the many female business owners dependent on this flawed research, has been unable to convince mass retailers to carry her Star Wars clothing for females in their stores. Eckstein said, "Nowadays, in the mass market, you cannot fail. It is not an option. Hasbro and Lego must guarantee to Target or Walmart that when they release a new product, it will be a success. They don't want to sell something for the girls in a traditional boys' market if it cannot guarantee sales." The research, although arguably biased, is what companies like Hasbro and Lego rely on, and it does not show that girl items will guarantee sales. Eckstein pointed out, "Star Wars was number one in toy sales last year and made over five-hundred million dollars, and they will say, 'Why fix what's not broken?' With Her Universe, I take it one step at a time. We've come a long way, though! The fact that Lucasfilm made a fourteen-year-old girl Anakin's Padawan is a huge step, and the people at Lucasfilm are working with me and helping me wherever they can."[4]

Gender-based marketing has a much stronger effect on children than it does on adults. Adults have the benefit of perspective, and we do not take things as literally as children do. When I see an ad showing a tall, willowy woman using a certain brand of perfume, I know logically that purchasing the same perfume will not make me tall and willowy. I can rationalize through the messages that the media is sending to me, but my young daughters cannot. Children are very literal, sometimes amusingly so, and other times frighteningly so. Paoletti told me that she really understood the impact of gender-based marketing when she looked at it from the point of view of the kids, not the adults. "I started looking at the kids. Children take marketing very seriously. They believe what they see on television, and they interpret things differently than adults. Even college kids, my own students, think they are very savvy, but they are still very influenced by marketing. Kids really hold on to and enforce gender stereotypes."

Because kids are the ones who really subscribe to gender stereotypes, retailers deliberately play up gender differences in bricks-and-mortar stores where kids tend to accompany parents who are shopping. When kids are removed from the equation, the shopping experience changes. "You can find more unisex clothing online," Paoletti observed, "because the online shopper is not the four-year-old; it is the adult at the computer. We are more likely to see and purchase gender-neutral options."[5]

Parents of small children who willingly cross gender boundaries are pained by the condemnation that their children tend to receive from other people. Just as children take marketing seriously, so do they take criticisms seriously. Even a young child with supportive parents may curtail his gender nonconforming interests as he grows increasingly aware of the world's disapproval. One worried mother told me, "I am troubled by the fact that my son, who likes everything (from his Star Wars stuff to his baby doll, from his trucks to his new *Princess and the Frog* sticker) is now getting old enough to notice some of the negative comments from friends, family, and even strangers when they see his Jessie doll (from Toy Story, because they think he should only have Buzz and Woody), or they hear him ask for a pink balloon at the grocery store, or he drinks out of a purple cup instead of one that is a 'boy' color, or they hear I'm taking him to a dance class. I always tell these people that we don't believe in boy colors/toys/activities and girl colors/toys/activities, so keep your comments to yourself, but I won't always be there to catch it. Soon he'll start to listen to them and be shamed out of enjoying things he loves . . . heartbreaking."

Laura Hanish, who focuses her research in the field of gender-based bullying in young children, shared with me her knowledge about the effects of gender-based toy marketing on kids.[6] "Beginning in preschool," she said, "we observe that children segregate by gender. Girls play with girls, boys with boys, and we see segregation of activities, too." I thought about how I have walked into preschool classes to see the girls playing house or dress up and the boys building tracks for their cars and trains. Hanish continued, "That kind of segregation has a developmental impact on children. As a girl spends more time playing with girls and less time interacting with boys, she develops an increasing interest in more gender-typical behaviors. At the same time, this limits her abilities to interact properly with boys. As the children get older, they develop gender-typical styles of interacting more often than gender-atypical behaviors. For example, girls are more submissive and boys are more aggressive. When a girl exhibits atypical-gender behavior, such as assertiveness or directiveness, this leads to conflict. Girls who are assertive tend to get victimized by their peers." When girls come together down the road with boys, Hanish explained, there is limited understanding of each other, which can lead to aggression and bullying. Now imagine a world where children are not directed into playing with certain toys or adopting certain behavior traits. In a diverse environment, girls and boys interact with each other more frequently, and they gain understanding of each other. Diversity is not just good in terms of race and religion; it is also good in terms of gender relationships.

The absence of gender-neutral clothes in bricks-and-mortar stores reinforces children's developmental desire to identify strongly with one gender, contributing to increased segregation by gender. This leads to the negative effects described by Hanish. We lose the continuum, and kids get shunted to one side or the other because there is no middle. Trucks and trousers for boys, dolls and dresses for girls—our children lose their individuality when they shop at mass retailers. Whereas making money is one motivating factor behind gendered marketing, there is another cultural issue at play: anxiety about gender roles. As Paoletti said, "Having limited choice forces kids into categories that they may not be entirely happy with. My theory, which I have not tested yet, is that kids who gravitate strongly toward gendered clothes are ones who feel strongly or who are more anxious about identifying with their gender. And if you have a boy who likes sparkly stuff but has received very strong messages that boys can't have that stuff, he will pick very masculine clothes. What makes a bully is fear."[7]

This theory fits in perfectly with a major story line on season two of the television show *Glee*. One of the characters, David Karofsky, was secretly gay, and he hid his torment behind an übermasculine appearance. Karofsky, played by Max Adler, was a big, macho guy who wore his football jacket every day and relentlessly bullied others, particularly an openly gay character named Kurt Hummel, played by Chris Colfer. I spoke with Max Adler about his role as the antigay bully on *Glee*.[8] Adler explained, "Karofsky was afraid of what he didn't know. Being a jock in rural Ohio, he was not exposed to different cultures. It was pumped into his brain that Kurt was wrong. Karofsky was homophobic and frightened. He saw Kurt and thought, 'If you are different, does that make me different? What does this mean for me?' Karofsky wanted Kurt out of his sight, so he didn't have to think about those scary things."

Karofsky may be a television character, but he has plenty of real-life counterparts. Jerry Pope, the college counselor I mentioned earlier who bonds with his students over hip-hop music, is one such example. Pope secretly knew he was gay from an early age, and he took his fear and rage out on kids who were different. Like Karofsky, Pope does not look like a stereotypical gay man, and nobody suspected he was gay. Even his own family was shocked when he came out as an adult. Pope, a tall, muscular athlete who looks like a typical frat boy, told me, "I viciously made fun of the theater kids and the gay kids, because I so desperately did not want to be gay. There was no one I related to, and I felt so isolated. I didn't have the Internet, so I didn't know anyone like me, a big athletic guy who was gay. I grew up in a rural area, and I thought I would never come out of the closet."[9] Even on modern-day television, many gay men are portrayed as feminine and theatrical, and the character of Karofsky is a welcome departure from the stereotypical gay man. Adler said, "You wouldn't believe how many letters I get from large, athletic gay men [like Pope] who have seen Karofsky on *Glee* and are so happy to see a gay character that represents *them*. It makes them feel less alone to know that not all gay men look or act like Kurt Hummel."

The Karofskys of the world grow up with a narrow definition of masculinity, wrapped up in a neat blue box with a blue bow, and it creates terror for the men who are different. Jerry Pope is working to actively counter the beliefs with which he was raised. He looked at me with honesty and said, "I am spending a life making amends. I was raised in a racist, sexist, homophobic community, and every day I am reprogramming myself to think differently, and I know that's true of a lot of other people—I am forgiving, like with Kobe Bryant, who used an antigay slur in the heat of a game. It was a teachable moment. He apologized, and I forgave him."

Many researchers are examining the explosion of interest around gender stereotypes, one of whom is Lyn Mikel Brown. We spoke about the pink and blue dilemma, and she observed, "We are in this postmodern moment about gender. Both boys and girls are crossing gender boundaries. It is very complex, and it raises a ton of anxiety among parents. Moms feel comfortable announcing little girls with pink and little boys with blue, because they feel they know what to expect. But no one really knows what to expect. Kids come out all over the spectrum." Marketers and media are taking advantage of this anxiety by making it really simple and saying, "this is boy" and "this is girl." "This is what's built into masculinity—it is kept in place by a denigration of femininity and homosexuality," commented Brown. "And girls are kept in place by sexualization."[10] Try as society might, kids are breaking free of the carefully constructed bonds that try to keep boys and girls in their respective places. There are little boys who insist on buying pink tennis shoes and little girls that insist on buying Star Wars water bottles.

Lego has ignited a furious controversy over gender-based marketing with the launch of Legos for Girls. The new line, featured in the January 2012 Lego catalogue, is called Lego Friends. The ladyfigs are slimmer than the traditional Lego minifigs, and they have curvy breasts. The Lego Friends live in Heartlake City, which thus far consists of a beauty parlor, a bakery, a café, a vet's office, a clothing design school, a sound stage, and an inventor's workshop. The toys come with accessories such as lipsticks, hairbrushes, and cupcakes. Unlike the "boy" sets, the Lego Friends do not require complete assembly before girls can begin to play with them, reducing the opportunities for girls to feel a sense of accomplishment at following the building instructions.[11] And while it is a nice addition to offer fun, pampering kits such as a beauty parlor and a café—because there are tons of kids who will really enjoy them—there is a noticeable underrepresentation of female leadership roles. Where are the female firefighters and teachers, the female police officers and the female mayor of Heartlake City?

In response to criticism from consumers, Lego explained that it conducted four years of market research with girls and their parents, and this is what girls want.[12] Girls do often like those things, but they have other interests, too! It is not surprising that the Lego Friends are what the girls want, because this is what Lego and other mass retailers have been telling the girls they should want. Children will listen. Children will agree when you constantly tell them that girls like parties and makeup while boys like adventure and building. And then when Lego asks the girls what they want to play with, and they answer, "princesses and jewelry, makeup and flowers," it is an answer Lego has helped to manufacture.[13]

Lego could have increased its product offerings to appeal to more girls in an integrative way. For example, the Lego Friends are the only line of Lego characters that do not have the classic blockish Lego shape, which makes the girls the "others." Why not create additional female minifigs that fit in with the existing lines of Legos? Why not make pink and purple bricks and simply mix them in with the red and blue and black bricks? What if a boy wants to use some pink or purple? Does he have to go to the—gasp!—girl aisle? What if he wants to build a bakery? A healthier strategy would be for Lego to put all their Lego kits side by side with gender-neutral packaging, thus allowing both girls and boys to choose the toys they want without feeling labeled. Add in the cafés and the beauty shops, but make them accessible to any interested child. In essence, bring back the strategy Lego used in 1981, when the company distributed a print ad that featured a little red-headed girl wearing blue jeans and a blue T-shirt who was proudly holding a Lego creation. The ad's caption said "What it is is beautiful." And in smaller letters, the Lego sets were referred to as "Universal Building Sets." Not "girl" sets or "boy" sets. Universal. Yes, what it was was beautiful.

Peggy Orenstein wrote about the Lego Friends issue, noting that although preschool girls and boys do prefer different types of play, which is developmentally normal, research shows that young children have brains that are more malleable.[14] This is the time for parents to be flexible with toy introduction, not rigid. "At issue, then," wrote Orenstein in an article for *The New York Times*, "is not nature or nurture but how nurture becomes nature: the environment in which children play and grow can encourage a range of aptitudes or fore-close them. So blithely indulging—let alone exploiting—stereo-typically gendered play patterns may have a more negative long-term impact on kids' potential than parents imagine. And promoting, without forcing, cross-sex friendships as well as a breadth of play styles may be more beneficial."[15] In the spring of 2012, The Lego Group demonstrated that it is listening to the concerns of consumers and held a meeting with the representatives from SPARK, a girl-fueled activist movement dedicated to ending the sexualization of women and girls in the media. Lego is currently working to address many of the issues raised and can serve as a role model for other companies on how to incorporate customer feedback into products that have already hit the market.

Chapter Fifteen

Stop Marketing Makeup and Sexy Clothes to Children

In the winter of 2011, Walmart announced that it was introducing Geogirl, a new line of cosmetics, specifically designed for girls eight to twelve years old.[1] The mass retailer wants a piece of the tween makeup market, which earns more than $24 million per year, with the top sellers to kids being lip gloss, eye shadow, and mascara.[2] When I heard about Walmart's expansion into kiddie makeup, my first thought was, *This doesn't help the movement to prevent bullying.* Parents may wonder, how is bullying at all related to makeup? The connection goes through sexualization.

According to the American Psychological Association's *Report of the APA Task Force on the Sexualization of Girls:*

There are several components to sexualization, and these set it apart from healthy sexuality. Sexualization occurs when

- *a person's value comes only from his or her sexual appeal or behavior, to the exclusion of other characteristics;*
- *a person is held to a standard that equates physical attractiveness (narrowly defined) with being sexy;*

- *a person is sexually objectified—that is, made into a thing for others' sexual use, rather than seen as a person with the capacity for independent action and decision making; and/or*
- *sexuality is inappropriately imposed upon a person.*

All four conditions need not be present; any one is an indication of sexualization. The fourth condition (the inappropriate imposition of sexuality) is especially relevant to children. Anyone (girls, boys, men, women) can be sexualized. But when children are imbued with adult sexuality, it is often imposed upon them rather than chosen by them. Self-motivated sexual exploration, on the other hand, is not sexualization by our definition, nor is age-appropriate exposure to information about sexuality.[3]

When mass retailers are marketing makeup to eight-to twelve-year-old girls, unhealthy sexualization is occurring.

"I like blush, lipstick, um, mascara," a nine-year-old girl said to ABC News during a report on children wearing makeup.[4] Of course she likes blush, lipstick, and, um, mascara. She is a kid. Katie asks me for makeup all the time. I hand her a tube of bubble-gum-flavored Chapstick and tell her to have fun. "I want something with *color*," Katie protests. I practically need to put a child lock on my makeup drawer to keep Annie Rose's groping little hands away from my powder and blush. And if you walk into an elementary school, be prepared to see little girls wearing lipstick and eye makeup. Toy, clothing, and makeup manufacturers have a name for this phenomenon: KGOY (Kids Getting Older Younger).[5] They market along strict gender lines: sexualized products for young girls and macho or violent products for young boys, pushing kids into gender-based stereotypes that harm their perceptions of each other. As soon as a twelve-year-old needs a bra, the clothing stores are right there pushing a bra to her younger sister, telling her that she, too, needs breasts to be sexy and attractive. Abercrombie & Fitch is one of many retailers that offers string bikini push-ups for girls age seven to eleven. Parents of little girls are left asking in bewilderment, where has childhood gone?

The retailers are quick to blame the parents, claiming that they are not forcing mom and dad to buy sexualized products. While there is parental accountability involved, it is not that simple. The stores enticingly market inappropriate items to young kids, and parents are in the difficult position of having to say no, not just to a single purchase, but to an entire glamorized lifestyle. Perhaps a parent has initial resolve and manages to escape the shoe store without buying high heels for her ten-year-old. But then the child begs her for a tube of lipstick at the grocery store, and a bottle of perfume at the drugstore, and a short skirt at the clothing store . . . the barrage is endless. In a moment of exhausted weakness, the mom purchases a pot of eye shadow, just for "fun." But the girl sneaks it out of the house and puts it on at school. Once one girl in the class starts wearing makeup, the other girls beg to wear it too.

Peggy Orenstein mulled the problem over with me.[6] She predicted that "what's going to happen is that the cool girls are going to start wearing makeup at age nine and ten, and then the kids who are being raised more healthily will end up being targeted and bullied for being uncool." Unfortunately, Orenstein's predictions are playing out. The "cool" girls *are* the ones who wear makeup, and the other girls are desperate to fit in. Worn down from picking their battles, some parents give in, and now we have a generation of nine-year-olds who wear mascara to school. What do we do with that as parents? Do we say, "I'd rather have my daughter be the mean girl than the picked-on girl"? Orenstein thinks the answer is to teach your girl how to value herself inside out and to provide her with skills for conflict resolution. "It's not easy," she commiserated, "but you try to make decisions based on what you know is long-term healthy."

For generations, little kids have played dress up at home, and for some, this includes applying Mom's makeup. Nothing unusual about that. And it is perfectly appropriate for kids to get their faces painted at carnivals, amusement parks, and the like. These activities are within the realm of a normal childhood. The trouble is that little girls are now applying blush, eye shadow, and mascara as part of their regular grooming before leaving the house. Can't a ten-year-old be free of the social pressure to feel suitably attractive before going to school? I know a woman who refers to putting on her makeup as putting on her "face." What does that tell her children? That without painting herself up, their mother doesn't even merit having a face? Makeup alone is not where young kids end their beauty regiments and procedures. There are now spa treatments, eyebrow waxing, facials, and massages marketed toward little girls between the ages of eight and twelve,[7] and there are plenty of parents who are willing to pay for these services. "I feel it's part of hygiene. I do all of these types of things myself, and I think they're better off starting young," one mother told ABC News.[8]

Part of good hygiene for a ten-year-old does not need to include facials and electrolysis. This doesn't mean it is harmful for a girl to get a manicure on a very special occasion, such as for a birthday treat or before a big event. It is fun and enjoyable! What it means is that kids who receive a weekly mani/pedi and regular spa treatments are at risk of feeling entitled at a very young age, and this contributes to discrimination against those girls who simply get their nails trimmed with Mom's clippers. We don't want kids to look down on other kids who are different, creating an "us" and "them" mentality, which allows kids to view each other as objects. Once that happens, kids (and adults) find it increasingly easy to taunt and torment someone who is "other." A nine-year-old with a freshly waxed upper lip is more likely to view a hairy-lipped peer as "other." But what is a parent to do if other kids are teasing her daughter for having a mustache? Leave her to suffer? It is a dilemma, a slippery slope of perfection, because if you allow a young girl to wax her lip hair in order to protect her from taunts, what do you do when she then wants to get a bikini wax?

Body hair has emerged as a surprisingly common reason why kids target others. An Indian mother told me, "There are some fair-haired girls in my daughter's fourth-grade class who make fun of my daughter for having a lot of dark hair on her forearms. She wants to wear long sleeves every day, even when it's hot outside." While it is true that kids with poor hygiene are at higher risk of being bullied, arm hair is not a hygiene problem. The pressure for girls to maintain hairless bodies has propelled children as young as eight to seek out painful treatments such as electrolysis and waxing for body hair. Just as disturbing is the behavior of mothers who want their daughters to look perfect. Diane Fisher, owner of Eclips Salon Day Spa and Eclips Kids in McLean and Ashburn, Virginia, both Washington, D.C. suburbs, told todayshow.com, "I had a mother who brought her daughter in, pulled up her shirt and asked us to wax the girl's back. The hair didn't seem to be bothering the little girl, but the mom was embarrassed and wanted it done," Fisher recounted. "I told the mom to wait until the child wanted it, but she refused." The girl with the hairy back was six years old.[9]

FOR A GLIMPSE INTO physical perfection at an early age, tune in to America's child beauty pageants, where little girls with pale skin are routinely spray-tanned and those with missing or crooked teeth are fitted for pearly white caps. The Learning Channel (TLC) released a commercial in the spring of 2011 announcing the return of its show *Toddlers & Tiaras,* and the announcer referred to the five-year-olds as "sassy superstars" but some viewers heard it as "sexy superstars." The commercial featured a young pageant star knowingly saying, "I'm real famous." The thirty-second commercial was a whirlwind of makeup, sexy dancing, and revealing costumes, summing up everything that many parents are trying to stave off.

Opposition to child pageants has propelled the foundation of community organizations such as Pull the Pin, which is trying to put an end to childhood beauty pageants. The people of Australia and New Zealand rallied strongly against plans by Universal Royalty Pageant, a child pageant based in Texas, to expand into their territory in July 2011. Psychiatrists from Down Under are displeased because pageants "encourage the sexualization of children and can cause developmental harm," according to the *Sydney Morning Herald.*[10]

Eden Wood, a well-loved sweetheart who earned the hearts of many on *Toddlers & Tiaras,* spent the first five years of her life performing on the show circuit. Her mother, Mickie Wood, has spent over $100,000 on Eden's costumes, beauty treatments, pageant expenses, and so forth, and estimates that they have won back $40,000 or $50,000 in prizes.[11] While most children do not compete in beauty pageants, this does not protect them from the social pressure to be attractive.

The long arm of sexiness reaches for all children and beckons them close. The music industry, where young and talented Eden Wood is now attempting to make her mark, is awash in images of sexiness linked with fashion. Music videos are all about big guns, big cars, big egos, and big tempers for the guys; big bling, big breasts, and big pouty lips for the gals (but little clothes). It has become normal for female pop stars to wear little more than corsets and short shorts or bikini bottoms during performances. Make no mistake about it, the superstars are doing more than just singing. They are selling, and not just cologne or perfume or a line of shoes. They are selling a lifestyle, one that is long on envy and sexiness and short on reality. Lyn Mikel Brown shared her thoughts with me about the complexity of this sexiness. "Being feminine in provocative ways is narrow and keeps us in stereotypes. Like Beyoncé's video, 'Run the World (Girls)'—she markets it as girl empowerment—but it's all about conforming to sexual stereotypes. Of course, look who is advising her: Jay-Z. Beyoncé is actually using highly sexualized power to promote a narrow version of femininity. It is the commodification of girls' and women's bodies and marketing to a heterosexual world."[12]

Beyoncé, like many successful singers, is a complicated figure to deconstruct. Although she is an example of the music industry's sexualization of females, she also uses her social capital in positive ways. For example, she has teamed up with Michelle Obama to combat childhood obesity in the Let's Move campaign. As part of the campaign, Beyoncé promotes a physically active lifestyle to kids through her song, "Move Your Body," and the music video takes place in a school cafeteria, where a flash mob of students begins dancing with Beyoncé. Considering the intended audience for the video, Beyoncé is dressed reasonably appropriately (no sexy lingerie, no bare midriff) in an off-the-shoulder white T-shirt and tight jean shorts. The clothing appeals to tweens and teens without crossing the line. The video is fun and engaging, with none of the usual trappings of sex, money, and power.

I mused with Brown about how the issue of sexualized marketing is really in the forefront of our social conscience right now. Every time I turn around, I see a blog post or a news article decrying the companies employing gender stereotypes and sexualized images in their marketing. Brown commented, "I think this stuff is so in-our-face right now because, in reality, things are changing. The changes create anxiety for the world, and marketers revert to the stereotypes to put girls in their proper place. And the young women participate in it because they experience the anxiety too. They wonder, 'Who am I?' Every time a Monster High doll or a Beyoncé video comes out, there is a bigger reaction."[13] Hundreds of parents and kids are trying to make sense of a changing world, and consumers are less likely to stand silently by when companies promote stereotypes.

The marketing team at Skechers learned this the hard way when they put out a commercial promoting their Skechers Shape-Ups shoes for Girls to preteen girls.[14] The commercial features Heidi, an animated girl character, singing onstage at a concert and prancing around in Skechers Shape-Ups. Another girl's voice narrates and sings, "Heidi's got new Shape-Ups, na na na na na na . . . got everything a girl wants . . . na na na from Skechers! She's got the height, got the bounce, yes she's looking good and having fun, because Heidi's got new Shape-Ups." In the most offensive part of the commercial, animated boy characters dressed as junk food try to pursue Heidi, to no avail. The commercial, which initially ran in the spring of 2011 on the Cartoon Network and on Nickelodeon, blatantly pushed the idea that girls who are tall and thin have everything a girl wants, and that wearing Skechers Shape-Ups will make girls look like Heidi. Furthermore, the commercial depicts food (and boys) as the enemy, setting up the type of harmful associations that contribute to eating disorders in young girls. Ten years ago, this commercial may have slipped under the radar, but as Lyn Mikel Brown pointed out, there is now a stronger reaction to these stereotypical cultural messages.

Some companies are at least making a show of listening to these reactions. As we learned, Mattel recruited the Kind Campaign to help the Monster High dolls reform their behavior (outcome still to be determined). But even if the dolls treat each other more nicely, there is still the damaging aspect of their physical appearance to overhaul. The animated characters are unrealistically thin and risk promoting anorexia to young girls who aspire to maintain the depicted body proportions. Despite their childish stick-like limbs, the dolls have large, alluring eyes that boast sultry eye makeup—a fashion-industry mix of childishness with sexuality. The female characters are dressed in supershort skirts with high-heeled shoes and boots.

The young girls who watch *Monster High* are led to believe that teenagers in high school should look like skinny, sexy supermodels preparing to strut down the catwalk during Fashion Week in Paris. There are real consequences to the girls who watch these programs, as evidenced by the American Psychological Association's *Sexualization of Girls*, which found that three of the most common mental-health problems among girls—eating disorders, depression or depressed mood, and low self-esteem—are linked to the sexualization of girls and women in media.[15]

I NOTICED THE WORD "sexy" first appear in Katie's vocabulary when we were shopping for some summer T-shirts and shorts. Katie pointed to a pair of high-heeled strappy sandals that she wanted, prominently displayed in the children's shoes area. "That pair is sexy," she commented. I explained to her that we would be buying flat sandals, and we began to search for a pair. Then we moved on to the clothes. "Ooh, that's sexy," Katie exclaimed. I was about to launch into a discussion of why she should not want to look sexy, when I remembered a passage I had recently read in Diane E. Levin and Jean Kilbourne's book *So Sexy So Soon: The New Sexualized Childhood and What Parents Can Do to Protect Their Kids:* "The lens an adult uses for looking at and understanding sexual issues is very different from the lens a child uses. Often when children say things that seem connected to sex and sexuality, they have very different meanings for the children than they have for adults."[16]

So I asked, "Katie, what does 'sexy' mean to you?"

She groaned and rolled her eyes. "Here we go again with the talks, Mom!"

"It's my job as a mom," I told her. "C'mon, c'mon, what do you think 'sexy' means?"

"Ummm, fancy?" she guessed.

"Nope. That is not what 'sexy' means," I replied. "When you say 'sexy' to mean 'fancy,' people will misinterpret you. 'Sexy' means wearing clothes or acting in a way that will increase people's feelings of attraction to you. They will want to kiss you on the lips. Not the way that little children kiss, but the way that older teenagers and adults kiss."

Katie raised her eyebrows and widened her eyes in surprise. But she still looked longingly back at the high-heeled sandals.

As we walked through the girls' clothing section, most of the Target brand clothes were age appropriate. Katie and I easily found cute, comfortable outfits, which was a relief after the shoe section. But then we wandered into the underwear display, and right next to "Hello Kitty" underpants were padded bras and bikini underpants for eight-year-olds. Since some children do develop breasts early, it is necessary and appropriate to offer bras for these young girls, but my concern was that the bras on display were enhanced push-up bras, visible reminders that there are eight-year-olds who feel pressured to look busty for a variety of reasons—in order to fit in, or to be sexy to the boys, or to look thin in the waist by comparison to the chest.

The proliferation of racy underwear marketed to children is drawing attention around the globe. In June 2011, the British Retail Consortium announced that it would be banning the High Street shops from selling sexualized clothing for children. Padded bras and thongs were deemed inappropriate for young children, as were clothes with suggestive slogans.[17] Sexualization is not a concern confined to children. Recall that in chapter 4 we examined the complexities of exaggerated sexiness among the Geek Girls. It is a common practice at Geek conventions such as Comic-Con for vendors to use scantily dressed Booth Babes to sell their wares. Maxim.com even ranked the Booth Babes by hotness at 2010's Comic-Com. Some

Geeks assert that it is inconsistent for a science-fiction convention to try to send a message of female Geek empowerment and simultaneously promote the objectification of women as Booth Babes.

I discussed this issue with Jennifer Stuller, programming director for GeekGirlCon.com, the first convention to be held specifically for female Geeks. "We wanted to create a safe environment for women and girls, a place where they would not have to feel uncomfortable," Stuller explained. That being said, she pointed out that many Geeks are perfectly comfortable with the Booth Babes, and some Geeks even double as Booth Babes. "But they are still using their bodies to sell merchandise," Stuller acknowledged, "and after many discussions and debates, we decided not to use Booth Babes, partly because GeekGirlCon is for children as well as adults."[18] GeekGirlCon had numerous panels and discussions, including one on how to put a stop to cattiness and competitiveness among female Geeks. Yes, even among the Geeks, there are queen bees and wannabes, and the prettier, sexier Geeks receive more attention and interest. The issue of physical attraction is pervasive in our society.

While girls feel the majority of society's pressure to be sexy at a young age, boys are also targeted. Jean Kilbourne, coauthor of *So Sexy So Soon*, pointed out some ways in which young boys are also forced to grow up too soon.[19] "Boys are not encouraged to present themselves as sex objects, but there is pressure on even little boys to be sexually precocious. There was a photograph in the paper of a five-year-old boy surrounded by buxom cheerleaders, and the caption said how lucky he was to be surrounded by these girls. It was creepy; he was portrayed as if he should be enjoying this like an adolescent. What does this say to imply a five-year-old boy should be titillated to be surrounded by these women? His most recent association with breasts should be food. The parents think it's funny to buy shirts that say 'pimp squad' or 'chick magnet' for toddler boys, but it creates anxiety." Hypersexualization in the media is a problem that affects young boys as well as girls. According to a study funded by the Geena Davis Institute on Gender in Media (GDI), animated male characters are more likely than their live action counterparts to have a large chest, small waist, and unrealistically muscularized physique.[20] Young boys who watch these excessively masculine animated characters are pressured to have disproportionately muscular bodies, and this contributes to the perception that smaller, skinnier boys are less masculine.

Kilbourne believes there are several factors influencing the increase in hypersexualization of children. She said, "I first noticed the sexualization of little girls more than thirty years ago. That's why I made the *Killing Us Softly* film in 1979. But it's gotten so much worse, and one of the reasons is the Internet." It is impossible for children not to be exposed to porn, Kilbourne pointed out, because people no longer have to go to a seedy bookstore to find it. Pornography is everywhere. Children stumble upon it before they are developmentally ready to see the graphic images. Kilbourne observed, "What used to be part of an adult mysterious world—sex—would gradually be unfolded, but now very little children are seeing extraordinarily brutal images and perversions in ads and mainstream venues. It is also found in the way celebrities dance or dress. It's a different world than it used to be, and that is part of what has created this push to be sexy."

Kilbourne went on to explain, however, that the primary driving force behind our culture's emphasis on sexy is that it makes people buy more products and services. She noted, "Marketers have found that this is a fabulous way to target children. It's not even about sex; it's about shopping. Marketers are trying to link sex with shopping, so they eroticize consumerism and hijack kids' sexuality. This creates lifelong consumers who have a powerful drive to shop, because they associate sexuality with shopping." The fashion industry preys upon the insecurities of consumers, convincing them that they need to purchase goods and services in order to remain youthful, slim, sexy, and cool. Kilbourne is doubtful that the marketers will ever change their tactics, because they have found something that works. Instead, she recommends, "Our only hope is to educate a critical mass of people to stop buying this sexy stuff. We educate people to pay attention to this and build and build and build on this and hope the same thing happened as with secondhand smoke. But that kind of social change takes time to occur." The conversations are taking place, and grassroots efforts have sprung up to make changes.

In 2011, the documentary *Miss Representation* premiered at the Sundance Film Festival and later aired on the Oprah Winfrey Network. The film "explores how the media's misrepresentations of women have led to the underrepresentation of women in positions of power and influence."[21] Kilbourne was one of many people interviewed in *Miss Representation*, and the film provides a blunt and disturbing look at how the media sexualizes girls and women. I watched the film with a friend of mine who has two teenage sons, and she was so affected by it that she contacted their high school to inquire about showing the film to students as part of a media literacy class. Arrangements are being made—a simple yet stirring example of how one parent can make a difference.

Some parents are so affected by social issues that they build entire careers around creating change. Melissa Wardy is one of those leading a grassroots campaign against gender bias and the sexualization of children. Wardy's daughter Amelia is named after Amelia Earhart, and when Amelia was a baby, Wardy wanted to buy her a T-shirt with an airplane on it. "I went everywhere, but no one carried a girl's shirt with an airplane on it." In May 2009, Wardy decided to open her own business, Pigtail Pals, and she offers empowering apparel for girls and boys. "I'm not antipink or even antiprincess, but I am antilimitation," Wardy explained. As a result, Wardy makes clothes for girls that depict female astronauts, doctors, pilots, firefighters, carpenters, and more.

Wardy began writing a blog, and she quickly took on the cause of combating the sexualization of young girls. The Pigtail Pals blog is a fountain of information, news articles, and postings about developments in the crusade to take back childhood.[22] Wardy keeps her readers up to date with all the recent developments, research, and controversies related to the portrayal of young girls in the media.[23] In August 2011, for example, JCPenney marketed a shirt to girls that said, "I'm too pretty to do my homework, so my brother has to do it for me," and Wardy led her readers in a public outcry against the shirt that ended with JCPenney eventually pulling the offensive item.[24]

To the delight of mothers like Wardy, Academy Award winner Geena Davis shares their concerns and is working with the entertainment industry to effect change. In 2004, Davis was watching children's television programming with her young daughter when she noticed that there were very few female main characters. Davis raised money to fund research into the problem and was so dismayed by the results that she founded the Geena Davis Institute on Gender in Media (GDI). I spoke with Madeline di Nonno, executive director of GDI, about the scope and goal of their research.[25] She told me, "Right now there is a three-to-one disparity between male and female characters in top-grossing children's films, and we would like to see that needle move. Television for preschool does a better job—they are almost at parity, but programming for kids age six to eleven has far more male leads." Di Nonno provided me with some of the key findings from various research studies funded by GDI:

- In TV for kids age eleven and under, females are almost four times as likely as males to be dressed in sexy attire.[26]
- Of all speaking characters in family films, 32.4% are female in G-rated films, 30% are female in PG-rated films, and 27.7% are female in PG13-rated films—far less than the proportion of females in our general population. And of the female characters shown, there was a strong focus placed on their physical attractiveness and unrealistic body proportions, more so than for male characters.[27]

How will the GDI use its findings to orchestrate change? The group hosts a media symposium every two years and brings together about three hundred of the most senior industry executives. After the GDI presented its data at the December 2010 symposium, di Nonno reported, "We conducted a survey, and we had a high response rate. The news was hopeful. Based on the results of the survey, 95.8% of content creators believe that, when appropriate to the story being told, gender balance is important, and 50% said it was achievable without much difficulty. We expect to see improvements by 2015 when we do our next quantitative study. This is how we know we are making an impact." In the meantime, the GDI has written the following recommendations for entertainment executives and creators:[28]

1. G-rated movies and certain TV categories need more females as main characters, minor characters, narrators, and in crowds.
2. G-rated movies and certain TV categories need more characters of color, especially female characters of color as main characters, minor characters, narrators, and in crowds.
3. G-rated movies need to create more female characters with aspirations beyond romance.
4. G-rated movies need to create more women and girl characters that are valued for their inner character.

Films and television serve as a good barometer for cultural change, and even incremental shifts in gender and racial balance can have a positive effect on the self-esteem of young girls. Through her work with the GDI, Geena Davis has become actively involved in efforts to legislate changes in the media. In July 2011, she joined Girl Scouts of the USA, Senator Kay Hagan (D–NC), and Congresswoman Tammy Baldwin (D–WI) to campaign for the Healthy Media for Youth Act. Hagan and Baldwin introduced the bill, which would promote healthier media messages about girls and women and would improve media literacy for young people.

Chapter Sixteen

Reassess the Role of Schools in Character Education

Bullying prevention involves nearly every aspect of our lives—families, pop culture, the Internet—and, to a huge extent, schools. It is not uncommon for educators to first receive serious anti-bullying training once they have already been teaching, but by then, it is often too late, because many teachers bring preformed ideas about what constitutes tattling and whining into their classrooms. They become impatient with the squeaky wheels who constantly report being victimized, particularly within the special education classrooms. Taunting and aggression are viewed as normative behaviors, and many overextended teachers overlook all but the most violent forms of bullying in order to focus on academic achievements. Our nation's schools, desperate for funds and pressured to deliver better test results, place a premium on test results, while shunting aside behavioral concerns.

Perhaps the tests should not just be academic in nature. Dorothy Espelage, professor of child development and associate chair in the Department of Educational Psychology at the University of Illinois, Urbana-Champaign, recommends measuring the social skills of kids as part of their schooling. Espelage told me, "If we evaluated kids and their social skills in the same way that we evaluate their academic skills, this would be a whole different discussion. If we as a country wanted to know who the bullies are, we could find out. We could track them. We track, for example, special education kids, and we have IEPs [individualized education programs] for special education. The problem is that nobody wants to know who the bullies are." Espelage observed that parents are more willing to say their kids are learning-disabled than mean, because who wants to admit they are raising a bully? "We do have a very supportive government right now when it comes to anti-bullying legislation, but even so, schools need to show bullying prevention can be tied to improved academics in order to get the federal government to fund more preventative initiatives," she commented.[1]

Espelage and her colleagues advise that bullying-prevention education should begin in the preservice environment. Teaching certification programs must be revised to include bullying as part of their core curriculum. Indeed, when I asked Michael Robey, the assistant superintendent of our school district, about his preservice training, he noted, "As I think back to all the college education that prepared me for teaching and then the advanced education that prepared me to become an administrator, there was not much that was discussed or practical from the bullying standpoint. There are courses for educating the exceptional child, but they don't hit at the heart of the matter."[2] The reason that the preservice environment does not focus on bullying prevention is that it has not been considered part of the job of teachers.

Ron Astor, who holds joint appointments in the USC School of Social Work and USC Rossier School of Education, shared his insights with me about the role of schools in bullying prevention.[3] He said, "One of our biggest problems is that our society is a little confused about the meaning of public education. College is the purpose now, in order to get a job and to better our economy—that is where the political mind-set of our country is. Our country is continually shifting between schools being the main economic fuel of our country to whether they ought to focus on moral and societal issues." Astor believes that we need to redefine our meaning of a school. "If society says, 'Your job is to teach math successfully,' then that means the mind of the teacher is only the four walls of the classroom where he teaches. The teacher is not working in the area of bullying," he explained.

My husband, Andrew, teaches math in a large, diverse public high school, and after speaking with Astor, I asked Andrew if he gets involved when he sees bullying. "Well," he mused, "sometimes. I work on managing my classroom so that we learn the math that we are required to learn, because that is my primary concern." It was just like Astor had said. I relayed the conversation with Astor to my ever-patient husband, who nodded his head and listened without rolling his eyes as I told him that he was all wrong in his approach to teaching and that bullying prevention should be in the top of his mind, not math. He did consider it, though, and in the months since that conversation, Andrew admitted that he has developed a more heightened awareness of bullying-related behaviors.

"A student told me that he liked my shirt today," he told me one evening a couple of months into the 2011–2012 school year, "and he wanted to make it clear that he wasn't saying it as a come-on, so he specified, 'no homo.' I told him that he cannot speak that way in my class, that it is unacceptable."

"What did he say?" I asked.

"He looked at me in horror and asked if I was gay," Andrew said. "And I responded that I wasn't, but even if I were, there would be nothing wrong with that."

Bullying-prevention experts have come to realize that enlisting the teacher's support is the best intervention against bullying, and Astor believes we must expand our definition of what a teacher does. He elaborated, "Bullying is extremely rare in the classroom of a good teacher that the kids respect. Much more bullying happens when a sub teacher is in place, because the sub is not connected. If you look at the playgrounds, bathrooms, halls, the Internet—the undefined public spaces where there are ratios of one to one-hundred adults to kids—that is where bullying occurs. If we staffed those locations better, we would eliminate bullying. We need people who are connected, not just a sub or a security guard, but good teachers who know the kids, in those places." Why in a classroom do we require a one to twenty ratio, Astor asked, but then pay someone minimum wage with no connection to the kids to keep a one to two-hundred ratio at recess? He recommends that organized recess would be better, because it is unrealistic to expect that kids without any structure, consequences, or supervision would actually behave the same way as they do in the classroom.

New Jersey is one state that is reshaping its schools to promote an anti-bullying curriculum. As mentioned earlier, New Jersey has put in place very strict anti-bullying legislation that requires all public schools to adopt comprehensive anti-bullying policies, increase staff training, and adhere to tight deadlines for reporting episodes. The law mandates that districts appoint a safety team at each school, made up of teachers, staff members, and parents, to review complaints, and it also requires school principals to begin an investigation within one school day of a bullying episode. Some school personnel have protested that these demands are unreasonable, claiming that they have neither the budget nor the time to spend on such stringent anti-bullying measures, but supporters argue that this is the only way to change the culture of schools.[4] At this time, it is too early to see if the New Jersey legislation is making an improvement, but the pushback is not surprising from overburdened school administrators who are already stressed out trying to meet requirements from No Child Left Behind.

When I played devil's advocate and pointed out to Astor that teachers—already exhausted and stretched thin—use lunch and recess as much-needed chances to get work done and asked where the schools would find money to pay for these increased services, Astor replied, "It all goes back to our society redefining the meaning of a school. If the purpose of the school is to create a caring environment, then these things become a central priority at the school." This will require the involvement of the school district and the school board, the legislators, the parents—it is a community-wide undertaking. A caring school does not give up on the bullies.

It is easy to tout the importance of caring for the bullies, but in reality, it is hard to muster feelings of love for some kids. The harsh truth is that kids with behavioral problems are often unpleasant. Ask

any teacher who has an aggressive, bullying kid in his or her classroom, distracting the other students, and the teacher will tell you
how much of a relief it would be to get that kid out of the class. Just
as there are certain teachers everyone wants to get, there are certain
students everyone wants to avoid. This happens with kids as young
as elementary school age. I spoke with teachers who admitted that
they sometimes see first graders whom it already feels too late to
help. If a kid is deemed a lost cause at age seven, how can a high
school teacher hope to make a difference? It is a question that plagues
teachers everywhere. It hurts the heart to imagine what has happened
in the early years to some of society's youngest members.

Michael Kelly, coauthor of *School Social Work: An Evidence-
Informed Framework for Practice,* stressed to me that a healthy
school culture will say, we still love these kids even though they are
bullies and even though they cause trouble. An unhealthy school culture will say, these are bad kids and we're afraid of them. When a
teacher is confronted with an unlikable, contentious student, it will
help to remember that there is more to the student than just the outward behavior. I remembered how Jerry Pope found a way to connect
with kids through their hip-hop music, using songs they liked to
build a relationship. Then he leveraged that relationship to try to talk
to kids about their future. "In a healthy school," Kelly explained,
"difficult kids get helped instead of labeled, and victims get helped
instead of ignored. Schools struggle with how to respond to bullying
because there are a lot of islands within poorly run schools, and this
leaves people feeling isolated. Teachers may feel bullied; parents may
feel bullied. Larger steps have to be taken. Principals need to ask,
'What does my entire school need to look like so this doesn't happen?'" he recommended.[5]

There is no uniform answer to this question. Schools around the
world struggle with similar issues, but there is no manual to provide
pat solutions. I spoke with Trudy Ludwig, author of *My Secret Bully,*
about the haphazard approach many schools take to address bullying, and she observed, "There are a lot of anti-bullying efforts in
our schools that don't work. And the reason why they do not work
is because bullying is not being addressed systematically in the

school-wide approach. I see wonderful slogans on walls in schools, but it doesn't change behaviors. We need to concretize behaviors because everyone has different ideas of what is bullying." Ludwig has seen many schools address bullying by putting out fires, which is not an effective way to reduce bullying. Michele Borba, who has written over twenty books on parenting, agrees wholeheartedly with Ludwig, telling me, "A huge mistake is a one-time bullying assembly. It has to be an ongoing intervention. New habits take at least twenty-one days of repetition; not a one-time flyer or a couple of days of assembly."[6] It is not enough to get a child to change her cruel ways for three or four days, because she has not internalized the new behavior yet. A teacher needs to reinforce the tenets of respect and tolerance throughout the school year.

Teachers who are truly connected to their students, as Ron Astor describes, will stop and address issues of bullying as they occur, sending a message to kids that bullying will not be tolerated or ignored. I remembered one man named Darnell who wrote to Katie, a man who is managing his classroom in a way that promotes empathy. Darnell explained: "I am a male elementary school teacher. I bet you don't see a lot of boys doing that. I work really hard at taking down these walls between what is considered boys and girls in my classrooms. I celebrate when boys wear pink shirts and girls wear Star Wars shirts. I will wear a pink shirt and as soon as someone comments on it, we discuss." Creating an empathetic classroom takes time, but much of the work is front-loaded. Empathy is a skill, and once students become more familiar with expressing and analyzing their feelings, it can be a quicker and more natural process to stop and discuss incidents of taunting or bullying.

A teacher who works intensely to establish a respectful environment from the very first day of class will spend less time over the course of the year, managing an unruly, distracted classroom. This is certainly the philosophy of Zachary Herrmann, an award-winning math teacher at Evanston Township High School who is known for creating a positive social structure in his classroom.[7] Herrmann, who received his master's degree in education from Stanford University, told me, "I think the first important thing to recognize when trying to promote specific behaviors or perspectives in a classroom is that you are actively projecting certain cultural values on to others. Even concepts such as tolerance and respect are culturally charged, and they mean different things to different people with different cultural backgrounds. Thus, the question is: Whose culture should the school promote?" Herrmann admits that this is a challenging question to answer and is one filled with controversy and a multitude of perspectives. Considering the social context within which we live in the United States, he believes the cultural values and perspectives necessary for active participation in a democracy are at least some of those worth teaching. He added, "Paramount to those cultural values and perspectives is tolerance of diverse backgrounds and experiences, appreciation for diverse perspectives, and the willingness to engage with others in civil conversation."

Herrmann shared his observation that all learning in the classroom takes place within a social context, and that learning can only take place to the extent that students feel safe. "Even those teachers who believe character education or the promotion of certain cultural values within the classroom is inappropriate for public school must concede that traditional classroom activities are more efficient and productive when they take place within a climate of mutual respect and tolerance," he explained, "and this often means the teacher must take an active role in helping develop these skills and perspectives." With the goal of teaching his students to practice social skills along with math skills, Herrmann uses a large amount of collaborative education projects in his classroom.

Students who learn to work collaboratively are better positioned for success in the workplace, where they may be assigned to projects with people they don't prefer. Stan Davis, author of *Schools Where Everyone Belongs,* likens the ideal school environment to the workplace environment. He told me, "School is a workplace, not a play-date, and you still have to work with, include, and be kind to people you don't like. We're trying to prepare your kids to succeed in the world of work. If you are mean in the workplace—if you refuse to work with black people or gay people—you can lose your job." Davis believes that parents and educators should emphasize to kids that everyone's job at school is to learn, and that when kids support each other, it helps them learn. "Saying 'You're all going to be friends' is lying to them," Davis said emphatically, "because they aren't all going to be friends. What they need to be is respectful and supportive. They have to learn how to talk about nonpersonal things with kids they don't like."[8]

I've often thought of the ability to make small talk as a necessary social skill for grown-ups, but after talking with Davis, I realized that it is a skill to teach my girls, too. "Katie and Annie Rose," I asked them curiously, "how would you have a conversation with someone you don't like, or with someone who isn't always nice to you?"

"I don't talk to people who aren't nice to me," Annie Rose replied.

"Okay, but pretend that you *had* to talk to someone like that, because she was sitting next to you at school. What would you say?" I persisted.

"Do you think our sixteenth president was the best?" Annie Rose suggested.

"Lovely weather we're having?" Katie suggested.

We talked about other ways of making small talk, such as inquiring about someone's weekend plans, what music or movies she likes, if she has a pet. We did some role playing. The girls argued over who got to play the more hostile person. My poor girls, who are subject to constant discussions about stereotypes, marketing, media, bullying, and social skills! Every time I read another well-researched book or speak with another expert, I feel compelled to act on the advice given. I have visions of my girls sitting in a therapist's office one day, complaining that their mother drove them crazy while writing a book about bullying. With so many tactics to try, I am trying to combine the most promising elements from everything I've learned. Apparently, schools are doing the same thing, each picking what seems most effective.

Anne Collier observed, "Different schools have different cultures, different policies. Some schools do social emotional learning (SEL), some do empathy training, some do Positive Behavior Intervention and Supports (PBIS), some do the Olweus program; we are cobbling together solutions because every school is different. There are some things we have arrived at, and it does take a whole school culture to really deal with bullying. It must change from the roots up. Doing the social norms approach helps kids see that the vast majority of kids don't bully. When kids understand that most kids don't bully, bullying actually goes down."[9]

There are hundreds of incredible grassroots initiatives taking place in schools across the country, but we must keep in mind the critical caveat that no school programs will work unless the principal and the teachers are completely dedicated to creating a school culture of acceptance.

This was a common refrain I heard from experts in the field. Stan Davis cautioned, "The key for all of these is that they will not work as curricula unless they reflect the actual day-to-day behavior of teachers in taking incidents seriously, modeling positive behaviors, building positive norms and expectations, and reinforcing the need for positive action in the moment. Without those day-to-day interventions on a consistent basis, a once-weekly curriculum lesson will have no meaningful effect."[10] As a parent, it is easy to be lulled into reassurance by knowing your school has bullying-prevention programs in place, such as Steps to Respect or Positive Behavior Intervention and Supports, both of which are used at Katie's school. But I didn't really understand how the programs were used on a day-to-day basis until I met with Katie's principal to ask all my questions, and she competently walked me through numerous scenarios. If your school has a bullying-prevention program in place, take the time to really learn the policies and procedures. If your teacher or principal cannot adequately explain the program and how it looks on a day-to-day basis, it may be the unfortunate case that the policy is there in name more than in spirit, and you can lobby for the school to do a better job.

Teachers who do not possess effective skills to address bullying are more likely to abandon the effort as a losing battle. Roberto, a survivor of bullying, recalled,[11] "I think my third-grade teacher did care, at least at first, but after a while she viewed the situation as hopeless, and she stopped trying to help me. I was the only Mexican kid in a class filled with blacks and Puerto Ricans, and they all bullied me. Eventually, I switched schools." Roberto's experience left him filled with anger and hatred for the kids who bullied him. "I met back up with the kids who bullied me when I was in high school, and it was awful. They wanted to fight with me all the time. Teachers knew what was going on, but they didn't know what to do about it. So they did nothing." Roberto now has a young daughter, and he takes an active role in making sure she is not bullied at school. "Things are better now than they used to be in the Chicago Public Schools," he said.

Where Do Schools Begin?

If your school does not yet have anti-bullying measures in place, and you would like to raise the issue with school leadership, please see appendix A for a brief description of some promising research-based approaches. One possibility is for your school to model its own organic program off one or several of these models. In some cases, these programs are modeled off each other and have very similar components. William Porter, one of the authors of *Bully-Proofing Your School,* reminded me, "Across all anti-bullying programs, research has shown the greatest reduction in bullying when programs are implemented in elementary school. No one has been able to replicate this same level of success in middle and high schools." The reason for this is that elementary school is when children are developing the critical social and emotional skills that help them resolve conflict. "The kids may actually use the skills more in middle school, but the time to learn them is in the early grades," Porter emphasized.[12]

One place for schools to start could be a simple assessment of the amount of bullying that goes on at school. Researchers have designed numerous questionnaires and surveys to help them understand the frequency and severity of bullying and to help them develop the most effective bullying-prevention programs. With the younger children, it is easiest to limit the survey to a shorter number of basic yes-or-no questions. Older children are able to answer more detailed questions that inquire not only about the presence of bullying but also the frequency and severity of the episodes. Please see appendix B for two basic samples of bullying surveys, one geared toward younger children, and one geared toward older children.

Be Wary of "Experts"

Dorothy Espelage, bullying researcher and educational psychologist, has studied all of the major anti-bullying programs developed for our nation's schools and believes that the three biggest factors for creating a successful bullying-prevention program are (1) teacher training, (2) parental involvement, and (3) the use of multimedia in implementation. A program that emphasizes these components has a better chance of reducing bullying. Due to the amount of media attention that bullying has received, schools need to use caution when hiring anti-bullying speakers, assemblies, and programs. It is a cottage industry with many people and organizations looking to capitalize on the urgency that schools feel as anxious parents pressure them to take action. An inexperienced person can do more harm than good, and anyone who offers immediate results should be viewed with skepticism. Changing a school's culture takes time.

Benefits of Grassroots Programs Unique to Each School

In lieu of anti-bullying programs, Lyn Mikel Brown advocated instead for active student involvement in creating a solution unique to each school.[13] She would rather see schools put their energy into initiatives that come from the bottom up than from the top down. Brown explained, "The kinds of conversations that will come up about gender and power intersect in different ways in different communities, so universal programs won't work. Instead, we need to know each community and start with the kids, and then adults need to be trained to listen well to the kids and incorporate the kids' initiatives." Brown is concerned that many bullying-prevention programs do not appreciate that by policing kids and having numerous consequences, they are not giving kids the tools to do their own work with their peers. "Kids need to be able to describe from their experience the difference between homophobia and racism, because a white school or a black school will have different cultural identities around racism and homophobia. Because of these differences, a national bully-prevention program that is marketed to everyone is not going to work."

Brown believes that what works in schools are civil rights teams, gay-straight alliances, and restorative justice. She provided me with a concrete example from a junior high school that has worked with a civil rights team, recalling that, "There was this group of tough little sixth graders in a boys' group who ended up talking about homophobia and all the 'that's so gay' comments in their school. The boys realized they were creating the problem, so they took action." First they conducted a survey in their school, and then they created a day where they wanted kids to pledge not to say "that's so gay" anymore, and finally they made a video of the project. "These little boys, who used to be in detention all the time, did all this themselves and are totally committed to having an impact on their school," Brown said, and pointed out that punishing the boys had done nothing to change their behavior. "The change came when the boys took their own initiative to make an impact."

Chapter Seventeen

Social and Emotional Learning

Parents hear educators talk about the importance of social and emotional learning (SEL). When I met with Katie's principal to ask about bullying prevention, I heard the acronym SEL over and over again. What exactly does SEL mean, I wondered, and how many other parents are nodding and smiling but secretly confused when their children's teachers use the term? If SEL is critical to bullying prevention, and those of us who do not have a background in social work are uncertain as to what SEL is, how can we play an effective role in helping our children acquire SEL skills? Let's break it down.

The Collaborative for Academic, Social, and Emotional Learning (CASEL) is the world's leading organization that focuses on social and emotional learning. In 1997 CASEL developed the basic definition of social and emotional learning by establishing five broad areas of social and emotional competence:[1]

- *Self-awareness*—accurately assessing one's emotions, values, strengths, and capacities.
- *Self-management*—managing emotions and behaviors, persevering in overcoming obstacles; setting and monitoring progress toward achieving personal and academic goals.

- *Social awareness*—showing empathy and understanding for others; recognizing and appreciating individual and group similarities and differences.
- *Relationship skills*—establishing and maintaining positive relationships based on cooperation; preventing and constructively resolving interpersonal conflict.
- *Responsible decision making*—making constructive choices about personal and social behavior.

Bullying prevention is just one component of a good SEL program. But even if your child is not involved in a bullying relationship, he or she is bound to experience social conflict. This is where SEL comes into play, smoothing the way for your child to be successful in school and in life. It is never too early to teach SEL, because social conflict begins in the preschool environment.

During my first conversation with anti-bullying author Rosalind Wiseman, I asked her if she could recommend some good books about social conflict for younger kids, and she told me, "One of the reasons I had to redo *Queen Bees* was because of that question. People are shocked that young children have such intense friendships. But really, it is normal, and I recommend that parents try not to be too horrified when kids go through painful breakups at six, seven, or eight years of age. They are just children going through social conflict." She went on to explain that at base, what you want is for a seven-year-old to be able to express her feelings after a conflict. "Developmentally, a first grader may not be able to say much more than 'I was sad,' but that is a good start."

Wiseman told me about her ten-year-old son who had recently had a fight with a good friend of his. "I asked him, 'How did you feel?' and my son said, 'I felt mad and glad. I was so mad at him for teasing me, and I was so glad that I got back at him by pushing him. But I also didn't know why I had acted that way.'" Wiseman was pleased, because a few years ago, her son would not have been able to express so much after a fight. "But now," she enthused, "he is learning to ask himself questions when he has conflicts with others." Wiseman advises parents, "Don't tell your kids how you would have done it. Ask how they feel. You are literally creating the foundation for how children resolve conflict."[2]

Wiseman explained that she wants to help her young son become emotionally intelligent, a popular practice among parents who are tuned in to the importance of social and emotional skills. I had heard the term "emotional intelligence" from a handful of people by this point, and I wanted to gain a better understanding of what it meant. Was it something people are born with? Can parents teach it? I called John Gottman, author of *Raising an Emotionally Intelligent Child*, and asked for a tutorial. He spoke with me about a technique called "emotion coaching" that parents can use to help kids learn to identify and understand their emotions.[3] Gottman described emotion coaching as a strategy that "allows kids to be more emotionally intelligent about their choices. Emotion coaching teaches kids not to feel isolated, so if something is upsetting them, they come to the person who is emotion coaching them." Since emotion coaching creates children who identify with the values of the family, Gottman cautioned that it can be problematic if the parents are bullies. "But in general," he said ruefully, "queen bee parents don't engage in emotion coaching. They are very dismissive."

Gottman believes the key to bullying prevention is to teach emotion coaching to parents before they have kids and before they raise bullies. When kids receive proper emotion coaching, they become more empathetic and socially skilled, but not necessarily more popular. Emotion-coached kids have *closer* friends, not *more* friends. If an emotion-coached child experiences bullying at the hands of her friends, Gottman explained, she would be more likely to find an alternative group of kids who share her values than to keep suffering in the wrong group. Emotion coaching may not protect kids from being targets, but it may prevent them from internalizing the harmful effects of being victimized.

Gottman's research has revealed that how children express their emotions varies developmentally quite dramatically, and this plays an important role in bullying prevention. The tactics that work during one phase of life backfire in another phase of life. Gottman elaborated, "If you are a preschooler, the socially competent thing to do is say 'I don't like what you are doing, and it hurts my feelings. I'm going to tell the teacher.' But when you are eight or nine up through middle school, that same behavior gets you bullied more. You have to act like you don't care, like you've had an emotionectomy." The norms in middle childhood require a child to be unobtrusive. In adolescence, it changes again, remarked Gottman, and you have to learn how to integrate emotions and express emotions with your real friends and disclose who you are, because exploring your identity is key to adolescence. You have to be good at discussing your emotions. Social behaviors change in different stages of development. Kids who receive emotion coaching are emotionally intelligent, and they learn which behaviors help them avoid bullying at each developmental level.

How to Be an Emotion Coach

Emotion coaching involves five steps, summarized briefly below:[4]

1. *Notice and be aware of the child's emotions.*
   - Parents must be emotionally aware themselves in order to help their kids be emotionally aware. Parents who fear losing control of their own emotions will find this more challenging and will need to do some self-work.
   - People who are emotionally aware can recognize when they are feeling an emotion; they can identify their feelings; and they are sensitive to the presence of emotions in other people.

2. *See the emotion as an opportunity for teaching or intimacy.*
   - Notice lower intensity emotions in self and kids. Emotions do not have to escalate to get noticed.
   - It is easier to acknowledge emotions as they occur and help the child learn to self-soothe.

3. *Validate the child's feelings.*
   - Be an empathetic listener.

- Treat feelings of sadness, anger, and fear as a healthy part of normal development.

4. *Help the child verbally label emotions.*
   - It is easy to teach kids how to label emotions.
   - Labeling helps uncomfortable, intense feelings become manageable and normal.

5. *Set limits while you help the child solve problems.*
   - Teach kids that all feelings are allowable, but not all behaviors are.
   - Just because you feel angry does not mean you can act however you want.
   - Solve problems with your child: set limits; identify goals; brainstorm for possible solutions; talk together to evaluate the possible solutions based on the family's values; and help your child select a solution.

An Emotion-Coaching Success Story

Gottman put me in touch with his colleague, Christina Sung Aie Choi, founder and director of the HD Family Therapy Center in Seoul, Korea, who has used emotion coaching to achieve dramatic results with adolescents in Korea.[5] Choi explained how grave the situation was when she first arrived. "I had twenty-two orphanage girls, all eighth graders, who were terribly behaved. They didn't care at all about authority. The only reason they came to school was to beat up other kids. So I volunteered to help, and the first thing I did was give them genuine respect." Choi formally welcomed each girl in front of the classroom every day. She used the respectful Korean greeting, and at the beginning, the girls felt awkward and asked, "Why are you doing that?" Choi also taught the other teachers to respect the girls, and she trained the staff on emotion coaching. "During the four months of us working with them," she said, "the girls grew to respect each other. Their relationships with teachers improved tremendously from rude and violent to respectful and caring.

And their relationships among themselves went from hostile and violent at the beginning to respectful by the time the semester was over."

Choi's eighth graders also achieved tremendous academic success during that time. Average grades went up twenty to thirty points out of a hundred. "I did a number of interventions with the girls, of which emotion coaching was the basis," Choi recalled. The girls practiced identifying and labeling their emotions, and they learned to solve problems in an empathetic manner. "We also did heartbeat work. When kids are under stress, their heartbeats are irregular, the flight-or-fight response, but when they breathe deeply and easily, within less than a minute, their heartbeats are more regular. Then we could interfere more calmly and solve problems in peaceful and effective ways." Choi practiced active breathing with the girls for three minutes every morning to prepare for a learning environment. On the days when they were really noisy, loud, or chaotic, she quickly changed the mode of their learning into games and ways to focus.

Choi described how, at the beginning, 90 percent of their time was spent on therapeutic activities and only 10 percent on academic work, but over time she changed the balance. "The entire school saw less bullying and violence, all as a result from the improvements in this one class of girls." The girls are now in the tenth grade and have continued to do really well. Choi told me proudly, "In a single semester of intervention, we changed the school." There are an additional 22,000 children in Korea, the Philippines, Mexico, Brazil, and Guatemala who are now benefiting from emotion coaching. Choi and her husband, Peck Cho—principal of the Boystown orphanages throughout the world—went to nineteen schools in those five countries to train caregivers and teachers on emotion coaching.[6] When given respect, the children will treat others with respect.

Classroom Empathy Building Exercises

The experts all agree that bullying is least likely to occur when we create an environment where students respect each other and develop feelings of empathy. A bully sees his or her victim as an "it," which allows the bully to be cruel without feeling guilty. By teaching the bully empathy, he or she begins to regard other people as valued human beings. In order to teach empathy, we need to allow children to learn how it feels to be different.

I remembered my own efforts to develop empathy for Katie after she was diagnosed with amblyopia. Every day, she cried and moaned about having to wear her patch, and although I tried to be sympathetic, the constant whining and arguing about it wore me down. Within a month or two, I started reprimanding her for being noncompliant about putting on the patch. And then, one morning, out of curiosity, I decided to put a patch over my own eye to see what it was like.

I *hated* it. I couldn't see well; I lost my peripheral vision. I felt unbalanced and uncomfortable. After about five minutes, I couldn't stand it any longer, and I ripped the patch off. I never again felt critical of Katie for moaning about her patch. The poor kid had to wear it for hours, and I could barely tolerate it for five minutes. I was tormented by the physical sensations of wearing the patch, and that was without the additional emotional difficulties Katie experienced, having to endure the stares of strangers.

Everything in my mind changed when I put myself in Katie's place. I felt badly about snapping at her to "just wear the patch already!" Social workers and teachers can run empathy-building exercises right in their classrooms, allowing students to step in one another's shoes, just as I did with Katie's patch. Role-playing exercises and simulations are a powerful tool in helping kids develop compassion. For how can we expect kids who are low on empathy to feel one another's pain if they have no way to relate to an unfamiliar experience?

Here are a couple of examples to see how empathy training can work to address bullying:

Scenario 1

Marissa is a fifth-grade girl with sensory disorders who experiences extreme discomfort in her feet. The only shoes Marissa can tolerate are a pair of unattractive brown lace-ups. Her female classmates, who have developed an interest in fashionable shoes, mock and taunt Marissa for wearing ugly, babyish shoes every day. Marissa and her family would like to try empathy training with the class, and Marissa is comfortable revealing why her feet are sensitive.

Empathy-Building Exercise

Have a social worker join the teacher in talking to the class about why Marissa wears specific shoes. Then, ask each student to take off his or her own shoes. Give the students four marbles to insert in their shoes, and have the students put their shoes on the wrong feet. Ask them to walk around the room and inquire about the comfort of their feet. Allow the children to remove the marbles from their shoes and have them replace the shoes on their proper feet. Discuss how Marissa feels when she is wearing any shoes other than her brown lace-ups.

Scenario 2

Cheung is a third-grade boy whose family recently immigrated to America from China. He struggles reading English aloud in class, and other kids taunt him for not understanding reading comprehension questions. The teacher and the social worker have spoken with Cheung and his family about doing empathy training, and the boy is willing.

Empathy-Building Exercise

Hand students a paragraph-long story where every third word is written in English. The rest of the words are written in Chinese. Ask the students how they would feel about being tested on the story or reading the story aloud. Encourage them to work together with Cheung to figure out what the story is about, and have the class work collaboratively to make a mural of the story.

EMPATHY-BUILDING EXERCISES ARE DESIGNED to allow us to feel the frustration or discomfort of another. One of the risks with empathy training, particularly in a case like Marissa's, is that the victimized child is viewed as very different from her peers, and her condition becomes her identity. To prevent this from happening, when leading an empathy exercise, it is important to stress to students how they are more the *same* than different. The goal is for students to feel compassion for each other's challenges while also finding common ground over which to relate. After pointing out that Marissa's feet are sensitive, the teacher can help Marissa and the class to discover common interests and similarities. Before doing empathy training at school, a teacher and social worker must speak with the targeted child and her family in order to assess their interest and get consent.

Empathy work can continue outside the classroom. One of the best places to practice compassion is in the lunchroom, because studies show that social groups are most easily identified in the school cafeteria. Teaching Tolerance, a project of the Southern Poverty Law Center, has developed an inclusion program called "National Mix It Up at Lunch Day," specifically to address the bullying that occurs at lunch. Schools that participate in Mix It Up do a variety of preparatory activities that culminate in a day where kids sit in diverse groups at lunch.[7]

Chapter Eighteen

Responding to the Bully

Kids live in a lot of different contexts. Home is one of them, but so are school, the neighborhood, and the peer context. The best-case scenario is when home, school, media, and peer groups—all the settings—discourage aggression, which minimizes bullying behaviors. If this isn't happening, advises Laura Hanish, then we need to get as many settings as possible to be supportive and to teach conflict resolution. And the earlier you do that, the better. As Hanish said, "It's really difficult to take a sixteen-year-old kid who has a long history of being exposed to aggression and try to change him. It's easier to start with a three- or four-year-old and intervene so you can provide different developmental pathways a child can move down."[1] The top priority is to recognize bullying behavior as early as possible in order to create a coordinated intervention effort.

The tricky part is knowing which intervention to use. Suspension, time-outs, expulsion—simply tossing a child who engages in bullying behavior out of the group does not fix the problem. In addition to removing the child from the prosocial environment of school, these punitive tactics avoid the very real psychological component of bullying. A 2001 study by Kirsti Kumpulainen et al. found that 13% of bullies and 18% of bully victims were diagnosed with a depressive disorder,[2] indicating that the aggressive kids are often in pain.

The association between depression and bullying is not to be taken lightly. An analysis of school shootings over the past thirty years has revealed that 79% of the attackers had a history of suicide attempts or suicidal thoughts and 61% had a history of a serious depression,[3] and over two-thirds of the attackers were victimized prior to the school shootings. What this means for bullying intervention is that any program designed to address bullying must include individual psychological care for students who bully others.

Without adequate, effective psychological care, children who act as bullies may continue to suffer psychological pain into adulthood. This was the case with Arthur, a tall, soft-spoken man who told me of his history with aggression.[4] "I was a terrible bully as a kid," he admitted. "I used both verbal and physical aggression. I would push other kids around, mostly picking on weaker and smaller kids. I was a big fat kid, and it made me feel better about myself to bully others." Arthur paused for a moment, remembering. "Plus, the cool kids didn't bother me; in a way, they approved. And quite honestly, I got a rush from bullying others." Kids who get a rush from bullying are well positioned to shift their need for stimulation into healthier activities. If you have a kid who bullies for the thrill of it, work with him or her to find another outlet. Teach your child about the endorphin rush that follows exercising, or the intense satisfaction that comes from playing a great song on the guitar. Maybe your child can start a daily run where he or she listens to music and burns off some energy. There are countless options—cooking classes, yoga, martial arts, skating, basketball, painting, knitting—that can provide an at-risk child with positive feedback.

In the absence of better alternative ways to cope with his emotions, Arthur continued bullying others. When he was nine years old, the school told his parents that he needed therapy. Arthur went to see a therapist every week for a year, at which point the school said it was enough. Arthur confided that he did not feel the therapy had really been effective, because he resumed bullying other kids all the way through high school. This is actually one of the problems with therapy; not all therapists are equally skilled, nor are all therapist-patient matches the right ones. Some people really work through their problems in therapy, and other people make no progress at all. If your child is in therapy and you see no improvements, talk with the therapist and get involved. Family therapy may be required in addition to individual counseling.

In Arthur's case, his parents knew that he continued to act aggressively. "One time in fifth grade, I brought a switchblade to school," he recalled. "I didn't intend to use it on anyone, but I planned to intimidate others with it. The principal saw me with it, and I was suspended for a few days. Everytime I was caught bullying, the interventions were punitive, and that didn't work. No one ever tried a positive intervention with me. When I reached high school, others bullied me a little bit, and I didn't like it. I started to see what it was like. But I wouldn't say I really changed then. I bullied others a little less, but I found a way to get my rush elsewhere. I smoked a lot of pot." It does not surprise me that Arthur turned to self-medicating with pot. He was in unresolved pain, switching from the balm of bullying to the balm of smoking dope. Some kids turn to alcohol or cigarettes or food.

Arthur wanted a better life, and he went on to get a degree in psychology in college, followed by a master's degree in learning disabilities. But despite his academic achievements, he was still terribly unhappy. "When I began studying for my PhD in educational psychology, I realized how completely miserable I was, and I made the decision to enter therapy as an adult. This time, it was really an insightful process," Arthur said, "and I finally understood why I had been such a terrible bully, and I was able to feel better. Now I have my doctorate, and my job is helping kids with problems maximize their potential in school." Arthur sought and received adequate psychological care, and he is now living a fulfilling life. But it would have been better if someone could have helped Arthur twenty years earlier, sparing him and the kids he bullied years of pain. To the credit of Arthur's school, they did take action when they noticed his aggressive behavior, requiring that he go to therapy, but it was not enough. The year of therapy as a child neither harmed Arthur nor gave him meaningful help. One problem was that there was no mechanism in place to follow up post-therapy, which allowed Arthur to slip back through the cracks and return to his aggressive ways.

There are some interventions that we now know cause harm, and it is critical for schools to avoid these tactics. "Peer mediation with a bully and a victim is contraindicated," explained Dorothy Espelage, editor of *Bullying in North American Schools,* "because in a true bully-victim dynamic, there is nothing to mediate. The bully is using power to harm the victim, and any attempts at mediation will make the situation worse for the victim."[5] Another intervention that should be avoided is grouping bullies together in special support groups. Putting bullies together has been shown to cause an increase in their aggressive behavior toward victims, because they try to out-bully each other in order to establish dominance.[6]

Other responses, such as zero-tolerance policies with the consequence of school expulsion, have proven to be failures. One of the problems with severe punishments for bullies, such as expulsion, is that victims and even school staff may be reluctant to report incidents of bullying. Susan P. Limber, national director of the Olweus Bullying Prevention Program, told me, "Zero tolerance sounded great to policy makers in the beginning—no tolerance for bullying—but it meant different things to different people, and over time, everyone has learned lessons from the field. Removing children who bully from the school does not help them."[7] Quite the opposite, in fact, because studies have indicated that school suspension tends to predict higher future rates of misbehavior and suspension among those students who were suspended.[8]

Often, but not always, kids who act as bullies come from families where people bully one another, and the aggressive behavior they have learned at home is reinforced by the media. David Shriberg, associate professor in psychology at Loyola University Chicago, spoke with me about the types of parenting styles that actually teach bullying to kids.[9] "Parenting styles characterized by extremes, such as authoritarian or military models, really shut kids out. If you approach discipline that way, and if you use violence or emotionally aggressive tactics to ensure compliance in your kids, you are modeling bullying. You learn that the way you get what you want is through controlling others." The best chance to prevent raising a bully is not to be a bully, but some parents have a history of severely dysfunctional relationships, and it is unlikely that there will be a change in dynamics.

The fact that some kids will never have positive parental role models is a critical reason to keep them in the prosocial environment of school instead of suspending them for bullying behavior. Counteracting a disastrous home environment might feel hopeless at times, but the hours at school can make a difference if the school community is caring. These children literally need to be taught how to treat others, in the same way that they need to be taught academic skills. Sometimes, merely pointing out the difference between good friends and bad friends can help a child recognize specific actions that he or she needs to change. Trudy Ludwig provides the following simple chart in her children's book, *Confessions of a Former Bully*, to help kids assess how they are doing:[10]

Good Friends	Bad Friends
. . . appreciate and like you for who you are.	. . . put you down to build themselves up.
. . . accept that you get to choose your own friends.	. . . tell you who you can be friends with.
. . . make you feel welcome in their group or activity.	. . . won't let you join their group or activity.
. . . have good things to say about you to their friends.	. . . gossip, spread rumors, or send hurtful email and text messages about you.
. . . use humor in a harmless way.	. . . hide behind the words "just kidding" or "no offense, but . . ." when saying something really hurtful.
. . . make you feel accepted and safe.	. . . make you feel unaccepted and unsafe.
. . . work things out with you when you have problems.	. . . refuse to admit when they do something wrong and keep doing it!
. . . are friends you can count on, every day.	. . . are nice one day and mean the next.
. . . really want to hang out with you.	. . . only play with you until "someone better" comes along.

Text copyright © 2010 by Trudy Ludwig. Used by permission of Tricycle Press, an imprint of Random House Children's Books, a division of Random House, Inc.

With practice, kids can measurably improve how they treat others. Maria, a former child bully, was one such girl who worked hard at becoming a better friend. She explained to me, "When I did bully someone, it was as a result of my temper, and it wasn't because I always intended to hurt her. I always felt bad afterward and would get a lot of guilt. I didn't want to let my temper control my actions, so I made an effort at learning to control my temper. As I grew older, I got better at it. In the end, I guess it was not wanting to feel guilt that helped me to stop hurting others physically and psychologically. I wasn't an evil child, I just needed to learn."

Maria believed that her anger was to blame for her bullying, but Barbara Coloroso would bring up another factor to consider. Coloroso told me, "Bullying is not about anger; it is about contempt. Kids who feel contempt for others have three characteristics that allow them to engage in bullying without feeling empathy or shame: (1) they have a strong sense of entitlement, (2) they are intolerant of others' differences, and (3) they feel a liberty to exclude people they view as inferior."[11] In Maria's case, she probably did have a quick temper, but it was coupled with contempt for the people she victimized. Bullies come in varying degrees, and Maria differed from more severe bullies in that she did feel shame after the aggressive acts. Maria accessed the pangs of conscience and used them as a powerful motivator to create new habits.

I recalled Coloroso's statement that bullying is about contempt when I received an email from an Australian man named Ross, a former bully who wanted me to know that Katie's story inspired him to write the following confession:[12]

In my second year of high school, for reasons unknown, other than he was possibly different in some way, I took a real dislike to a student a year behind me. And I picked on him. I recall one day giving him such a hard time that he lost it and lashed out, hitting me once. So, full of righteous indignation, I went after him and gave him a pounding. A teacher appeared on the scene, breaking things up. Still full of myself, I angrily claimed the other had hit me. Other students, however, quickly told the real story, that I had been the instigator. I wasn't exactly one of the popular crowd anyway (anyone seeing the irony?). So I was in trouble, my then less-than-stellar reputation among the teaching staff dropped that much lower, the victim went on his way, and I left him alone after that.

I did not give him much thought for several years until my younger sister commented one day that this young fellow had attempted to kill himself, partly because everyone "hated" him.

That revelation really floored me. I was one of those arse-wipes who had helped drive this kid toward suicide, even though I had left him alone for several years. By then I was at a senior high school and hadn't even seen the kid for more than a year. But, my God, did I feel guilty.

The next year, that same student now appeared at the same senior high school. So I made a point of saying "g'day" to him. The look of mixed relief and gratitude on his face made me feel even worse. Out of a sense of guilt, I kept saying "hello" anytime I saw him around the school. It eventually ceased being a thing of guilt and instead became just a natural thing to do. Did we become friends? Not really. But I think he appreciated knowing there was at least one person around who was going to at least make some sort of effort. And my greeting was always answered with a big, toothy smile.

That was thirty years ago. I have no idea where that young man ended up or how he is doing. I hope he is doing alright. Chances are that he's actually doing better than me. But I like to think that I have never forgotten the lesson that he didn't ever realize he had taught me. I like to think I haven't picked on anyone since.

Ross, fueled by his own feelings of contempt and inferiority, picked on a boy who was different. Unlike Maria, Ross did not feel guilty immediately after the acts of bullying. Ross most likely felt a stronger sense of entitlement than Maria, and this protected him from his own conscience for a longer period of time. Distance and maturity softened Ross and positioned him to experience true feelings of contrition upon learning of the boy's suicide attempt. This is where Ross diverges from lifelong bullies—he recognized the consequences of his actions, and his genuine remorse spurred him to make conscious improvements in the way he treats others. Arthur, Maria, and Ross are hopeful examples of how people can change. Unfortunately, not all bullies are capable of feeling true remorse. Ludwig said, "Some kids come into this world and are raised without an internal moral compass. I tell those kids, 'Even if you don't think it is wrong to hurt someone else, you should treat them respectfully out of self-preservation—what if the kid you bullied comes in with a gun one day?'"[13]

In some cases, a child who acts like a bully needs intense help in all aspects of his or her life. At Washington Elementary, which uses PBIS, Steps to Respect, and Second Step to guide bullying prevention, there are several students in Tier 3 (the individualized intervention level) who are at extremely high risk for aggressive behavior. For these students, Washington offers a Wrap Program. Kate Ellison, the school's principal, explained, "A wrap means that home, school, and the community all 'wrap' around the child to offer support. I will go to a family's house, as will our teachers and social workers, if that's what it takes to get more connection between home and school. There is value to connecting with families in their home space."

The family of the "wrapped" child drives the wrap and identifies the support systems that they want to include in the wrap. For example, one boy's family chose the involved parties to be the child, the family, the YMCA, the school, the church, a social worker, a teacher, a behavioral specialist, and the principal. "We met with the child and talked about his strengths and needs and how to meet those needs," Ellison said, "and when we ask, the community of Evanston really steps up and participates." At Washington, the members of the wrap meet every six weeks to review data and to see how the goals are being met. The school coordinated four wraps for its most at-risk students in the 2010–2011 school year, and all had positive results. Ellison told me, "Wraps go on as long as we need them; it could last for a child's entire academic career here at Washington."[14]

Chapter Nineteen

Responding to the Victim

Your young child comes to you sobbing that the other kids are being mean to her. Or maybe your middle schooler complains of headaches every day and begs to stay home from school, but you know it is because he is being bullied. Perhaps your high school student has begun anxiously checking her text messages and spending hours at her computer, emerging red-eyed from crying, and you suspect she is being cyberbullied. What if your kid has some behavioral quirks, and you know that he can be "irritating" to other kids? What do you do? What do we all do?

One mom wrote me to say: "My son has high functioning autism and ADHD. He has been bullied ever since starting school in preschool. One child in preschool told him to pull down his pants and pee on the playground and then the other child 'spanked' him on the bare butt in front of all the other children. Bullies are very hard to stop. J is twelve now (maturity level of about an eight-to nine-year-old) and is trying to avoid bullies through humor. One of the aspects overlooked is that sometimes victims' actions are almost guaranteed to attract bullies. Not that I am blaming victims, I just think that social training needs to be addressed for kids who need it. For example: J talks almost nonstop and says some things people think are really odd (if they don't know him well especially), in part because he is very literal and not great at understanding idioms/slang."

J's mom brings up a very complicated idea—do kids "invite" bullying by acting differently than others? Stan Davis is one bullying expert who is working to combat that type of thinking. He spoke passionately to me about the need to stop assigning responsibility to the victim, insisting that "we as a society must give up on the adult idea that if someone did something to you, it must be because *you* did something wrong. Adults think that the only people who get picked on are too passive or too annoying, and if we react to a kid's report of injury from that frame of mind, we have a problem." Davis commented that this mentality is exactly how the police used to react to reports of rape. Police would ask a rape victim what she was wearing. "We have lobbied to change that way of thinking," he said. "Sure, it was a task, but it was successful, and now police would never say to a rape victim, 'Well, what were you wearing?' We need to do the same thing with bullying." Davis stressed that mean behavior is the fault of the person who does it. "I tell parents that their child is teased because there are people who think making fun of someone who is different is acceptable, not because your child has an awkward social style. This requires a big conceptual change: teasing tells us about the person who did it and nothing about the person who was teased."[1]

By removing the blame from the victim, we can shift our focus to the perpetrators and work on teaching them empathy and compassion. This will not be an easy shift, and it has long-reaching implications for the self-confidence of the targets. For how can we convince the victims that they did nothing wrong if even their own parents and teachers approach bullying from the standpoint that behavioral quirks invite bullying? This does not mean we should abandon efforts to teach quirky kids how to engage in normal social interactions. Getting through life requires children and adults to manage social dynamics. Children with autism, ADD, ADHD, and other disorders need extensive assistance building their social skills. Some children do not have *any* diagnosed disorders, yet they still cannot gauge social situations well. In an ideal classroom, children who have trouble with social situations will be encouraged to develop their skills, and children who are socially adept will be encouraged to support and include others in a nonjudgmental way.

"My social radar is off," Josie admitted to me, as she recounted her struggles to make friends.[2] Starting in second grade, Josie floundered in social situations, and the other students picked up on her discomfort. By fifth grade, she was the target of vicious taunting. Josie remembered, "At the lunch table, the ringleader would say, 'Okay, Josie, turn around. Everyone who thinks Josie is fat, raise your hand.' It was awful." Josie's classmates started a game where they would call her Medusa, and the whole class would freeze whenever they saw her. The message of "you don't belong" was loud and clear. Josie's mom tried to talk to the teacher, who responded that her job was to teach and not to babysit. "I don't know how to be a regular member of a group," Josie told me. "I either have to be the one in control—the leader of the group—or else the group eventually turns on me."

I asked Michael Thompson how we incorporate social-skills training for quirky kids who "don't fit in" without making them feel as if we are blaming the victim, and he responded, "Kids who lack social skills should be invited to join friendship groups by school counselors who are well liked and popular with kids. If a child joins a group with a popular counselor, then it isn't blaming the victim. Developing social skills is straightforward learning, and it can be done in a group composed of a counselor, other kids who lack social skills, and a few good-hearted altruistic leaders (not popular kids, but altruistic kids) from the class."[3]

Not all kids who are bullied lack social skills, however. Sometimes kids are victimized by their peers, simply because they look different or come from a different background, and offering them social skills training is not what they need. All parents feel a measure of helplessness when they have a child who is being victimized, and they agonize over what to do. Barbara Coloroso, internationally known for her work in bullying prevention, provides very clear advice to parents in *The Bully, the Bullied, and the Bystander* about what to do if your child is bullied:[4]

Don't
- Don't minimize, rationalize, or explain away the bully's behavior.
- Don't rush in to solve the problem for your child.
- Don't tell your child to avoid the bully.

- Don't tell your child to fight back.
- Don't confront the bully or the bully's parents alone.

Do Tell Your Child:
- "I hear you; I am here for you; I believe you; you are not alone in this."
- "It is not your fault."
- "There are things you can do."

And then:
- Report the bullying to school personnel.
- Bring the facts to the meeting in writing.

I thought back to the time when I confronted Jake in the schoolyard about calling Katie Piggy and realized I had violated #5 of Coloroso's *Don't* list. I wish I had known back then all the things I have learned in this journey! In terms of reporting the bullying to school personnel, many students are afraid to tell their parents that they are being bullied because they dread being labeled a tattler. Sometimes children confide to their parents on the condition that their parents promise not to report the problems to the school. The fear of being labeled a tattletale is a serious inhibition to effective bullying prevention. Research by Stan Davis and Charisse Nixon shows that only 42% of students who had been bullied at a moderate, severe, or very severe level went forward with reporting the bullying to a school official. Of those who told what was happening, only 34% reported that things got better. In fact, an alarming 29% reported that telling a school official made things worse.[5]

Davis pointed out, "Kids are taught systematically not to tell an adult about being mistreated. There are actually teachers who have told special education kids that they don't listen to tattles. My analogy is this: you see someone weaving on the highway and you call 911 to report it and the police say, 'Do you just want to get that person in trouble?'" Davis advocates that schools change this mind-set by teaching students that reporting the truth is a good thing. Furthermore, teachers should tell the aggressor that he has no reason to get angry when the victim reports the bullying, because it was the aggressor who made the choice to do the mean thing.

Davis stressed just how deep-seated the fear of tattling is, telling me, "In national studies, fifty percent of kids said they would tell an adult if they thought there would actually be a school shooting the very next day. *Only fifty percent.* The rest are afraid they would be tattling. To combat this, there are several things we should start doing when students report being victimized: (1) a kid's report to us should be welcomed and dealt with effectively, and we must do everything possible to keep it from happening again; (2) we should take the report as an indication that this victim needs some nurturing from us, and *we* are responsible for checking back with the kid to see if it gets better; and (3) it's our job to make sure every kid feels connected at school, by making sure that other kids spend time with the victimized kid at school."[6] Davis is one of those leading the effort to create more caring, compassionate schools.

The Youth Voice Project, conducted by Davis and his colleague, Charisse Nixon, is the first-known large-scale research project that solicits *students'* perceptions about strategy effectiveness to reduce peer mistreatment in U.S. schools. Davis and Nixon believe the findings should help guide educators, parents, and youth in applying effective prevention and intervention efforts to reduce bullying. Over thirteen thousand students in grades five through twelve have been surveyed thus far, and the results show that some of the most common advice given by adults is viewed as *not helpful* and in some cases even *harmful* by the students themselves.[7] How did it happen that so many experts were offering unhelpful advice? It's a frightening thought for all of us who turn to experts. I asked Davis for his insights.

"We did this research for two reasons," Davis explained. "First, we were concerned that the advice everyone was giving the kids was an adult opinion of what an adult thinks ought to work." He pointed out that kids aren't living in the same experience we did, and adults give advice based on our own memories, which are inaccurate. "The second reason," he continued, "is that we wanted to get away from the idea that the adults are the experts. We wanted to ask the kids what helps them." Many anti-bullying programs advise kids to tell the aggressor "Stop," but in the Youth Voice Project surveys, kids reported that telling the bully "Stop" only worked about 20 percent of the time. Davis stressed that saying "Stop" didn't work 80 percent of the time, so it is time to try something else. Given that thousands of kids have now shared what *does* work for them, Davis and Nixon want to disseminate that information. One important thing to note is that the children surveyed were in grades five through twelve; therefore, this research is best applied to children ages ten and up.

In the Youth Voice Project, surveyed students were most likely to report that the following strategies *made things better:*[8]

- Told an adult at home.
- Told an adult at school (large differences in this rating between schools).
- Made a joke about it.
- Told a friend(s).

whereas the following strategies *made things worse:*[9]

- Hit the bully(ies) or fought them.
- Made plans to get back at them.
- Told the person or people to stop.
- Did nothing.
- Told the person how I felt.
- Walked away.
- Pretended it didn't bother me.

Basically, strategies aimed at accessing support from others made a positive difference, while strategies aimed at trying to change the behavior of the aggressors made things worse. Telling an adult at school was described as making things better only *slightly more* often as making things worse and largely depended on how the adult handled the report. How should adults respond to reports of bullying? According to victimized students, the following actions by adults were most likely to *make things better:*[10]

- Listened to me.
- Checked in with me afterwards to see if the behavior stopped.
- Gave me advice.
- Kept up increased adult supervision for some time.

whereas the following actions by adults at school were most likely to *make things worse:*[11]

- Told me to stop tattling.
- Told me to solve the problem by myself.
- Told me if I acted differently this wouldn't happen to me.
- Ignored what was going on.

A sympathetic ear seems to be the greatest source of comfort, and it is something we can teach our educators to provide in lieu of judgment. Sometimes, simply listening can be harder than it sounds. I have found that it is difficult for me to listen without also trying to offer advice when my girls are upset. As a parent, it is hard to resist the urge to try to "fix" things that are wrong. I remember my own mom asking me, "Is there anything you want me to do about it?" when I complained about a problem. Often, the answer was, "I don't want you to do anything. Just let me rant." But now that I am the mom, I feel compelled to *do* something when my kids are hurting. Listening doesn't feel like enough, even when it is.

Besides listening and offering empathy, what else can we do to help victims of bullying? We have heard a common theme from both victims and experts: find an activity outside of school. Jodee Blanco, a survivor of school bullying and author of the bestselling memoir, *Please Stop Laughing at Me,* told me, "One of the main pieces of advice I give parents is to find their child an alternative social outlet outside of school. It will give the child a lifeline. And you never want to say to your kid, 'They're just jealous.' It's a cliché. Avoid the clichés because they insult the child. Instead, do what's practical and necessary, and get your kid into an activity that helps."[12]

Finding the right outlet can change your child's entire school experience. This was the fortunate outcome for Wes Shockley, who was bullied consistently from early childhood into high school.[13] He explained, "In my sophomore year, while waiting for my bus, another student kept picking on me. This was a continuation from my freshman year. Something about me always seemed to draw his attention, and I never figured out what it was. He was always pushing and shoving me and making threats." One day, a bystander intervened and pulled Shockley aside to give him some support. Shockley recalled, "He talked with me for a while about learning to be confident and standing up for myself. It turned out he studied judo, and it caught my interest. That summer I started Tae Kwon Do near my home. Then junior year came, and the bully was at it again. I talked to my instructor who said he would teach me 'defense only,' never to antagonize or provoke."

Shockley's instructor taught him some defensive moves, and he also told Shockley's dad about the situation. Shockley had been too embarrassed and afraid to confide in his parents, but this opened the door for their first discussion about the trouble he was experiencing. Shockley continued, "At school the next day, the bullying started again, so I decided to stand my ground. After the first shove, I assumed a defensive stance. This caught the bully off guard. After a moment of hesitation, he decided I wasn't worth his time. I was so surprised. Then I realized, 'I did it!' I defended myself without having to throw a single punch!" Shockley's confidence level went up much higher. "I was standing taller. I was more socially able and started letting people in and making good friends." Today, Shockley is a skilled, experienced martial-arts instructor who holds a Shodan in the Vietnamese art of Cuong Nhu and teaches self-defense to many victims of bullying.

What if your child has been the target of a physical attack or lives in terror of being assaulted? How can a parent bear to watch a child's constant anxiety? There *are* ways to empower kids who are at risk for bodily harm. This does *not* mean we should teach our kids that "if someone hits you, you should hit back." On the contrary, kids should take every step possible to remove themselves from situations that are potentially violent. But the truth is, if another kid corners you in the schoolyard and starts pounding away, you want to know how best to protect yourself from serious bodily injury. With self-defense in mind, I asked Shockley what parents can do to help their vulnerable sons and daughters. "My best advice for parents," he said, "is to find a good martial arts school for their child. Defense takes practice and time. The hard part of this is finding a good school. Word to the wise," he cautioned, "martial arts programs are *not* federally regulated. This is a buyer beware market." Shockley recommends that "the trick is to observe the instructor. Is he or she all about his or her own image or helping others? Is he or she consistent with the schedule? Does he or she feel like a bully?" He tells parents and kids to shop around and take advantage of trial programs at a school before signing on, emphasizing, "Do not ignore community center programs. Some of the best instructors I know operate out of a community center or YMCA. They teach because they love to."

Defensive Techniques to Use in the Moment of a Physical Attack[14]

In the moment of a physical attack, many things happen. The nervous system is in overdrive, and a person experiences a flood of adrenaline. The heart rate, respiration rate, and blood pressure all increase. This is referred to as fight or flight—a person's autonomic response to danger. We are all born with this response system, and it is difficult to overcome these feelings of panic unless you train your body through regular practice.

For those who are not yet trained, Shockley recommends the following postures and techniques to use for self-defense during a physical attack, stressing that parents must remind children to employ these methods for *defense only:*

- Make lots of loud noise. Draw attention to yourself. Bullies or assailants do not want to be seen. Scream "Stop hitting me! . . . Help! . . . Stop hitting me!"
- Keep your chin low to protect the throat.
- Do not close your eyes! You have to try to see what is coming.

- Make two fists and hold them in front of you with the palms of the hands *facing each other*. Making fists protects the fingers from being jammed or hyperextended.
- Do not turn the palms to face your own body, as this weakens the body mechanics and causes your arms to collapse during incoming attacks.
- Shield your face and body as best you can from incoming blows by maneuvering your forearms up or down and turning your waist side to side. You can also drop your elbows to protect your ribs.
- To defend against an attack to the midsection or groin, drop one or both fists down as if using a hammer. Try to envision this posture as a standing fetal position. (Parents, you can practice this with your children by having them hold the position while you try to tap them lightly on the head, the ribs, the abdomen, etc. Start with slow movements at first, then faster movements over time.)
- If you must strike back, which is always a last resort, open your hand and use your palms. You risk injury when your fist is not trained, and your wrist may collapse and break. Other safe tools to use for striking back would be the elbows. Knees are an option if the attackers have your arms pinned. Pinching is also a viable technique when you are stuck in a bear hug. Above all, use these techniques only to make the attackers stop. When they do stop, discontinue attacking. Always avoid causing permanent injury.
- Parents, if your child employs any of these techniques, even in self-defense, be prepared for your child to still be at risk for suspension or expulsion from school. Most schools have a zero-tolerance policy for fighting, no matter who started it.

Speaking Out Against Bullying

Victims of bullying often emerge as passionate advocates for those who share their plight. Just as Wes Shockley enjoys training others in need of protection, so, too, does Victoria Stilwell, who is the star of the television series *It's Me or the Dog*. Stilwell suffered at the hands of a classic "mean girl" when she was in high school, even losing her lifeline—her best friend—to the mean girl's dominating influence for a painful period of time. Eventually, the best friend developed pangs of regret and solicited her boyfriend's help in stopping the mean girl from attacking Stilwell. Guided by her intuition about human nature, Stilwell developed a career as an animal trainer and has become famous for protecting canine victims from bullying owners. Stilwell told me earnestly, "My experience with bullying is one of the many reasons why I am not into the old style message of dominating your dog into submission so it behaves. That is bullying your dog. I ask people, 'Do you want your dog to follow you because it wants to, or do you want your dog to follow you because it fears what will happen if it doesn't?' Their eyes open up; they didn't know." Although thousands of people subscribe to positive training, many people remain resistant to Stilwell's alternative training techniques, preferring to use force and punishments with their pets. Authoritarian styles, whether used in parenting or pet training, are problematic because they are based in fear and control.

Stilwell observed, "People who are insecure and out of control themselves are the ones who feel the need to dominate an animal in order to control it. I believe in taking the humane route and using positive reinforcement, which is also how I think people should treat children."[15] Just as Shockley finds healing power in teaching martial arts to beaten-down children, Stilwell finds it therapeutic to teach pet owners how to restore healthy relationships with their dogs. The cases of Shockley and Stilwell illustrate how much strength victims of bullying have to offer others. If your child has experienced bullying, encourage him or her to reach out to others in the same position. There is strength and comfort in numbers.

Chapter Twenty

Restorative Justice

Children who act as bullies are unlikely to change their behavior unless they change the way they think. But changing the way people think is not easy to do, not without accessing their deep inner beliefs about who they are and who others are. Punitive measures do not encourage children to question their core values, nor do such sanctions enable children to view their victims as whole people. Understandably, when parents learn that their child is being bullied, they have a knee-jerk reaction—usually an urge to see the bully punished. There is a better way to repair broken relationships, and it is called restorative justice. To gain a better understanding of the philosophy behind restorative justice, I spoke with Brenda Morrison, director of the Centre for Restorative Justice.[1] Morrison shared some background with me. "Initially, anti-bullying programs were too focused on individuals. There was assertiveness training for victims and anger management training for bullies. Now we know it is a relational dynamic. What bullies typically need is more structure with very clear expectations about how they should manage their behavior, and what victims need is more peer support."

From a restorative justice perspective, Morrison explains, it is best to separate the behavior from the person, because we don't want the child to become the label. In the United States, many responses to bullying are based on external sanctions such as the school's code of conduct. Bullying behavior leads to office referrals, suspension, and expulsion, and punishment is the big motivational leader to deter behavior. "By contrast," Morrison said, "restorative justice is not about punishment and rules; it is about values and relationships." Restorative justice is a shift away from third-party decision making that imposes rules and sanctions, replacing it with first-party decision making that involves reparation of relationships and dignity.

Morrison, like Stan Davis, is a big proponent of helping kids feel connected to their schools. "Connection to schools and peers is a protective factor for violence, emotional distress, early sexual behavior, and drug and alcohol use," she said, "and we best maintain good connections in the classroom. But sometimes mistakes happen. After there is an incident—an 'oops,' we like to call it—then we use restorative justice to talk about how it feels—an 'ouch.' We work through the problem or the harm." Given the right skill set, kids can often stop a conflict before it escalates, but Morrison noted that when the conflict is more intense, kids do need another person to step in. "We do it as a collective in a classroom instead of sending kids off to the principal's office, and we work on the relational ecology. The social emotional programs fit in really well with restorative justice."

Restorative justice is making its move into schools, but at this time, the process of restorative justice is most widely used in criminal cases, where it can be used to repair the harm that a criminal offender has inflicted on his or her victim. Morrison pointed out that restorative justice makes good economic sense in addition to good emotional sense. "When someone enters the criminal justice system, it is a very expensive process. In England, for every one pound spent on restorative justice in the criminal context, the country saved eight pounds on criminal justice expenses. Restorative justice reduces the occurrence of the problem behavior, and recidivism rates drop," she said. Morrison believes that doing early intervention in the form of restorative justice in schools will prevent bullies from becoming criminals.

"It's not about a violation of rules; it is about a violation of people," she commented. "Institutions only focus on the violator and not on the violated, but restorative justice gives a voice to people, especially the victim. Victims regain their sense of safety from restorative justice, and they experience reduced symptoms of post-traumatic stress disorder (PTSD). None of the other interventions address PTSD." Victims are also more likely to come forward when they know that restorative justice awaits their bully instead of punitive sanctions. Punishments create a chilling effect on victims' reports, as they are terrified of the bully retaliating, and silence grounded in fear makes symptoms of PTSD worse. There is a negative ripple effect from crime that can harm other people beyond the victim, such as parents and neighbors, and restorative justice allows for healing within the community of those most affected.

In March 2011, Morrison was one of many experts invited to the White House Conference on Bullying Prevention. Following the conference, the Office of Safe and Drug-Free Schools hired Morrison to do a webinar on restorative justice. The response was so positive that she returned to Washington, DC, in August 2011 to give another talk called "Restorative Justice and Bullying: Prevention Not Punishment." Currently the two evidence-based programs that receive the most government support are PBIS and SEL, but restorative justice is starting to come up in many policy discussions.

One of the concerns raised by those unfamiliar with restorative justice is that they think it is a form of peer mediation, a practice that has been shown to be harmful in bullying. Morrison acknowledged, "A lot of people learn about restorative justice in the criminal justice system, and they think we are going to make the bully face the victim. What they don't realize is that in schools, the restorative justice process is more about building a community of support around each person, and we would only have face-to-face conversations when it feels safe to do so." I asked Susan Limber of the Olweus Bullying Prevention Program to clarify their opinion of restorative justice, and she responded, "We have been public about saying 'don't mediate peers,' but restorative justice does not mean peer mediation. Where there is the time and the training to do restorative justice appropriately and the parties are willing, then I think it is a beneficial thing, a very good thing." Given that the Olweus program guides the thinking of many who work in bullying prevention, it is important to understand that Olweus is supportive of restorative justice when done properly.

To get an idea of how restorative justice works locally, I met with Susan Garcia Trieschmann, committee chair for Restorative Justice Evanston, and Arika Barton, restorative justice coordinator for Evanston Police Department Youth Services Program.[2] Youth offenders in Evanston can either go through the juvenile court system, or they can do restorative justice, when the conditions are appropriate. Barton described how a typical peacemaking circle works. "Everybody sits in a circle, and a ceremony takes place in the middle. No one is in charge, but there are two facilitators to keep things on track. We use a talking piece, like a stress ball or a teddy bear, and a person can talk for as long or as short as is comfortable. The others must listen with their hearts instead of preparing rebuttals or retorts. Respect is the guiding principle." Barton stressed that the most important component in maintaining safety in the circle is confidentiality, and that whatever is said in the circle stays in the circle. To that end, participants sign a confidentiality agreement.

I asked Barton if she had any instructive examples of how restorative justice has been used to repair a bullying relationship among elementary school children. She began telling me about one of her most memorable cases. "We had a situation with two third-grade boys. Kid A, who had poor social skills, had been teased previously by the older brothers and cousins of Kid B. Kid A retaliated by bullying Kid B, the younger brother of the perpetrators. But Kid B was innocent—a nice kid—and he suffered. Kid A was big and strong, and Kid B was small and scrawny." The parents of Kid B kept complaining to the school, but the school did nothing about it. Kid A gave Kid B an especially hard time on the school bus, which was unsupervised. As the weeks went by, the parents of Kid B grew more and more distraught. Finally, after a particularly brutal episode, the parents of Kid A called the police, and Kid B was formally arrested. This is when Barton became involved. She suggested that the families try restorative justice, and everyone was receptive to it, which is a key component of the process. It does not work unless both the offender and the victim are willing participants.

Barton continued her story, "I did a peace circle with Kid A and his mother and Kid B and his father and two facilitators. First, I did a five-minute teaching component, and then everyone signed a confidentiality agreement. I did an opening question to allow each boy to introduce himself as a person, not as a bully or a victim." In the comfort of the circle, Barton recalled, the kids each talked for fifteen or twenty minutes. They spoke about their favorite sports and their favorite teachers and the flavors of ice cream they like. "We learned a lot about these kids, but nothing having to do with the conflict. It's okay to talk about something besides the conflict initially. It's about connection. It puts everyone on a level playing ground. So after one or two talking rounds, then we talked about the incident. We gave the victim the chance to talk first. We asked, 'What was the incident, what hurt you, how do you feel about it?' Then everyone had a chance to react or respond to what they heard." The offender then offered his perspective of the story, explained Barton, and was given the same questions and the same opportunity to talk.

Although an apology is not required in the circle, Barton was touched to see that Kid A chose to apologize to Kid B. After the boys talked, the mom of Kid A provided some background about Kid A, revealing some of the reasons why he acts aggressively. Barton noticed that the dad of Kid B listened intently and nodded with new understanding. After everyone spoke, they made a plan to prevent the harmful action from happening again.

"Who makes the plan? How does that part of the process work?" I asked.

Barton replied, "The peace circle is a component but does not require restorative justice. The actual restorative justice is often planned during the family group conferencing, which is a more formal, structured meeting with a true defined victim and offender, and it requires an agreed-upon way of righting the wrong. It's not a punishment; it's more about restoring a person. For example, in the event of theft, we don't just make people pay for stolen goods. We find a way to repair the harm. If a kid knocks down a fence, we get him a mentor with a carpenter to help him rebuild a fence. If kids cover a wall with graffiti, we have them clean it and then enroll them in art classes, because they are good artists."

Interestingly, when Barton asks the offenders what the reparative action should be, the offenders usually suggest harsher things for themselves than the victims recommend. In the case of the two third-grade boys, the circle was "amazing," said Barton. "Even though we didn't need to make a contract, it turned out that Kid B's dad is a dance instructor, and Kid A loves to dance. The boys decided that the reparative action would be for them to take a dance class together. The two of them have not had a problem since then." I was very touched by the image of these two boys learning new steps together, rewriting their choreography from a dance of violence to a dance of friendship. Although Kid A has learned to view Kid B as a person and not as an object, Kid A still struggles in his relationships with the world at large. Barton told me, "Kid A reoffended with a different person, and he is still a work in progress. He has taken anger-management classes, and he still sees the social worker at the school." The promising news? Kid A has never again bullied Kid B.

The fact that Kid A reoffended at all is very much the exception rather than the rule. The Evanston Police Department follows every youth restorative justice case at six months and again at a year to see if they have reoffended. Barton said, "Our success rate is ninety-eight percent. That means ninety-eight percent of our cases do not go on to reoffend. The national average success rate for traditional juvenile offenders is forty-eight percent. Only forty-eight percent of the cases that go to juvie court do not reoffend." The reduced recidivism rate for restorative justice has profound implications for a child's future, because repeat offenders usually increase the severity of their crimes. "First they bully," Barton explained, "then they move to aggressive battery, and then they get caught with a gun." The kids who go through restorative justice have a far more hopeful future than the kids who go through court sanctions.

Still, restorative justice is not for everyone, Barton cautioned. Trieschmann concurred, telling me, "The person we look at closely before doing restorative justice is the victim. Is he or she ready to face the offender? If a victim is unable to even discuss the crime, we can't do restorative justice. Sometimes it takes six months to prepare for a peacemaking circle. The offender needs to be invested in the process, too, because if we do restorative justice and then the bully revictimizes the same victim, we have done more harm than good. If the offender is denying guilt, for example, there is no way restorative justice will work. So we do preconferencing to meet with the offender and the offender's family and the victim and the victim's family to see if restorative justice is appropriate."

Trieschmann and Barton are currently working with Washington school principal Kate Ellison to bring restorative justice to the elementary school students. Trieschmann explained, "At a school like Washington, restorative justice means introducing the philosophy of communicating from the heart. Kids attend the circle to learn to listen, not just to talk. We introduce the concept of listening to kindergarten and first graders, and by the time the kids are in second or third grade, they can use the circle to repair wrongs. The children will reach a point where they can ask to 'circle this' when they have conflicts. In Evanston Township High School, for instance, we are using the restorative ideals in the peer jury. It is not a program in the schools; it is a philosophy."

I found the idea of schoolchildren circling up to discuss conflict an intriguing one. The image of not just two children but an entire class participating in a peacemaking circle is much more positive than the image of several kids being sent to the principal's office. Morrison, who has implemented restorative justice in classrooms, told me that there are three steps in using the circle to resolve issues at school:[3]

1. Build understanding.
2. Talk about how you were affected socially, emotionally, and physically by the incidents.
3. Talk about how to make it better.

Morrison shared one class's restorative justice story with me. "We had a fifth-grade classroom that used peacemaking circles to talk about conflicts," she said. "There was a box, and if someone had an issue, he or she could put a note in the box requesting a circle. When the class circled up, those who felt most affected by the incident could choose to sit in the inner circle and talk, and the rest of the class would make an outer circle around them to listen and learn." In this classroom, there was one boy who acted out frequently. He acted aggressively, she explained, because he did not feel safe anywhere. For two-thirds of the year, he physically sat outside of the inner circle because it did not emotionally feel safe to him. Morrison continued, "Then one day, this little boy put a note in the box, saying he was ready to talk about his anger. For the first time, he chose to sit in the inner circle and revealed to the class a little bit about himself and why he gets so angry. He gave the class members permission to tell him when he was getting too angry. This was a huge step for him, and it changed the tone of the class for the rest of the year."

In a fascinating application, Morrison has also used restorative justice to successfully heal broken parent relationships. As many school teachers and principals can attest, the parents of students can cause huge amounts of damage when they become emotionally involved in conflicts at school. In June 2011, Morrison was called in to work with a school that was experiencing a crisis among the parents. "It started with a sixth-grade girl who had been bullied all year," she began, "even though the school was doing everything possible to improve the situation. One day, the mother of the victimized girl reached her own tipping point, because her daughter was so emotionally distressed. The mom completely lost it and went marching into the school with her other two kids in tow, and she terrorized the students in the class. She had kids hiding under desks and crying, and the teacher lost total control of the classroom."

The next day, many kids skipped school, and rumors spread like crazy. The gossip really took on a life of its own and threatened to destroy the parent community of the school. Morrison said, "With the support of the school's principal, I convened a restorative justice circle just for parents. They were the only ones who could possibly stop the rumor mill. Parents came to the school and voluntarily joined the circle. They disclosed what was happening to them as a result of the incident and how they were affected. It was incredible. There was remarkable healing and reconciliation. After the circle, people who lived on the same streets as one another and had never talked before went to one another's houses and had heart-to-hearts. My point in telling you this story is that we often think reconciliation is just between victim and offender, but sometimes parents need a voice."

When parents are denied an opportunity to discuss controversial issues face-to-face, it is not uncommon for them to bring conflicts to the Internet, where they debate problems on the school Listserv or in Google groups. If you are a parent and you are learning about a bullying situation by reading conversation threads online, *stop!* Go to the source, call the school, make sure you get accurate information before fanning the flames. Without face-to-face interaction, there is a heightened risk for miscommunication. Rumors tend to get even worse, and parents grow angrier and more self-righteous in an online environment. Implementing a peacemaking circle for parents is one way to manage particularly contentious situations, as evidenced by the positive outcome with the sixth-grade class. The school administrators did an excellent job of thinking outside of the box when faced with a spiraling crisis.

Chapter Twenty-One

Strategies That Ease the Negative Effects of Taunting

Not every child who acts as a bully will be amenable to participating in restorative justice with the victim. And most of the time, peer victimization happens far from the eyes of caring adults who can jump in and assist the target. Where does this leave targeted kids? How do we help them cope with bullying in the moment that it is happening, particularly verbal taunts? There are concrete strategies that kids can use to help them get through the day. You may find that merely having a strategy in mind provides your bullied child with enough confidence to leave for school without a struggle.

It is not just in school that children can use these techniques. One area of bullying that is often overlooked by parents is sibling bullying. Although it is normal for brothers and sisters to taunt each other, it is not normal for one sibling to persistently terrorize another. If your kids fight and squabble and disagree, they are displaying normal social behavior. Annoying, yes, but normal, as I try to remind myself when Katie and Annie Rose are tearing each other to shreds over who had what toy first. It is different, however, if you have one sibling who makes it his or her mission to constantly beat down, berate, insult, condescend, scorn, intimidate, and injure another sibling. Then the situation needs to be addressed, because sibling bullying can be just as traumatic as peer bullying. If you can teach your victimized child some techniques to cope with the taunting, the aggressive sibling will no longer elicit the desired response, and the tormenting is likely to cease. Additionally, Barbara Coloroso recommends that you examine how you treat your children to analyze what role you may be playing in the situation. Do you favor one child or overlook misbehavior by one child? If jealousy is at the root of the problems, find a way to make your jealous child feel valued and special while helping empower your victimized child.[1]

Judy Freedman, author of *Easing the Teasing: Helping Your Child Cope with Name-Calling, Ridicule, and Verbal Bullying*, has spent over thirty years as a school social worker working with children who are teased, and she wrote a detailed guide for parents and children based on her surveys and conversations with thousands of students. The manner in which a child responds to teasing greatly influences the frequency and duration of the attacks, and Freedman has assembled a collection of techniques that students have reported to be the most helpful. I remember holding Katie's dear face in my hands as she wept after being taunted about her Star Wars water bottle, and I felt at a loss as to what she could have said in response. Fifteen months later, it feels so good to now know some tools to teach Katie to use in the event of future episodes. Parents have a keen need to protect their kids, but perhaps our best way to protect them is to teach them to protect themselves when we aren't around. Below is a brief description of how and when to use some of the most popular strategies.[2]

Self-Talk or Cognitively Reframing the Event

Self-talk teaches a child (1) not to let the teasing upset her, and (2) that the teasing may be completely untrue and not worth worrying about. For very young children, age four or five, it might start with something as simple as saying to themselves, "I am not going to get mad or cry" when the teasing starts. This can help with impulse control, especially for kids who immediately react to being teased with a hysterical response. Children who reward their aggressors with exaggerated emotional responses often suffer further victimization.[3] If you have a six-year-old son who bursts into tears and cries every time other kids call him "stupid," you can teach him to say to himself, "I know I'm not stupid, so it doesn't matter what they say. I am going to take a deep breath and remember it isn't true and not yell and scream."

Freedman recommends that the most important self-talk older kids can use is, "I don't like when kids say mean things to me. I hate when kids make fun of me, but I'm going to handle it. This is not the end of the world." Internalizing this coping message is critical to prevent bullied kids from feeling a sense of hopelessness. Kids who can feel unhappy about being teased while simultaneously reassuring themselves that it gets better are less susceptible to suicide. A real-life example of this is Carla, the girl who was the victim of a sexual cyberbullying attack and ended up leaving high school at the age of sixteen. Remember, Carla used the following self-talk: "I told myself that the other kids were being juvenile and didn't want to face their own problems, and I became an easy target."[4]

This technique is also referred to as "cognitively reframing the event" by Stan Davis and Charisse Nixon, and it is one of the most effective strategies a child can use to feel better.[5] Dr. Sheri Bauman shared an excellent example of a girl who used cognitive reframing, or self-talk, to comfort herself.[6] "The victim was a girl who was overweight and bullied. The kids from school made a mean webpage about her and photoshopped a photo of her face onto a whale. The mean kids asked her in front of everyone, 'What did you think?' and she said, 'Bad job photoshopping.' She told herself, 'These are not the type of people I want to base my self-image on. I can have web access but do not need to read or look at everything sent to me. I will give no reaction to that mean content.' And the kids stopped bothering her," Bauman said with satisfaction.

Even if the kids had continued to post cruel things online, the targeted girl had made a decision not to look at the webpage, which would have continued to protect her from feeling unhappy. With cyberbullying in particular, it is critical to teach kids that they can cognitively reframe the bullying and make a decision that it is not worth looking at every mean post. Using self-talk restores a feeling of control to kids who have no control over what takes place on the Internet.

Ignoring

This one is very complex. Many adults say that you should *never* ignore it when you are being bullied, but if you actually ask the kids who are being bullied, they say it can work sometimes. Of course, as Stan Davis told me, "*Everything* works sometimes."[7] In my own interviews with former bullying victims, about half explicitly recommended ignoring as a tactic that worked. One victim, Erik, qualified it by telling me, "but ignoring name-calling is very different from ignoring flat-out violence to one's self." Freedman writes, "In my experience, ignoring works quite well in isolated incidents."[8] Isolated incidents, by nature, are not the same as bullying, so ignoring might better be recommended as a strategy for random occurrences of teasing or taunting.

To effectively ignore, the target should not look at or respond to the teaser, nor show any emotion, and, most important, should move away to join other kids when possible. This technique may not work in places like a school bus where the target is a trapped, captive audience. And ignoring may not deter someone who is very determined to get a rise out of you; it may just egg them on and make them try harder. Your child may spend several weeks doggedly ignoring his tormentor before the other child finally gives up and stops the taunting.

I think there needs to be an important distinction between ignoring the actual taunting when it occurs and ignoring it afterward. Even if your child elects to ignore the bully in the heat of the moment, be sure that he knows how important it is to report what happened to an adult once he has reached a safe place. Ignoring should never mean keeping silent and not accessing help when help is needed. The thought of a child who feels unable to ask for help makes my stomach hurt.

The "I" Message

Using the "I" message is designed to tell someone how you feel about their actions without putting them on the defensive. Instead of saying, "You made me upset by calling me names," your child can say, "I feel so upset when you call me names." This makes it easier for the other person to empathize with her. An additional benefit of the "I" strategy is that it teaches the child who is speaking how to recognize and label her emotions. This strategy works best in structured settings, such as in the classroom or during supervised activities and is particularly useful with young children in preschool and elementary school.

The "I" message will backfire, however, if the aggressor is a cruel kid deliberately trying to get an emotional response from the target, because upon hearing "I feel upset," the aggressor will feel rewarded. Teach your child to know the motivation of his or her tormentor in order to assess when this technique is appropriate. This technique is probably the least effective in middle school, when kids need to display little emotion in order to fit in successfully. Davis told me that for kids in fifth through twelfth grades, "Telling the bullies how you feel was most likely to be reported as having a negative effect. It made things worse."[9]

Although this strategy may not help older kids deal with peer victimization, it can be very effective in helping older children communicate with adults who tend to be overly aggressive; for example, a teenage member of the baseball team might say to his harsh coach, "I feel discouraged when you tell me that I can't hit the ball to save my life." Or a kid might say to a demanding parent, "I feel frustrated when you criticize my performance in school. I am really doing my best." Bullying does not just occur among peers and siblings, and it is necessary to give kids tools for managing difficult adults.

Turning the Tease Around: Reframing and Accepting the Tease as Positive

When a child reframes a tease and takes it as a compliment or as a positive, it takes all the fun away from the teaser. Problem solved. If you are trying to upset someone, and he thanks you for your comment, what more is there to say? Last year Katie had her hair braided into cornrows while on vacation, and she was very anxious to go back to school with her new braids. She was afraid that Jake, the boy who had called her Piggy, would make fun of her braids. We helped her prepare for the possibility of being teased by teaching her to reframe it. Before she left for school, we engaged in some role-playing. "Your braids look stupid," I said, pretending to be the taunter. "Thank you for noticing my new braids," Katie responded. When I picked Katie up from school, she reported with a big smile that Jake had noticed her braids, but only to comment, "Cool braids." Maybe the fact that Katie felt more self-confident about the braids helped deter the potential for taunts.

How else could a child reframe a tease? Say a girl tells her younger sister, "Your messy hair looks like a bird's nest." The little sister could respond with "I love baby birds! Bird's nests are awesome." Or if an older brother tells his younger brother, "That drawing looks like scribble scrabble," the younger brother could respond, "Scribble scrabble is fun to draw!" If a boy says to his neighbor, "You suck at riding your bike. I saw you fall," the neighbor could respond with "I sure have gotten good at falling. And check out all the awesome Band-Aids on my scrapes!"

Agreeing with the Teaser

This strategy will work if the target has enough self-confidence to accept the tease in a matter-of-fact manner without feeling defeated. Developmentally, it might be better suited to older kids who can understand how to do this. For example, if a middle schooler is overweight, and she is aware of it but still maintains a healthy self-image, she may respond to a taunt of "You are so fat" with "Yes, I am overweight." If the target is a boy who pitched badly in the previous day's baseball game, and the teaser is telling him, "Are you going blind? Cause you couldn't see the strike zone," the target could reply, "I really pitched poorly yesterday; you are right."

This technique was used successfully in adolescence by James Arnold Taylor, who voices Obi-Wan Kenobi in *Star Wars: The Clone Wars*. Taylor is five foot four, and when kids used to mock him for being short, he simply responded, "You are right. I am a very short guy."[10] If the teaser was looking for Taylor to protest or fight the tease, he was not getting the reaction he sought. Parents could teach a child with glasses to respond to taunts of "You have four eyes!" with "That is true. And I need all four of them to see." Or if kids are taunting a boy for having long hair, he could reply, "Yep, my hair sure is long. I think I have the longest hair in our class."

So?

Replying, "So?" to a tease is a similar strategy to agreeing with the tease, but it is even easier to do. Even the youngest children can use this response. It removes the momentum from the aggressor and conveys a lack of distress on the part of the target. The target needs to say "So?" without attitude or anger. It should simply be a statement of noncommittal agreement in order to be effective. If someone taunts a girl who has a buzz cut by saying, "You look like a boy," the girl could respond with, "I have short hair. So what?" If a competitive sister tells her sibling, "You messed up the piece in our piano recital," the other sibling could say, "So? I missed a few notes. Big deal." Seeing that the target is unmoved by the taunt, the teasers are likely to abandon the effort to be provocative. There is not much else to say. The teaser is unlikely to keep hammering the issue if the target shrugs her shoulders and says, "Yeah, so?"

Complimenting the Teaser

It can be very disarming for an aggressive child to receive a compliment from the target. This strategy is difficult for very young children to master, but by first or second grade, it can be very useful. If a student taunts a boy who has a speech impediment, the boy could respond, "I hope I can learn to speak as well as you. You speak really clearly." A girl who is mocked for being fat in gym class could say to her bully, "You are in really great shape. What exercises do you recommend to keep so fit?" If an older brother tells his younger brother, "You throw like a girl," the younger brother could say, "You have such a great arm. Would you show me how to throw like you?" In some cases, such as with the brothers playing catch, this technique can turn an aggressive child into an ally.

Another example of converting a teaser into an ally would be if a mean girl tells a fellow student, "You are stupid for missing that question in class," and the targeted girl replies, "You always know the right answers. What are your tips for remembering the things you read?" By enlisting the advice of the person doing the taunting, the target shifts the dynamics at play. Of course, there is always the possibility that the aggressor could reject the target's efforts. For example, the mean girl might say, "Nothing I suggest will help you memorize the answers because you are so stupid." If that happens, at least the target has tried the technique, and she can make a note of whether or not it worked. It may be that the mean girl felt compelled to make a comeback to save face, but she might still leave the target alone after that.

Humor

Humor is a very effective tool for those who are able to use it. Children who taunt others are looking for tears or anger in response, but certainly not laughter. A child who can genuinely laugh at himself or make others laugh will not remain a desirable target for very long. For example, if a boy tells his brother, "Don't you ever take a shower? You smell worse than a dog," the brother could drop to the ground and pretend to be a dog, barking and crawling around on all fours. A girl who is taunted for being the last to finish a relay race could reply, "My sister did a magic trick on me to turn me into a sloth. I guess it worked!" A boy who is taunted for having red hair could say, "When I was a baby, it was green. Red doesn't seem so bad!" Judy Freedman wrote about one boy who was taunted for having a large nose. He responded by sniffing and wiggling his nose, which made the taunting stop.[11] Most kids who are taunted simply desire for the mean behavior to stop, and if they can use humor to achieve relief, all the better.

Chapter Twenty-Two

Creating Witnesses and Allies out of Bystanders

Bullying rarely takes place in a vacuum. Usually, there are three parties in the bullying triad: the bully, the bullied, and the onlookers. Starting at an early age, all three parties must be addressed in order to successfully prevent a bullying problem. Barbara Coloroso believes that there is also a fourth party to bullying: the potential defender of the victim. She told me, "We need to identify that fourth party and cultivate those defenders." Defenders should be taught to recognize cruel behavior, developing a keen eye for the difference between normal social conflicts and bullying. When kids observe another child suffering deliberately at the whims of a bully, they should do something about it. Ron Astor advises that "it should be a normative expectation that the peer group responds to someone in need or in pain by saying, 'That is mean, don't do that.'" This is exactly what happened at Evanston Township High School in response to the Evanston Rats website, and the students reversed a harmful situation. Sometimes it simply takes one or two students to step up and say something to the bullies, and this enables other kids who secretly oppose the aggressive behavior to feel more comfortable expressing their support for the victims. What often surprises kids is how *good* it feels to do something nice for others.

Even the youngest kids are capable of learning how to be good bystanders. I remember when Katie was only three years old, and—

perhaps in a weird piece of foreshadowing—one of her favorite songs was "Billy the Bully" by popular kids' artist Justin Roberts. She liked the song so much that we wrote to Justin Roberts, and he performed the song for Katie at a local concert. The song talks about Billy the Bully and Margaret the Mean, who pick on the other kids *one by one by one by one*, hurting them day after day with punches and with words. And then, *the smallest girl in the smallest grade, someone hardly known named Sally McCabe*, stands up at lunchtime to say enough was enough. *She raised her finger in the air to say that bullying was so last year.* And even though the bullies laugh at her, the song concludes by telling us that, *one by one by one by one*, the other kids join little Sally in standing up to the bullies. *It happened one by one by one by one; it started one by one by one by one.*

I contacted Justin Roberts to ask him more about "Billy the Bully," which is an excellent song to play for grade-school children as a way to foster a discussion about being a good bystander. "It was easy to write about the bullies, from physical to verbal abuse, because we all remember it from our own childhoods," Roberts explained, "but then I wasn't sure what to do to resolve the situation." Roberts had an image of an outside figure standing up to the bullies, but he was concerned that "if this happened in reality, she would probably get beaten up, so I decided to add in the idea of other kids joining her one by one." Roberts writes all his songs from a kid's point of view, and, therefore, he did not want it to be preachy or authoritarian. "So I wrote a song where a kid would be the one to solve the problem," he said.[1] Roberts hit on a key concept in resolving bullying—it works best if it comes from the kids themselves, not from a top-down authority. Recall, this is exactly why Stan Davis and Charisse Nixon conducted the Youth Voice Project, in order to get away from the idea that the adults are the experts.

How important is the role of the bystander? Absolutely crucial. Brenda Morrison told me, "When bystanders passively watch, those who are doing the bullying get the message that the behavior is acceptable, and even entertaining. This peer attention actually reinforces the bullying behavior, and research has shown us that the size of the peer audience is correlated with the duration of the bullying event—the more peers who watch, the longer the bullying episode lasts." Morrison went on to explain that when bystanders do intervene, about half the time they use inappropriate aggression toward the kids who are bullying (i.e., physically attacking or using rude language), and about half the time the bystanders are appropriate (i.e., getting a teacher or pointing out that the bullying behavior is hurtful). "What is really interesting," she said, "is that in the majority of cases, the bullying stops within ten seconds when peers intervene, regardless of the method used." It is not *how* they intervene but the fact that they intervene at all that causes the bullying to cease.[2]

Tattling Versus Reporting

Sometimes the safest intervention for bystanders is to report the incident to an adult once they are out of harm's way. Being a good bystander does not mean your child has to walk up to a bigger, stronger kid who is in the act of bullying and tell him to stop, because this may result in your child receiving a pummeling too. The message we want our kids to receive is "*stand together* against bullying" more so than "*stand up to* bullying," because there can be risks involved when individuals stand up to bullies.

The problem with reporting, as we have heard, is that kids have been conditioned to think that *telling* is the same as *tattling*. Since the earliest of ages, kids have heard, "Don't be a tattletale." I'm guilty of saying it to my own girls, when they come shrieking to me that one or the other is committing some minor transgression. "Is she in danger? Are you in danger? Then I don't need to hear about every last little thing!" I have huffed in exasperation. Instead, when young people tell us about unimportant concerns, bullying expert Justin Patchin recommends that we simply thank them for letting us know and return to our other tasks.[3] Given the negative associations with tattling, older children loathe to be labeled as snitches, crybabies, and tattletales. I wrote about this stigma earlier as it applied to the direct targets of peer victimization, but it also applies to the reports of bystanders. In fact, in the Youth Voice Project, a whopping 80 percent of students who witnessed peer victimization chose not to tell an adult at school.[4] To help bystanders understand the concept that it is okay to report harmful behavior, parents and teachers can provide the following distinction:[5]

- If telling an adult will only serve to get another child *in trouble,* that is *tattling.*
- If telling an adult will serve to get you or another kid *out of trouble,* even if it might get the person doing the harmful behavior in trouble, that is *reporting.*

Here are some examples to help explain this to your child.

Younger Kids

Tattling: Sheila sees Jasper sneak a second cookie from the box during snack time. If Sheila tells the teacher, this would be tattling, because Jasper is not harming anyone else, and eating one additional cookie will not harm his own body.

Reporting: John snatches Carlos's lunch bag and proceeds to eat Carlos's food. If Carlos tells the teacher, this would be reporting, because it is harmful for Carlos not to have any lunch. He will be hungry and will have trouble concentrating. Additionally, someone should be checking to see why John stole Carlos's lunch. Is John coming to school hungry?

Older Kids

Tattling: Lena overhears a couple of boys making plans to feign illness the next day, so they can skip school and go to the Red Sox home opener. If Lena tells the teacher, that would be tattling, because the boys are not harming anyone.

Reporting: Jerome overhears a couple of boys making plans to surround a gay fan from the rival team after their high school's homecoming game, with the intention of beating the boy up. If Jerome tells, this would be reporting, because the other fan is in danger.

Victims' Perceptions of the Effectiveness
of Peer Interventions

In chapter 19, we saw some of the results of the Youth Voice Project surveys. Specifically, we learned which strategies employed by the victims made things worse versus better, and which responses from adults in whom the victims confided made things worse versus better. Now we will look at what happened after victimized students confided in their peers. What helped? What hurt? Stan Davis and Charisse Nixon learned that the following responses by peers were likely to make things better for the victim:[6]

- Spent time with me
- Talked to me
- Helped me get away
- Called me
- Gave me advice
- Helped me tell an adult
- Distracted the bullies
- Listened to me
- Told an adult

whereas the following responses by peers were likely to make things worse for the victim:[7]

- Blamed me
- Made fun of me
- Ignored the bullying
- Confronted the bullies
- Asked the bullies to stop

When I spoke with Davis about his research findings, he pointed out that "the peer actions reported as most helpful, such as supportive listening, are also the safest actions for the peers. Calling a student at home to see if he is okay is a low-risk intervention, and it brings comfort to the victim."[8] *One by one by one by one,* as Justin Roberts sings, kids can learn to support each other.

Bystanders who stand silently by and do nothing to help afterward bear some of the responsibility for the bullying, even if they did not initiate the aggression. Likewise, kids who pass along rumors or who forward mean text messages are just as culpable as the person who started the rumor or wrote the initial text. Barbara Coloroso commented, "There are no innocent bystanders," and recommends that bystanders go through the same restorative process as the bullies. She explained to me, "It's the three *R*s: restitution, resolution, and reconciliation. For example, if a girl forwarded a rumor in a text, she must start with restitution—fixing what she did. She should contact the people to whom she sent the text and tell them it wasn't true and ask them not to pass it along. Next step is resolution, which means finding a way to make sure the incident doesn't happen again. The girl needs to ask herself why she forwarded the rumor and learn from the incident. Finally, she must engage in reconciliation, which is a process of healing with the person she harmed. Maybe she can invite the person to have lunch with her or they can spend some time together."[9]

Teaching kids how to shift from being a witness to being an ally takes practice. In the middle of witnessing a bullying episode, many kids may feel uncomfortable about what is happening yet do not want to put themselves in the socially awkward position of saying something. Some kids may consider intervening but decide it is not safe for them personally. How do we harness these good intentions? We allow kids to practice strategies ahead of time, when they are not in the middle of a high-adrenaline real-life situation. Davis likens this to fire drills—by practicing what to do in case of a fire, people are more likely to respond appropriately amidst the terror of an actual fire.[10] We provide kids with a wide range of positive actions—a toolkit of options—from which to choose. This could be as simple as the decision not to forward a vicious text message or as complicated as quickly organizing a group of people to pull a child who is being beaten to safety. Kids who practice running through a mental list of options, evaluating those options, and choosing a strategy that best fits the situation will be empowered as bystanders to do the right thing. Anne Collier reminded me, "The more kids see others doing the right thing, the more they want to do the right thing too."[11]

Most kids want to be connected to their schools, and they want school to be a positive environment. We saw this happen at Evanston Township High School, when the kids decided to shift their focus from the cruelty of the Evanston Rats to the warmth of the Evanston Mice. I like to envision it as a pendulum swinging, moving away from the contagion of bullying and toward the contagion of kindness. "Being mean feels yucky," Annie Rose told me, "but sometimes I do it. Sometimes I call people the S word" ("stupid"—her idea of the worst possible epithet). "But then," she continued, "my whole body is sorry. Yes," she decided, "I like it more when I'm nice. It's better."

Even in Katie's own peer group, we saw a small but fascinating change in terms of bystander behavior. In December 2011, her school held the second annual Proud to Be Me Day, which was inspired by Katie's experience with the Star Wars taunting. Katie wore a Star Wars shirt, and a boy began heckling her about how Star Wars was for boys. But *this year,* another boy who was standing nearby overheard the comment, and he defended Katie. "She can wear a Star Wars shirt if she wants," he told the taunting child. Katie came home and told me about it, and I made a point of thanking the boy who acted as a positive bystander the next time I saw him. He blushed, ducked his head, and smiled. "You're welcome, Katie's mom," he told me, flashing a grin.

There are several significant online movements that encourage older kids and adults to be good bystanders both online and offline. One movement started by Cartoon Network[12] is called "Stop Bullying: Speak Up," and it is geared toward teaching kids to say something as soon as they witness cruelty. The corresponding Facebook page for "Stop Bullying: Speak Up" has nearly one million followers and encourages the following steps for those who want to stop bullying: (1) speak up; (2) take the pledge; (3) take action; and (4) spread the word. Given the amount of time kids spend online, it makes sense to reach them through sites like Facebook. Each time a kid sees that one of his or her friends has chosen to "like" an anti-bullying page, it serves as a public statement encouraging good bystander activity. In many ways, the ability of people to track one another's every move on Facebook is disturbing and Big Brotherish, but there is a silver lining when it spurs peer groups to take a stand against bullying!

When It Isn't Bullying

Sometimes bystanders may see social interactions that look like bullying but in fact are not. Kesha Burch-Sims told me, "I have a high percentage of African American clients, for whom there is a cultural legacy of 'signifying' and 'playing the dozens' and other types of quick-witted laughing and joking." To a group of students unfamiliar with playing the dozens, this game of trading insults may appear aggressive. "But playing the dozens is not like bullying," explained Burch-Sims, "because playing the dozens does not have a power differential. One kid is snapping at another and then the other kid comes right back. By contrast, bullying is a consistent degradation of a person. Bullying is not a rite of passage."[13]

There are other times that social interactions may be mistakenly labeled as bullying. Exclusion, in particular, is a tricky one. On its own, exclusion is not always bullying, no matter how painful it might feel. Michael Thompson shared an example with me. "A woman told me about her sixth-grade daughter who desperately wanted to join a group of cool girls, and they would not let her join. Every day she asked if she could sit with them at lunch, and they always told her no. The mom was convinced that the popular girls were bullying her daughter."

Thompson asked the girl's mom, "'Are they picking on her in the halls? Do they point at her or whisper about her during lunch? Are they going after her?' And the mom said, 'No, but they won't let her join them, and she is so upset.' This is a case where it may be damn painful, but it isn't bullying."

Just because the sixth-grade girl really wants to be with the popular girls doesn't mean they want to be with her. As Thompson said, "It's the same reason why I can't call Julia Roberts to have lunch with me. We can't always be with the superstars. Later in life, if you do that, you are a stalker." Thompson believes that one of the most important lessons in sixth grade is to learn to work with the friends who want you. A harsh lesson, to be sure. I can still close my eyes and instantly remember the days in eighth and ninth grades when I desperately wanted to be included by the "cool girls." The longing for their approval was practically a physical desire. I yearned to feel their girlish arms around my shoulders, pulling me close in a gesture of acceptance, as we made our way through adolescence. But sometimes I was pushed away, and when it happened, the sting of rejection could be breathtakingly painful.

Thompson told me, "School is a laboratory of social learning. Some experiments are with love and inclusion, and others are experiments in meanness and nastiness. Kids are learning how to use social power."[14] If a concerned bystander witnesses the popular group excluding a particular girl, yet there is no additional aggression directed at the girl, the best action the bystander can take is to reach out to the rejected girl and offer her companionship.

When Bystanders Band Together and Become the Attackers

Sometimes children who learn about being good bystanders misinterpret the call to duty. For example, let's say that two girls, Allie and Christina, are in an argument about Allie's boyfriend Jonah. Allie thinks that Christina was flirting with Jonah, and Christina is vehemently denying it. Christina begins to yell at Allie, "If anyone even speaks to Jonah, you get mad, like you own him, and other people can't even talk to him!" Allie's friends rush in, under the guise of being bystanders who want to help out, but the way they respond is to attack Christina, calling her a "slut who was throwing herself at Jonah." Allie's friends begin spreading rumors about Christina and post mean comments on her Facebook page. In this case, Allie and Christina had been experiencing a social conflict, and the other girls turned it into a situation where they began bullying Christina. They may say they were defending Allie, but their actions were aggressive. Being a good bystander does not mean that one person's friends intervene in a social conflict by ganging up on another person. Let us teach our children the proper meaning behind the words "good bystander," rather than giving them a manipulative way to defend cruel actions.

Chapter Twenty-Three

Cybersupporting Instead of Cyberbullying: A Real-Life Happy Ending

In the preceding chapters, we have heard from all manner of experts about how to ease the pain of bullying. But what happens if a student cannot find relief? Imagine the bleakest of bullying situations: A gay child, let's call him Joseph, lives in a rural town and is being bullied at school. He has no friends to lend him support. His school does not have any anti-bullying policies or procedures in place, and his teachers treat him dismissively. He is terrified to tell his parents he is gay, because they hold strong religious beliefs that are not compatible with having a gay son. Joseph is drowning in a sea of isolation and hopelessness, and he thinks that suicide is the only way to obtain relief.

There is one more option, one more way to reach out and seek a kindred spirit. For all of our concerns about cyberbullying, the Internet has demonstrated a far more inspiring phenomenon—a term I call cybersupporting. If cyberbullying is the use of electronic media to degrade, humiliate, torment, and harass a person, then cybersupporting has emerged as the very opposite. It is the use of electronic media to boost, support, inspire, and provide confidence to another person. A person who feels different needs only log in to the Internet to find someone who shares his or her interests.

Just as cyberbullying often occurs alongside other forms of in-person bullying, increasing the pain of its punch, so, too, does cyber-supporting lend itself to in-person interactions, amplifying the aid it provides. A sympathetic person might read a blog post and start writing about it online, garnering additional supporters. Eventually, the online activism can translate into speeches, written publications, and activist work. Directionality is irrelevant. A person who speaks about a cause may decide to supplement his or her work with a web-site or a blog, and the online component becomes a full cybersup-porting movement.

One of the best known cybersupporting campaigns that has translated into activism work is the It Gets Better Project. Created by Dan Savage and Terry Miller in the wake of too many tragic suicides by gay children in the fall of 2010, the It Gets Better Project consists of YouTube videos made by gay and straight people alike, specifi-cally to speak words of reassurance and encouragement to gay teens.

Savage's original goal was to get one hundred users to upload videos to YouTube offering support to gay and lesbian kids in crisis. The project took off like wildfire, and as of August 2011, the site had over twenty-five thousand user-created videos that have been viewed more than forty million times. People from all walks of life—politicians, CEOs, celebrities, ordinary citizens—have recorded mes-sages of support for LGBT kids who are enduring bullying.

The San Francisco Giants were the first major league sports team to join the It Gets Better Project, followed by the Chicago Cubs, the Boston Red Sox, and the Baltimore Orioles. When major league sporting teams speak out against gender stereotyping and antigay bullying, the message has a stronger chance of reaching the ears of those who really need to hear it. It increases the pressure on athletes who have used slurs publicly (such as Kobe Bryant, who was fined one hundred thousand dollars in 2011 for calling referee Bennie Adams a "fucking faggot" on live television in a heated moment).

Popular culture today transcends a single media outlet, and we are seeing evidence that some forward-thinking television shows are leveraging their popularity to spread a wider anti-bullying message. After watching the final episode of the 2011 season of *Glee,* I saw a commercial in which *Glee* actress Lauren Potter, who has Down's syndrome, urged viewers to stop using the "*R*-word" ("retarded"), as part of contemporary lingo. *Glee* actors and actresses have participated in several cybersupporting campaigns: They are promoting www.thinkb4youspeak.com, which urges people to stop using words like "that's so gay" or "that's retarded" as part of everyday conversations, and they have uploaded videos to www.itgetsbetter.org.

Max Adler, who plays the formerly homophobic bully Dave Karofsky on *Glee*, spoke with me about why he decided to make an It Gets Better Project message.[1] After the episode in which Karofsky revealed that he was a tormented closet gay, the It Gets Better Project asked Adler if he would upload a message. Adler embraced the opportunity to cybersupport gay people, commenting, "I figure it comes with the territory of being an actor, an athlete, or a musician. When you are in the spotlight, why not direct those eyeballs to something that needs to change? I took my cues from watching people like George Clooney and Angelina Jolie talk about social change. If I can get on someone's computer screen who may not meet a gay person and tell them gay people are okay, maybe they will listen to me, and it's a start."

We talked about the phenomenon of a television show launching a national conversation about anti-bullying. It was an evolving process that grew organically out of the Internet. Adler enthused, "The blogs, the posts, the communities—people connected over the storyline, and it became something more than a TV show." It has been particularly moving for Adler to see how his portrayal of Karofsky affects gay people. Adler receives letters from around the world, and his voice filled with emotion as he read me one letter that really touched him:

> *Max,*
>
> *Proud to say I am a gay man. I've come to accept that this is me and it's okay. I've been struggling with it since high school. I was picked on about being gay since elementary school. I didn't have friends because the other kids would brand me, and no one would talk to me. I*

finally accepted it. During that struggle I hurt myself,
dropped out of college, stopped pursuing my lifelong
dream, and quit talking to all my friends.

But now that I have finally realized it is the beauty in
me, I will be reenrolling in school next semester to get my
degree in music education and further hope to get my
doctorate. I'm just so glad I can finally see the light in
things. My vast amount of knowledge has showed me that
life is nothing like how I was raised. I was taught to be
racist. I was abused on many occasions by my stepfather. I
was actually told by my stepfather when I was younger
that if I ever told him I was gay, he would kill me. No
exaggerations.

But since I've read so many books and watched shows
like Glee *and characters like yours, I now see what is right*
and how I was raised is not.

"It's letters like that," Adler said, "that really mean a lot to me." In a twist during season three of *Glee*, Adler's character, Dave Karofsky, is on the receiving end of antigay bullying. A so-called friend from his new school discovers that Karofsky is gay, and launches a vicious hate campaign against him. Within days, Karofsky is so overwhelmed by despair that he tries to hang himself. Gay teens feel that the actor really understands their pain. To demonstrate how online cybersupporting can translate into offline actions, consider the fact that Adler now speaks publicly in support of gay rights.

Another public figure who has become famous as a heterosexual cybersupporter of gay rights is British rugby star Ben Cohen. The England Rugby World Cup winner has blogged about the importance of addressing homophobia, and his website frequently features articles about combating antigay bullying, particularly in the world of professional sports. Cohen, who has over 180,000 Facebook followers, uses his popularity to garner additional cybersupport for the cause. He credits his father, Peter Cohen, as being a huge influence in his decision to speak out against bullying. Peter Cohen witnessed a group of men attacking an employee outside a nightclub the family owned in Northampton in 2000, and when he stood up for the employee, the bullying group turned on him too. Peter Cohen was brutally attacked, and he died a month later from his injuries.[2]

Ben Cohen greatly admired his father's desire to stand up for others, and he wanted to find a way to honor that. He began to speak out about bullying and focused his attention on gay rights, telling me, "My gay friends have been incredibly supportive over the years, even when I wasn't performing so well on the pitch, so I felt I wanted to give something back, and this was the most obvious and worthwhile way of doing that." In 2011, he created a foundation called the Ben Cohen Standup Foundation to promote speaking out against bullying and concurrently launched his Acceptance Tour. Cohen's initiatives demonstrate how an effective cybersupporting campaign can lead to positive actions outside of the Internet. Of the tour, Cohen said, "It gave us a chance to meet people and get our message of tolerance out there. We started in the UK in Manchester and London at 'Beer with Ben' nights and then went over to Atlanta, New York, Washington, and Seattle. We worked with gay/gay-friendly rugby clubs in each city. It was great because each club arranged different types of events so there was plenty of variety." Cohen reported that the foundation is now well under way with events and partnerships popping up all over the place on both sides of the Atlantic. "We are planning visits to schools and colleges, making anti-bullying videos with the students, holding bullying-awareness summits in several cities."

Cohen recognizes the power of the Internet as a way to educate people and change their attitudes, calling it "a huge step forward" and admits that even he was not aware of the suffering experienced by gay people until some of his fans began writing to him about their lives. "There are millions of people out there who are not aware of the issues that some people go through on a daily basis—from feelings of self-doubt to being bullied into harming themselves.

"At the end of the day, it's not about being gay, lesbian, black, white, fat, thin—it's about being a human being and having the right to be true to who you really are. My message is about equality for all and the right to be happy and to live a fulfilled life. That's what I want for myself and my family and everyone else."[3]

With Cohen's words in mind, let us return to the scenario in the beginning of the chapter, the story of young Joseph who is being bullied at school and cannot bear to face another day. One night, Joseph logs on to his computer after everyone is asleep, and he starts searching for information about being gay, feeling suicidal, and needing help. He comes across a link for the It Gets Better Project and clicks on it. He is astonished to see thousands of videos urging him to hang in there, telling him that his life is worth living, that he is a good and valuable person. While watching one of the videos, he learns about a suicide-prevention organization called the Trevor Project.

Fingers trembling, Joseph clicks on the link: www.thetrevorproject .org. He learns that he can call "the Trevor Lifeline," a nationwide, around-the-clock crisis and suicide prevention lifeline for LGBTQ youth. A real person will talk to him and hold all he says in confidence. For the first time in months, Joseph has a new feeling, one that he is almost afraid to acknowledge. The dark cloud of winter has settled so deeply around Joseph that he can barely see the coming spring. Yet here is evidence of pale green shoots breaking through the brittle earth. Hope, as tender and beautiful as the first signs of life, began to stir in Joseph's heavy heart. He sits in front of his computer, tears streaming down his face, as he realizes that he is not alone in the world after all. Joseph picks up the phone and starts to dial, sobbing with relief and pain, barely able to speak when the other line picks up. "Please help me," he finally chokes out. Even though his school, his family, and his community have all failed him, Joseph has access to cybersupporting services. It starts with a website. It ends with a life saved.

Most of the people who participate in cybersupporting campaigns are older teens and adults, but that is starting to change. Children enjoy many positive social experiences through the Internet and are learning that they can make a difference in the world, especially for their own peer group. Anne Collier told me, "There is a new sociology of childhood emerging that looks at kids as whole beings in their own right with different contexts. They have their own communities and their own interests based on where they are in their lives."[4]

We see kids reaching out and supporting each other every day. I saw it with my own little girl. In a time when parents are all fired up about the Internet tearing their kids down, I experienced quite the reverse: my child was lifted up and bolstered by online support. Katie received email messages from many young children who wrote to her through their parents' accounts as a way of connecting. When people participate in a cybersupporting campaign, they feel better about themselves, and the original intended recipient of the campaign becomes just one of many people who benefit from the outpouring of love and positivity. One of my favorite emails we received was from a mother who wrote how her child was also bolstered by the support directed at Katie:

> I would like to tell you about my daughter, Maya. She is eight years old. She loves her friends and school. She adores her little brother. She loves horses, '80s heavy rock music, Jack Skellington, Transformers, books, and she is starting to like Star Wars.
>
> Because she is sensitive and likes a lot of "boys' toys," she gets teased a lot. Especially by the boys in her class. While she doesn't have a hard time standing up for others, she usually doesn't say anything back. But she gets very upset. Even though we have talked about it a few times, she hasn't felt confident enough to do anything or say anything. We do buy a lot of her favorite stuff in the boys' section, and I know this makes her feel like those boys may be right.
>
> But today was a different day. Today, my son Lance (four), Maya, and I wore our Star Wars clothing on behalf of you. And guess what happened to Maya? Yes. The boys in her second-grade classroom laughed at her and told her that Star Wars was for boys only. Her response to them was, "I don't care." And they stopped. She said that she didn't really care what they said.
>
> Why the change, you may ask? What happened? Simple. Your story. As soon as I read Jen's post at Epbot

last month, I went and read everything I could about Katie and her story, and when Maya got home, I shared it with her. She was upset about the boys at first, but then she was jumping in excitement when I read to her some of the responses that you got. "AMAZING," she said. "That's so exciting, Mom." Since then, she has been waiting for today. To wear her Star Wars T-shirt and hoodie to show her support for Katie.

Your story has helped my Maya find a way to stand up for herself. And be proud of who she is!

I like to imagine young Maya, marching off to school in her Star Wars gear—no longer feeling trepidation about being taunted—but instead feeling confidence in her convictions. Maya has never met Katie, but they are forever connected through cyberspace, partners in playtime. They both have the force of millions behind them, rooting for the triumph of kindness over cruelty and individuality over conformity. Kids are the most important demographic of this force, and they have united to help each other with actions great and small.

All we have to do is look around us, and we will see kids taking a stand against cruelty. Kids who find one another through online groups such as *Wipeout Homophobia* on Facebook, where bullied teens and adults connect across continents to share stories of sadness and hope. Kids who cheer the launch of anti-bullying organizations such as Lady Gaga's Born This Way Foundation, combining their love of community with their love of individuality. Kids who responded with warmth and support to teenage bullying victim Jonah Mowry when he uploaded details of his plight in a heartbreaking YouTube video. Kids who write blogs for groups like SPARK, taking on companies like Lego and Disney in their efforts to break down stereotypes. Kids who know that by changing just one life for the better, they have changed the world. Kids who make amazing things happen.

Conclusion

This book was an exploration of how we can prevent taunting and bullying. How do we curtail these harmful behaviors? By creating a culture of acceptance from the earliest age. By teaching kids respect and empathy. If children learn to view one another with empathy, their differences no longer become fodder for taunting and bullying. When a bully learns empathy, his potential victim becomes a person instead of an "it." This is particularly challenging in cyberspace, where the fact that a bully is not face-to-face with her victim intensifies the viciousness of the attacks. Empathy all but disappears in cyberspace, not just for children but also for adults. Who among us hasn't witnessed abusive personal attacks in the "comments" section of many online articles, be they about sports, politics, entertainment, or parenting? Adults who do not know each other engage in bullying online, and then they wonder why the next generation thinks it is acceptable to tear one another apart on Facebook.

We can teach empathy by teaching our children to be educated consumers of media and video games and by staying connected with them as they absorb cultural messages. If your son is watching a violent show, turn it into a teachable moment. Talk about it so that he does not think that violent behavior is normative and acceptable. If your daughter is watching a show where other kids tease a girl who is geeky, turn it into a teachable moment. Recently, we watched *The Princess Diaries* starring Anne Hathaway with our daughters. Halfway through the movie, there was the inevitable makeover scene where Anne Hathaway was changed from an ugly duckling into a beautiful princess.

I grew increasingly uncomfortable as I watched the hairdresser transform Hathaway's frizzy hair into a sleek, straight fountain of hair, coupled with the removal of her thick glasses in exchange for contacts. What message was this sending to my older daughters, one who wears glasses and the other who has curly hair? Did they think they would only be pretty if we tamed their hair and ditched their glasses? I toyed with turning the movie off, but instead my husband and I paused it to have a "teachable moment." We talked about the issues for a few minutes and then resumed playing the movie.

A deeply caring environment at home goes beyond monitoring television shows and watching them with your child to find teachable moments. It also means teaching our children how to independently deconstruct television shows or music where people treat each other like worthless objects. Celebrities, the media, and corporations have tremendous influence over our kids. Instead of merely dismissing many of them as "bad examples," we can take the opportunity, when appropriate, to partner with them and promote a culture of acceptance. Enlist the help of our cultural icons in ending the hypersexualization of girls and the übermasculinization of young boys. Very few things in this world are truly black and white, and it is our job as the adults to demonstrate flexibility and forgiveness.

At the same time as we teach empathy to the bullies, we need to stop sending the victims the message that their own behavior or traits are bringing on the attacks. This requires a fundamental change in the way adults view bullying. A child is not bullied because he is gay or autistic or overweight. A child is bullied because a bully has decided that the target is unacceptably different and less worthy of respect. We must teach the targets how to cognitively reframe the bullying so that they do not think the abuse is their fault or something they deserve.

Groundbreaking new research by Stan Davis and Charisse Nixon has shown that when a victim learns to think about the bullying in new ways—"This bullying is not happening because I am overweight. It is happening because the bully is choosing to act in a mean and hateful way, and that is his fault, not mine"—then the effects of the mistreatment are greatly diminished. Davis and Nixon's research also shows that many bullied kids find relief when they tell an adult or a peer, but many are reluctant to do so. Our job as educators and parents and friends is to teach victims how to access help from adults and peers. Tell someone. Call someone. Write to someone. Text someone. Help will come. Someone will be there, and you will not have to bear this burden alone.

We need to empower the bystanders and witnesses to speak up or go get help, and we need to teach them that silence or laughing or joining in makes them accountable too. If even a single witness reaches out to a victim, the tide can change. Others will join in, and the balance of power shifts. The situation diffuses, and the bullying will cease.

How do we teach these skills? By creating caring environments in all of the different worlds our children inhabit: the home, the school, the neighborhood, the Internet, the playing fields, and all the places in between. Increasing the adult supervision of high-risk bullying areas is part of the picture. But our budget-strapped schools will be the first to admit that it is impossible to always have a connected, respected teacher in every corner, and time-pressured parents will protest that they cannot be everywhere. This is why our kids need better social skills. We don't want to create a "helicopter parent" approach to bullying prevention. Yes, adult monitoring and intervention are critical, but so is the ability of children to resolve conflict on their own. If we swoop in and rescue our kids every time someone picks on them, we inadvertently teach them that they cannot take care of themselves.

There is a dance to social interactions, an ever-shifting choreography that requires balance and skill and practice. Let us teach our children how to speak up for themselves and carry themselves with confidence. Let us teach our children how to break the code of silence and call each other out on cruelty. Let us teach them strategies to cope with teasing, taunting, physical abuse, and cyberbullying. Even after the bullying has occurred, there are strategies for reconciliation that can be employed if the circumstances are appropriate. Restorative justice, for example, can be used to repair the harm that a bully has inflicted on his victim, and it is a much more effective option than simply suspending a child who has bullied a peer.

Bullying is a multifaceted problem, and thus it requires a many-pronged solution. It is not enough to monitor our children's media use, teach empathy to the bullies, empower and support the victims, and provide children with social skills and conflict-resolution skills. We have to step back and analyze our own culpability in creating a culture that has fostered attitudes of entitlement and condescension toward those who are different. It is uncomfortable to explore our own secret inconsistencies and stereotypes. One mother told me she initially recoiled at the sight of her preschool son in a dress, before she ultimately decided that he should be allowed to play dress up if that is what makes him happy. Many people disagree with her, and issues of gender nonconformity are particularly controversial. Gender-based bullying is rampant, and it stems from a myriad of places. Even within gender-based bullying, not all victims receive equal defending. The world was quick to defend Katie's right to be a Star Wars–loving girl, but a princess-loving boy is unlikely to receive such universal support. Some people say Star Wars is for everyone and princesses are just for girls. But if you walk into a toy store, Star Wars toys are clearly displayed in the "boys' section" and princesses are relegated to the pink "girls' section". Gender-based toy marketing contributes to gender-based stereotypes and creates situations ripe for bullying.

None of us is without blame. None of us is without strengths. If we keep these two truths in mind, we are well positioned to take on the problem of bullying with grace and maturity. Every person has a voice that deserves to be heard, even the marginalized and the mute. We just need to listen, and change will occur.

Acknowledgments

This book would not have happened without the help, support, and encouragement of many people. Thank you to my agent, Mollie Glick, for attentively escorting me through the process of taking an initial idea and turning it into a book. Thank you to my editor, Roger Freet, for the excellent guidance, feedback, and support as I researched and wrote *Bullied*.

To Dorothy Espelage, for writing the foreword to *Bullied*, for helping me out so much with the research, and for all the incredible work you do to help victims of bullying.

To the many experts, advocates, authors, and professionals who graciously spent time educating me and talking with me, including but not limited to Lyn Mikel Brown, Rosalind Wiseman, Rachel Simmons, Anne Collier, Peggy Orenstein, Jo Paoletti, Barbara Coloroso, Mike Kelly, Judy Freedman, Laura Hanish, Ron Astor, Trudy Ludwig, John Gottman, Christina Sung Aie Choi, Annie Fox, Stan Davis, Sheri Bauman, Michael Thompson, Justin Patchin, Jean Kilbourne, Brenda Morrison, Madeline di Nonno, William Porter, Susan Limber, Michael Robey, Kate Ellison, Arica Barton, Susan Trieschmann, Kesha Burch-Sims, Michele Borba, Josh Golan, Lauren Parsekian, Molly Stroud, Maria Wynne, Eric Witherspoon, Melissa Wardy, David Shriberg, Wes Shockley, Jodee Blanco, Cheryl Kilodavis, Sarah Buttenwieser, Zachary Hermann, Will Crawford, Keith Robinson, Jerry Pope, Sarah Hoffman, Joslyn Gray, Nicole Knepper, Bedford Hope, Al Yellon, and Jim Margalus.

A huge round of appreciative applause goes to the actors, actresses, athletes, and musicians who were so willing to let me interview them, including Felicia Day, Ben Cohen, Peter Mayhew, Victoria Stilwell, Max Adler, Catherine Taber, James Arnold Taylor,

Ashley Eckstein, Tom Kane, Chase Masterson, and Justin Roberts.

To the Star Wars fans, the science fiction fans, and the Geek community, none of this would have happened if you had not shared Katie's story. An extra special thank-you to Jen Yates and the *Epbot* readers, to Bonnie Burton and Lucasfilm, to GeekGirlCon and Jennifer Stuller, and to J. D. Adams at Duckon.

To Jimmy Greenfield, for helping me navigate the media maelstrom when Katie's story went viral, and to the ChicagoNow bloggers, for being such great colleagues.

To the readers of my blog, and especially to the wonderful community of *Portrait of an Adoption* followers on Facebook, thank you for giving me a forum in which to develop this project and for cheering me (and my family) on throughout the process.

Thank you to the astonishingly brave kids and adults who told me about their painful histories with bullying. Your real names are in my heart, and I think of you with more respect and gratitude than you can ever imagine.

To my incredible parents, Barbara and Allan Goldman, and to Andrew's amazing parents, Ralph and Nancy Segall, thank-you for your endless love, assistance, and support. Thank you to my extended family and friends, especially my grandma, Ruth Gulinson, for all of your caring and enthusiasm.

Thank you to my sisters, Lisa, Jenny, and Lindsey, and my sisters-in-law, Kim and Julie, for being my closest network, along with my very dear friends and extended family members. An extra thank-you to the Goodman family for all your love, to Jen Goldstein and Meagan Novara for all the Wednesday afternoons together, and also to Jen for so willingly driving Annie Rose all over town while I was writing, to Sylvia Gates for watching baby Cleo every Friday, and to Jen Preschern for being my unofficial research assistant.

Muchas gracias por amar a Toña y Griselda mis chicas mientras yo estaba muy ocupada trabajando. Son sus bebés, demasiado!

Thank you to Katie, Annie Rose, and Cleo for being my inspiration and joy and laughter.

And most of all, thank you to my husband, my partner, my match, Andrew. I love you every day in every way.

Bibliography

ABC Local News. KTRK-TV/DT. September 29, 2010. "Parents: Bullies Drove 13-Year-Old to Suicide." abclocal.go.com/ktrk/story?section=news/local &id=7695982.

ABC News. December 6, 2011. "Lady Gaga Takes Anti-Bullying to White House." abcnews.go.com/WNT/video/lady-gaga-takes-anti-bullying-white-house-15100813.

Alexander, B. "The Bullying of Seth Walsh: Requiem for a Small-Town Boy." Time U.S. October 2, 2010. www.time.com/time/nation/article/0,8599 ,2023083,00.html.

Alphonse, L. M. "Epic T-Shirt Fail: 'I'm Too Pretty to Do My Homework, So My Brother Has to Do It for Me.'" Shine from Yahoo! August 31, 2011. shine.yahoo.com/parenting/epic-t-shirt-fail-quot-im-too-pretty-to-do-my-homework-so-my-brother-has-to-do-it-for-me-quot-2537106.html.

American Psychological Association. 2007. *Sexualization of Girls.* www.apa .org/pi/women/programs/girls/report.aspx.

Aronson, E., N. Blaney, C. Stephin, J. Sikes, and M. Snapp. *The Jigsaw Classroom.* Beverly Hills, CA: Sage, 1978.

Baldry, A. C., D. P. Farrington, and M. M. Ttofi. "Effectiveness of Programmes to Reduce School Bullying: A Systematic Review." Swedish National Council for Crime Prevention. Brottsforebyggande radet–Bra, 2008.

Ball, B., and B. Rosenbluth. "Expect Respect—Program Overview: A School-Based Program for Preventing Teen Dating Violence and Promoting Safe and Healthy Relationships." Austin,TX: SafePlace, 2008. www.safeplace .org/document.doc?id=27.

Bauman, S. *Cyberbullying: What Counselors Need to Know.* Alexandria, VA: American Counseling Association, 2011.

Beland, K. "Second Step: A Violence Prevention Curriculum." Seattle: Committee for Children, 1992.

Blanco, J. *Please Stop Laughing at Me . . . : One Woman's Inspirational Story.* Avon, MA: Adams Media, 2003.

Borba, M. *Nobody Likes Me, Everybody Hates Me: The Top 25 Friendship Problems and How to Solve Them.* San Francisco: Jossey-Bass, 2005.

Boyle, C. "'Bullied' Staten Island Teen Kills Self." *NY Daily News*. January 3, 2012. www.nydailynews.com/new-york/staten-island-teen-kills-jumping-front-bus-family-cites-bullies-article-1.1000243.

Branch, J. "Two Straight Athletes Combat Homophobia." *New York Times*. May 13, 2011. www.nytimes.com/2011/05/14/sports/two-straight-athletes-combat-homophobia.html?pagewanted=all.

Brooks, K. "Bullied Greensburg Student Takes His Own Life." WXIN-TV. Fox 59. September 13, 2010. www.fox59.com/news/wxin-greensburg-student-suicide-091310,0,1101685.story.

Brown, L. M., S. Lamb, and M. Tappan. *Packaging Boyhood: Saving Our Sons from Superheroes, Slackers, and Other Media Stereotypes*. New York: St. Martin's, 2006.

Canning, A., M. Pflum, and K. Hagan. "Bikini Waxing for Tweens! Have Spas Gone Too Far?"ABC Good Morning America. May 19, 2008. abcnews.go .com/GMA/BeautySecrets/story?id=4881675&page=1.

CBS News. March 29, 2010. "Cyberbullying Continued After Teen's Death." www.cbsnews.com/stories/2010/03/29/earlyshow/main6343077.shtml.

CBS News. April 7, 2009. "Parents Sue School After Son's Suicide." www .cbsnews.com/stories/2009/04/07/earlyshow/main4925059.shtml?tag=curre ntVideoInfo;videoMetaInfo.

Collier, A., and L. Magid. "A Parents' Guide to Facebook." *Connectsafely.org*. February 2012. www.connectsafely.org/pdfs/fbparents.pdf.

Coloroso, B. *The Bully, the Bullied, and the Bystander: From Preschool to High School—How Parents and Teachers Can Help Break the Cycle of Violence*. New York: HarperCollins, 2008.

———. *Kids Are Worth It! Giving Your Child the Gift of Inner Discipline*. New York: HarperCollins, 2002.

Committee for Children. "Steps to Respect: A Bullying Prevention Program." Seattle: Committee for Children, 2001.

Connolly, J., D. Pepler, W. Craig, and A. Taradash. "Dating Experiences of Bullies in Early Adolescence." *Child Maltreatment* 5 (2000): 299–310.

Curry, C. "Staten Island Teen Bullied Before Taking Her Life." ABC News. January 12, 2012. abcnews.go.com/US/staten-island-teen-bullied-suicide-family/story?id=15287910#.TwnBq9WOeDO.

Davis, S., and C. Nixon. "Youth Voice Research Project: Victimization and Strategies." 2010. www.youthvoiceproject.com/YVPMarch2010.pdf.

de Becker, G. *Protecting the Gift: Keeping Children and Teenagers Safe (and Parents Sane)*. New York: Dell/Random House, 1999.

Doll, B., and S. Swearer. "Cognitive-Behavioral Interventions for Participants in Bullying and Coercion." In *Cognitive Behavioral Interventions in Educational Settings: A Handbook for Practice*. Edited by R. Mennuti, A.

Freeman, and R. Christner. New York: Brunner-Routledge, 2006. 183–201.

Eisenberger, N. I., and M. D. Lieberman. "Why Rejection Hurts: A Common Neural Alarm System for Physical and Social Pain." *Trends in Cognitive Sciences* 8 (2004): 294–300.

Eliot, L. *Pink Brain, Blue Brain: How Small Differences Grow into Troublesome Gaps—And What We Can Do About It.* New York: Houghton Mifflin Harcourt, 2009.

Espelage, D. L., and M. K. Holt. "Bullying and Victimization During Early Adolescence: Peer Influences and Psychosocial Correlates." *Journal of Emotional Abuse* 2 (2011): 123–42.

Espelage, D. L., and S. M. Swearer, eds. *Bullying in North American Schools.* 2nd ed. New York: Routledge, 2011.

Espelage, D. L., K. C. Basile, and M. E. Hamburger. "Bullying Perpetration and Subsequent Sexual Violence Perpetration Among Middle School Students: Shared and Unique Risk Factors." *Journal of Adolescent Health* 50, no. 1 (2012): 60–65.

Espelage, D. L., M. K. Holt, and R. R. Henkel. "Examination of Peer-Group Contextual Effects on Aggression During Early Adolescence." *Child Development* 74 (2003): 205–20.

Faris, R., and D. Felmlee. "Network Centrality, Gender Segregation, and Aggression." *Journal of the American Sociological Association* 76 (2011): 1.

Franks, L. "Life and Death at Suicide High." Daily Beast. May 30, 2010. www .thedailybeast.com/articles/2010/03/31/life-and-death-at-suicide-high.html.

Freedman, J. *Easing the Teasing: Helping Your Child Cope with Name-Calling, Ridicule, and Verbal Bullying.* New York: McGraw-Hill, 2002.

Frey, K. S., M. K. Hirschstein, J. L. Snell, L. V. Edstrom, E. P. MacKenzie, and C. J. Broderick. "Reducing Playground Bullying and Supporting Beliefs: An Experimental Trial of the Steps to Respect Program." *Developmental Psychology* 41, no. 3 (2005): 479–91.

Gabarino, J., and E. deLara. *And Words Can Hurt Forever: How to Protect Adolescents from Bullying, Harassment, and Emotional Violence.* New York: Free Press, 2002.

Garrity, C., K. Jens, W. Porter, N. Sager, and C. Short-Camilli. *Bully-Proofing Your School: Administrators' Guide to Staff Development in Elementary Schools.* 3rd ed. Longmont, CO: Sopris West, 1994.

Gladstone, G., G. Parker, and G. Mahli. "Do Bullied Children Become Anxious and Depressed Adults? A Cross-Sectional Investigation of the Correlates of Bullying and Anxious Depression." *Journal of Nervous and Mental Disease* 194 (2006): 201–8.

Goldman, C. "Dear Lego, I Have a Girl." ChicagoNow.com. December 22, 2011. www.chicagonow.com/portrait-of-an-adoption/2011/12/dear-lego-i-have-a-girl/.

Goldman, C. "Pink Is Not the Enemy." Minnesota Women's Press. February 10, 2012. www.womenspress.com/main.asp?SectionID=124&SubSectionID=684&ArticleID=3988.

Goleman, D. Social Intelligence: The New Science of Human Relationships. New York: Bantam, 2006.

Gottlieb, L. "How to Land Your Kid in Therapy." Atlantic. 2011. www.theatlantic.com/magazine/archive/2011/07/how-to-land-your-kid-in-therapy/8555/.

Gottman, J. Raising an Emotionally Intelligent Child: The Heart of Parenting. New York: Simon and Schuster, 1997.

Graham, S., and J. Juvonen. "Self-Blame and Peer Victimization in Middle School: An Attributional Analysis." Developmental Psychology 34 (1998): 587–99.

Greenspan, S. Playground Politics: Understanding the Emotional Life of Your School-Age Child. Reading, MA: Addison-Wesley, 1993.

Gruber, J. E., and S. Fineran. "The Impact of Bullying and Sexual Harassment on Middle and High School Girls." Violence Against Women 13 (2007): 627–43.

Hamburger, M. E., K. C. Basile, and A. M. Vivolo. Measuring Bullying Victimization, Perpetration, and Bystander Experiences: A Compendium of Assessment Tools. Atlanta, GA: Centers for Disease Control and Prevention, National Center for Injury Prevention and Control, 2011. www.cdc.gov/violenceprevention/pub/measuring_bullying.html.

Hamilton, R. "I Was a Bully." Words by Ross. November 18, 2010. wordsmiff.blogspot.com/2010/11/i-was-bully.html.

Hanish, L. D., A. Hill, S. Gosney, R. A. Fabes, and C. L. Martin. "Girls, Boys, and Bullying in Preschool." In Espelage and Swearer, eds. Bullying in North American Schools.

Hawkins, D. L., D. J. Pepler, and W. M. Craig. "Naturalistic Observations of Peer Interventions in Bullying." Social Development 10 (2001): 512–27.

Haynie, D., T. Nansel, P. Eitel, A. Crump, K. Saylor, K. Yu, et al. "Bullies, Victims, and Bully/Victims: Distinct Groups of At-Risk Youth." Journal of Early Adolescence 21 (2001): 29–49.

Hinduja, S., and J. W. Patchin. Bullying Beyond the Schoolyard: Preventing and Responding to Cyberbullying. Thousand Oaks, CA: Sage/Corwin, 2009.

Hoffman, J. "A Girl's Nude Photo, and Altered Lives." New York Times. March 26, 2011. www.nytimes.com/2011/03/27/us/27sexting.html?_r=2.

Horne, A. M., C. D. Bell, K. A. Raczynski, and J. L. Whitford. "Bully Busters: A Resource for School and Parents to Prevent and Respond to Bullying." In Espelage and Swearer, eds. Bullying in North American Schools.

Hu, W. "Bullying Law Puts New Jersey Schools on Spot." New York Times.

August 30, 2011. www.nytimes.com/2011/08/31/nyregion/bullying-law-puts-new-jersey-schools-on-spot.html?emc=eta1.

____. "Legal Debate Swirls Over Charges in a Student's Suicide." *New York Times*. October 1, 2010. www.nytimes.com/2010/10/02/nyregion/02suicide.html.

Hunter, G. H. "Students' Perceptions of Effectiveness of a Universal Bullying Intervention" (unpublished manuscript, 2007). Athens: Univ. of Georgia.

Jackson, L. A., J. E. Hunter, and C. N. Hodge. "Physical Attractiveness and Intellectual Competence: A Meta-Analytic Review." *Social Psychology Quarterly* 58, no. 2 (1995): 108–22.

James, S. D. "Gay Buffalo Teen Commits Suicide on Eve of National Bullying Summit." ABC News. September 21, 2011. abcnews.go.com/Health/gay-buffalo-teen-commits-suicide-eve-national-bullying/story?id=14571861#.TvNVQ9WOeD1.

____. "Gay Teen Jonah Mowry Says Bullying Made Him Stronger." ABC News. December 5, 2011. abcnews.go.com/blogs/health/2011/12/05/gay-teen-jonah-mowry-says-bullying-made-him-stronger/.

____. "When Words Can Kill: 'That's So Gay.'" ABC News. 2009. abcnews.go.com/Health/MindMoodNews/story?id=7328091&page=1.

Kelly, M., J. C. Raines, S. Stone, and A. Frey. *School Social Work: An Evidence-Informed Framework for Practice*. Oxford, UK: Oxford Univ. Press, 2010.

Kerr, N. L., and J. M. Levine. "The Detection of Social Exclusion: Evolution and Beyond." *Group Dynamics: Theory, Research and Practice* 12 (2008): 39–52.

Kindlon, D., and M. Thompson. *Raising Cain: Protecting the Emotional Life of Boys*. New York: Ballantine, 1999.

Knack, J., H. L. Gomez, and L. A. Jensen-Campbell. "Bullying and Its Long-Term Health Implications." In *Social Pain: Neuropsychological and Health Implications of Loss and Exclusion*. Edited by L. A. Jensen-Campbell and G. MacDonald. Washington, DC: American Psychological Association, 2011. 215–36.

Konigsberg, R. D. "Lego Friends for Girls: Have They Stooped to Stereotype?" Time. January 2, 2012. ideas.time.com/2012/01/02/lego-friends-for-girls-have-they-stooped-to-stereotype/.

Kowalski, R. M., S. P. Limber, and P. W. Agatston. *Cyber Bullying: Bullying in the Digital Age*. Malden, MA: Blackwell, 2008.

Kumpulainen, K., E. Rasanen, and K. Puura. "Psychiatric Disorders and the Use of Mental Health Services Among Children Involved in Bullying." *Aggressive Behavior* 27 (2001): 102–10.

Lamb, S., and L. M. Brown. *Packaging Girlhood: Rescuing Our Daughters from Marketers' Schemes*. New York: St. Martin's Press, 2009. 271.

Levin, D. E., and J. Kilbourne. *So Sexy So Soon: The New Sexualized Childhood and What Parents Can Do to Protect Their Kids.* New York: Ballantine, 2008.

Lieberman, M., and N. Eisenberger. "Pains and Pleasures of Social Life." *Science* 323 (2009): 890–91.

Limber, S. P. "Implementation of the Olweus Bullying Prevention Program in American Schools: Lessons Learned from the Field." In Espelage and Swearer, eds. *Bullying in North American Schools.*

———. "Research on the Olweus Bullying Prevention Program." In *Olweus Bullying Prevention Program.* 2009. www.clemson.edu/olweus/Research_OBPP.pdf.

Limber, S. P., R. M. Kowalski, and P. W. Agatston. *Cyberbullying: A Preventive Curriculum for Grades 6–12.* Center City, MN: Hazelden, 2009.

Low, S. M., B. H. Smith, E. C. Brown, K. Fernandez, K. Hanson, and K. P. Haggerty. "Design and Analysis of Randomized Controlled Trial of Steps to Respect." In Espelage and Swearer, eds. *Bullying in North American Schools.*

Ludwig, T. *Confessions of a Former Bully.* New York: Tricycle/Random House, 2010.

Maag, C. "A Hoax Turned Fatal Draws Anger but No Charges." *New York Times.* November 28, 2007. www.nytimes.com/2007/11/28/us/28hoax.html?_r=1&oref=slogin.

Madigan, L. "Cyberbullying: A Student Perspective." 2010. www.illinois attorneygeneral.gov/children/cyberbullying_focus_report0610.pdf.

Marr, N., and T. Field. *Bullycide: Death at Playtime.* Oxford, UK: Wessex, 2000.

Masten, C. L., N. I. Eisenberger, L. A. Borofsky, J. H. Pfeifer, K. McNealy, J. C. Mazziotta, and M. Dapretto. "Neural Correlates of Social Exclusion During Adolescence: Understanding the Distress of Peer Rejection." *Scan* 4 (2009): 143–57.

Mayhew, P., and A. Mayhew. *My Favorite Giant.* San Diego: Wandering Sage, 2011.

McGee, N., and T. Moss. "Girl Was 'Teased and Taunted,' Family Says." *News-Gazette.* November 14, 2011. www.news-gazette.com/news/courts-police-and-fire/2011-11-14/girl-was-teased-and-taunted-family-says.html.

Monnot, C. "The Female Pop Singer and the 'Apprentice' Girl." *Journal of Children and Media* 4, no. 3 (2010): 283–97.

Moss, H. "Skechers' Shape-Ups for Girls Called Out by Internet." *Huffington Post.* July 10, 2011. www.huffingtonpost.com/2011/05/10/skechers-shape-ups-for-girls_n_859781.html.

Nigam, H., and A. Collier. "Youth Safety on a Living Internet." *National Telecommunications and Information Administration*. 2010. www.ntia .doc.gov/reports/2010/OSTWG_Final_Report_060410.pdf.

O'Connell, P., D. Pepler, and W. Craig. "Peer Involvement in Bullying: Insights and Challenges for Intervention." *Journal of Adolescence* 22, no. 4 (1999): 437–52.

Olweus, D. *Bullying at School: What We Know and What We Can Do*. Oxford, UK: Blackwell, 1993.

Orenstein, P. *Cinderella Ate My Daughter: Dispatches from the Front Lines of the New Girlie-Girl Culture*. New York: HarperCollins, 2011.

____. *Schoolgirls: Young Women, Self-Esteem, and the Confidence Gap*. New York: Doubleday, 1994.

____. "Should the World of Toys Be Gender-Free?" *New York Times*. December 29, 2011. www.nytimes.com/2011/12/30/opinion/does-stripping-gender-from-toys-really-make-sense.html?_r=1&scp=2&sq=peggy%20 orenstein&st=cse.

Paoletti, J. "The Children's Department." In *Men and Women: Dressing the Part*. Edited by C. B. Kidwell and V. Steele. Washington, DC: Smithsonian Institution Press, 1989. 22.

____. *Pink and Blue: Telling the Boys from the Girls in America*. Bloomington: Indiana Univ. Press, 2012.

Park, N. "Child Pageants Bad for Mental Health." *Sydney Morning Herald*. May 25, 2011. news.smh.com.au/breaking-news-national/child-pageants-bad-for-mental-health-20110525-1f430.html.

Patchin, J. W., and S. Hinduja, eds. *Cyberbullying Prevention and Response: Expert Perspectives*. New York: Routledge, 2012.

Perkus, A., and E. Van Sciver. "NY Suicide Prompts Cyberbullying Awareness." *Wayland Student Press Network*. March 31, 2010. waylandstudentpress .com/2010/03/31/ny-suicide-prompts-cyber-bullying-awareness/.

Perry, D. G., J. C. Williard, and L. Perry. "Peers' Perceptions of Consequences That Victimized Children Provide Aggressors." *Child Development* 61 (1990): 1289–1309.

Pipher, M. *Reviving Ophelia: Saving the Selves of Adolescent Girls*. New York: Ballantine, 1995.

Pollack, W. *Real Boys: Rescuing Our Sons from the Myths of Boyhood*. New York: Random House, 1998.

Price, D. D. "Psychological and Neural Mechanisms of the Affective Dimension of Pain." *Science* 288 (2000): 1769–72.

Rao, V. "Too Young? Preteen Girls Get Leg, Bikini Waxes." Today Style. August 13, 2008. today.msnbc.msn.com/id/26182276/ns/today-style/t/too-young-preteen-girls-get-leg-bikini-waxes/.

Richards, B. S. "Lego's Listening, but They're Not Quite Hearing Us." Spark Summit. December 21, 2011. www.sparksummit.com/2011/12/21/3675/.

Rigby, K. *Children and Bullying: How Parents and Educators Can Reduce Bullying at School.* Boston: Blackwell/Wiley, 2008.

———. "Peer Victimization at School and the Health of Secondary School Students." *British Journal of Educational Psychology* 69 (1999): 95–104.

Rose, C. A., D. L. Espelage, S. R. Aragon, and J. Elliott. *Bullying and Victimization Among Students in Special Education and General Education Curricula* (unpublished manuscript, 2010).

Roth, D. A., M. E. Coles, and R. G. Heimberg. "The Relationship Between Memories for Childhood Teasing and Anxiety and Depression in Adulthood." *Journal of Anxiety Disorders* 16 (2002): 149–64.

Savage, D., and T. Miller. *It Gets Better: Coming Out, Overcoming Bullying, and Creating a Life Worth Living.* New York: Penguin, 2011.

Shariff, S. *Cyber-Bullying: Issues and Solutions for the School, the Classroom and the Home.* New York: Routledge, 2008.

Shipman, T. "High Street Shops to Ban Padded Bras and 'Sexually Suggestive' Clothing for Young Girls." Daily Mail. June 4, 2011. www.dailymail.co.uk/news/article-1394123/High-street-shops-ban-clothes-sexualise-little-girls.html.

Simmons, R. *Odd Girl Out.* New York: Harcourt, 2003. 3.

Sjostrom, L., and N. Stein. *Bullyproof: A Teacher's Guide on Teasing and Bullying for Use with Fourth and Fifth Grade Students.* Wellesley, MA: Wellesley College, 1996.

Smith, S. L., and M. Choueiti. "Gender Disparity on Screen and Behind the Camera in Family Films." The Executive Report. Los Angeles: Geena Davis Institute on Gender in Media, 2010. www.thegeenadavisinstitute.org/downloads/FullStudy_GenderDisparityFamilyFilms.pdf.

Smith, S. L., and C. A. Cook. "Gender Stereotypes: An Analysis of Popular Films and TV." Los Angeles: Geena Davis Institute on Gender in Media, 2008. www.thegeenadavisinstitute.org/downloads/GDIGM_Gender_Stereotypes.pdf.

Sourander, A., L. Helstela, H. Helenius, and J. Piha. "Persistence of Bullying from Childhood to Adolescence: A Longitudinal 8-Year-Follow-Up Study." *Child Abuse and Neglect* 24 (2000): 873–81.

Sourander, A., P. Jensen, J. Ronning, S. Niemala, H. Helenius, L. Sillanmaki, et al. "What Is the Early Adulthood Outcome of Boys Who Bully or Are Bullied in Childhood?" *The Finnish 'From a Boy to a Man' Study. Pediatrics* 120 (2007): 397–404.

Spoor, J., and K. D. Williams. "The Evolution of an Ostracism Detection System." In *The Evolution of the Social Mind: Evolutionary Psychology and Social Cognition.* Edited by J. P. Forgas, M. Hselton, and W. von Hippel. New York: Psychology Press, 2007, 279–92 .

Stein, N. *Classrooms and Courtrooms: Facing Sexual Harassment in K–12 Schools.* New York: Teachers College Press, 1999. 11.

Swearer, S. M., S. Y. Song, P. T. Cary, J. W. Eagle, and W. T. Mickelson. "Psychosocial Correlates in Bullying and Victimization: The Relationship Between Depression, Anxiety, and Bully/Victim Status." *Journal of Emotional Abuse* 2 (2001): 95–121.

Thompson, M., L. Cohen, and C. O'Neill Grace. *Best Friends, Worst Enemies: Understanding the Social Lives of Children.* New York: Ballantine, 2001.

____. *Mom, They're Teasing Me: Helping Your Child Solve Social Problems.* New York: Ballantine, 2002.

Twenge, J. M., and W. K. Campbell. *The Narcissism Epidemic: Living in the Age of Entitlement.* New York: Free Press/Simon and Schuster, 2009.

Vaillancourt, T., J. Clinton, P. McDougall, L. Schmidt, and S. Hymel. "The Neurobiology of Peer Victimization and Rejection." In *The Handbook of Bullying in Schools: An International Perspective.* Edited by S. R. Jimerson, S. M. Swearer, and D. L. Espelage. New York: Routledge, 2010. 293–304.

Vanallen, A., V. Weber, and S. Kunin. "Are Tweens Too Young for Makeup?" ABC News. 2001. abcnews.go.com/US/tweens-young-makeup/story?id=12777008.

Van Cleave, J., and M. M. Davis. "Bullying and Peer Victimization Among Children with Special Health Care Needs." *Pediatrics* 118 (2006): 1212–19.

Vossekuil, B., R. A. Fein, M. Reddy, R. Borum, and W. Modzeleski. *The Final Report and Findings of the Safe School Initiative: Implications for the Prevention of School Attacks in the United States.* Washington, DC: U.S. Secret Service and U.S. Department of Education, 2002.

Way, N. *Deep Secrets: Boys' Friendships and the Crisis of Connection,* Cambridge, MA: Harvard Univ. Press, 2011.

Werner, E., and R. Smith. *Overcoming the Odds: High Risk Children from Birth to Adulthood.* Ithaca: Cornell Univ. Press, 1992.

Wesselmann, E. D., D. Bagg, and K. D. Williams. " 'I Feel Your Pain': The Effects of Observing Ostracism on the Ostracism Detection System." *Journal of Experimental Social Psychology* 45 (2009): 1308–11.

Willard, N. *Cyber-Safe Kids, Cybersavvy Teens: Helping Young People Learn to Use the Internet Safely and Responsibly.* San Francisco: Jossey-Bass, 2007.

Wiseman, R. *Queen Bees and Wannabes: Helping Your Daughter Survive Cliques, Gossip, Boyfriends, and the New Realities of Girl World.* New York: Crown, 2002.

Workplace Bullying Institute. "Results of the 2010 WBI U.S. Workplace Bullying Survey." www.workplacebullying.org/wbiresearch/2010-wbi-national-survey/.

Ybarra, M. L. "Linkages Between Depressive Symptomology and Internet

Harassment Among Young Regular Internet Users." *CyberPsychology and Behavior* 7, no. 2 (2004): 247–57.

Ybarra, M. L., D. L. Espelage, and K. J. Mitchell. "The Co-occurrence of Internet Harassment and Unwanted Sexual Solicitation Victimization and Perpetration: Associations with Psychosocial Indicators." *Journal of Adolescent Health* 41 (2007b): S31–S41.

Resources

ONLINE RESOURCES

- Geena Davis Institute on Gender and Media, www.thegeenadavisinstitute.org

- Hardy Girls Healthy Women, www.hghw.org

- SPARK, www.sparksummit.com

- Girls Leadership Institute, www.girlsleadershipinstitute.org

- Common Sense Media, www.commonsensemedia.org

- Cyberbullying Research Center, www.cyberbullying.us

- Net Family News, www.netfamilynews.org

- The National Center for School Engagement, www.schoolengagement.org

- Positive Behavioral Interventions and Supports, www.pbis.org

- SafePlace's Expect Respect, www.safeplace.org/expectrespect

- Anti-Defamation League School Lessons, www.adl.org/education/curriculum_connections

- Gay, Straight, Lesbian & Education Network, www.glsen.org/cgi-bin/iowa/all/home/index.html

- American Civil Liberties Union LGBT Project, www.aclu.org/lgbt

- Gay and Lesbian Alliance Against Defamation, www.glaad.org

- It Gets Better, www.itgetsbetter.org

- The Trevor Project, www.thetrevorproject.org

- National Sexual Violence Resource Center www.nsvrc.org

- The Kind Campaign www.kindcampaign.com/index.php

- The Lives of Girls and Boys: Initiatives on Gender Development and Relationships, lives.clas.asu.edu/index.html

- National Association of School Psychologists' Cyberbullying Resources, www.nasponline.org/resources/cyberbullying/index.aspx

- Intervention Central, Behavioral Interventions, www.interventioncentral.org/index.php/behavorial-resources

- Steps to Respect and Second Step, www.cfchildren.org

- Girl Scouts Healthy Media blog.girlscouts.org/2010/10/watch-what-you-watch.html

- Girl Scouts Tips for Parents About Talking with Girls About Reality TV, www.girlscouts.org/research/pdf/real_to_me_tip_sheet_for_parents.pdf

- Campaign for a Commercial-Free Childhood, www.commercialfreechildhood.org

- Teaching Tolerance, www.tolerance.org

- Center for Media Literacy, www.medialit.org

- Media Education Foundation www.mediaed.org

- I-SAFE, www.isafe.org

- Connect Safely, www.connectsafely.org

- Restorative Justice in Schools, www.safersanerschools.org/articles.html?articleId=387

- Reporting on State Anti-Bullying Laws, bullypolice.org

- Self-Defense and Empowerment Training for Kids, www.kidpower.org

- Facing History and Ourselves, www.facinghistory.org

- Cooperative Learning: The Jigsaw Classroom, www.jigsaw.org

- The Autism Society of America, www.autism-society.org

- Autism Speaks, www.autismspeaks.org

- Equal Rights Advocates, www.equalrights.org

- Office of Civil Rights, U.S. Department of Education www.ed.gov/offices OCR/index.html

- Bullying Prevention in Canada, prevnet.ca

READING RECOMMENDATIONS FOR CHILDREN

Picture Books for Ages 4–8

How My Family Came to Be: Daddy, Papa and Me, by Andrew Aldrich. New Family Press, 2003.

The Bully Blockers Club, by Teresa Bateman. Albert Whitman and Company, 2004.

A. Lincoln and Me, by Louise Borden and Ted Lewin. Scholastic, 2001.

Violet the Pilot, by Steve Breen. Dial, 2008.

Ballerino Nate, by Kimberly Brubaker Bradley. Dial, 2006.

Simon's Hook: A Story About Teases and Put-downs, by Karen Gedig Burnett. GR Publishing, 2000.

How to Lose All Your Friends, by Nancy Carlson. Puffin, 1997.

The Meanest Thing to Say, by Bill Cosby. New York: Scholastic, 1997.

Ella the Elegant Elephant, by Carmela D'amico and Steve D'amico. Arthur A. Levine Books, 2004.

King and King, by Linda De Haan and Stern Nijland. Tricycle Press, 2003.

Oliver Button Is a Sissy, by Tomie dePaola. Harcourt Brace Jovanovich, 1979.

The Sissy Duckling, by Harvey Fierstein. Simon and Schuster Books for Young Readers, 2002.

Tough Boris, by Mem Fox. Harcourt Children's Books, 1994.

The Princess Knight, by Cornelia Funke. The Chicken House, 2004.

Elena's Serenade, by Campbell Geeslin. Atheneum Books for Young Readers, 2004.

The Sneetches and Other Stories, by Theodor Geissel (Dr. Seuss). Random House, 1961.

Chrysanthemum, by Kevin Henkes. Greenwillow Books, 1991.

Horace and Morris but Mostly Dolores, by James Howe. Atheneum Books for Young Readers, 2003.

The Little Bit Scary People, by Emily Jenkins. Hyperion Books for Children, 2008.

Just Like Josh Gibson, by Angela Johnson. Simon and Schuster Books for Young Readers, 2007.

My Princess Boy, by Cheryl Kilodavis. Aladdin, 2010.

My Travelin' Eye, by Jenny Sue Kostecki-Shaw. Henry Holt and Co., 2008.

How to Be a Friend: A Guide to Making Friends and Keeping Them, by Laurie Krasney and Marc Brown. Little Brown and Co., 2001.

Nathan Blows Out the Hanukkah Candles, by Tami Lehman-Wilzig and Nicole Katzman. KAR-BEN Publishing, 2011.

Tacky the Penguin, by Helen Lester. Walter Lorraine Books, 1990.

Stand Tall, Molly Lou Melon, by Patty Lovell. Scholastic, 2002.

Nobody Knew What to Do: A Story About Bullying, by Becky McCain. Magnetix Corporation, 2002.

Have You Filled a Bucket Today? by Carol McCloud. Ferne Press, 2006.

Say Something, by Peggy Moss. Tilbury House, 2004.

Enemy Pie, by Derek Munson. Chronicle Books, 2000.

King of the Playground, by Phyllis Reynolds Naylor. Atheneum, 1991.

The Boy Who Cried Fabulous, by Lesléa Newman. Tricycle Press, 2007.

It's Okay to Be Different, by Todd Parr. Little, Brown Books for Young Readers, 2009.

Thank You, Mr. Falker, by Patricia Polacco. Philomel, 1998.

Don't Laugh at Me, by Steve Seskin and Allen Shamblin. Tricycle Press, 2002.

The Juice Box Bully: Empowering Kids to Stand Up for Others, by Bob Sornson and Maria Dismondy. Ferne Press, 2010.

This Is Gabriel Making Sense of School, by Hartley Steiner. Trafford Publishing, 2010.

Stop Picking on Me, by Pat Thomas and Lesley Harker. Barron's Educational Series, 2000.

Am I Really Different? by Evelien Van Dort, Floris Books, 1998.

Why Does Izzy Cover Her Ears? Dealing with Sensory Overload, by Jennifer Veenendall. Autism Asperger Publishing, 2009.

Words Are Not for Hurting, by Elizabeth Verdick. Free Spirit Publishing, 2004.

William's Doll, by Charlotte Zolotow. HarperCollins, 1972.

Text-Rich Picture Books and Chapter Books for Ages 8–13

Parents and guardians should preread these books to make sure the content is age-appropriate for younger readers.

The Strange Case of Origami Yoda, by Tom Angleberger. Amulet Books, 2010.

Blubber, by Judy Blume. Yearling, 1974.

Vive La Paris, by Esmé Raji Codell. Hyperion Paperbacks for Children, 2007.

Blue Cheese Breath and Stinky Feet, by Catherine DePino. Magination Press, 2004.

The Hundred Dresses, by Eleanor Estes. Scholastic, 1973.

Real Friends versus the Other Kind, by Annie Fox. Free Spirit Publishing, 2009.

I Am Jack, by Susanne Gervay. Tricycle Press, 2009.

The Liberation of Gabriel King, by K. L. Going. Puffin, 2007.

Hot Issues, Cool Choices: Facing Bullies, Peer Pressure, Popularity, and Put-downs, by Sandra McLeod Humphrey. Prometheus Books, 2007.

The Popularity Papers, by Amy Ignatow. Amulet Books, 2011.

Stick Up for Yourself! Every Kid's Guide to Personal Power and Positive Self-Esteem, by Gershen Kaufman, Lev Raphael, and Pamela Espelano. Free Spirit Publishing, 1999.

Drita, My Homegirl, by Jenny Lombard. Puffin Books, 2006.

Confessions of a Former Bully, by Trudy Ludwig. Tricycle Press, 2010.

Just Kidding, by Trudy Ludwig. Tricycle Press, 2006.

My Secret Bully, by Trudy Ludwig. Tricycle Press, 2005.

Trouble Talk, by Trudy Ludwig. Tricycle Press, 2008.

Mr. Peabody's Apples, by Madonna. Callaway, 2003.

Nothing Wrong with a Three-Legged Dog, by Graham McNamee. Yearling, 2001.

Secret of the Peaceful Warrior: A Story About Courage and Love, by Dan Millman. H. J. Kramer, 1991.

Esperanza Rising, by Pam Munoz Ryan. Scholastic Paperbacks, 2002.

Riding Freedom, by Pam Munoz Ryan. Scholastic Paperbacks, 1999.

Friendship: How to Make, Keep, and Grow Your Friendships, by New Moon Books Girls Editorial Board. Crown Publishers, 1999.

Call Me Hope, by Gretchen Olson. Little, Brown and Co., 2007.

Mr. Lincoln's Way, by Patricia Polacco. Philomel, 2001.

If You Believe in Mermaids . . . Don't Tell, by A. A. Philips, Dog Ear Publishing, 2007.

Bullies Are a Pain in the Brain, by Trevor Romain. Free Spirit Publishing, 1997.

Loser, by Jerry Spinelli. Joanna Cotler Books, 2002.

Maniac Magee, by Jerry Spinelli. Little, Brown and Co., 1990.

Feathers, by Jacqueline Woodson. Putnam Juvenile, 2007.

Tomboy Trouble, by Sharon Dennis Wyeth, Random House Books for Young Readers, 1998.

Super Tool Lula: The Bully-Fighting Super Hero!, by Michele Yulo. BookLogix Publishing Services, 2011.

Chapter Books for Ages 12–17

Parents and guardians should preread these books to make sure the content is age-appropriate for younger readers.

The Strange Case of Origami Yoda, by Tom Angleberger. Amulet Books, 2010.

Twisted, by Laurie Halse Anderson. Speak, 2008.

Thirteen Reasons Why, by Jay Asher. Penguin Group, 2007.

Hate List, by Jennifer Brown. Little, Brown and Co., 2010.

Staying Fat for Sarah Byrnes, by Chris Crutcher. Greenwillow Books, 1993.

The Skin I'm In, by Sharon Flake. Jump at the Sun/Hyperion Books for Children, 1998.

The Secret Fruit of Peter Paddington, by Brian Francis. Harper Perennial, 2005.

Charlie's Story, by Maeve Friel. Peachtree Publishers, 1997.

The Misfits, by James Howe. Atheneum Books for Young Readers, 2003.

Totally Joe, by James Howe. Atheneum Books for Young Readers, 2007.

Teen Cyberbullying Investigated: Where Do Your Rights End and Consequences Begin?, by Thomas A. Jacobs. Free Spirit Publishing, 2010.

The Astonishing Adventures of Fanboy and Goth Girl, by Barry Lyga. Graphia, 2007.

Drowning Anna, by Sue Mayfield. Hyperion, 2002.

Luna, by Julie Anne Peters. Little, Brown Books for Young Readers, 2006.

Stargirl, by Jerry Spinelli. Alfred A. Knopf, 2000.

The Revealers, by Doug Wilhelm. RR Donnelley and Sons Co., 2011.

Parrotfish, by Ellen Wittlinger. Simon and Schuster Books for Young Readers, 2011.

Story of a Girl, by Sara Zarr. Little, Brown Books for Young Readers, 2008.

AUDIOVISUAL RESOURCES

Emotional Lives of Boys

Raising Cain: Exploring the Inner Lives of America's Boys, by Michael Thompson and Powderhouse Productions. PBS Video, 2005.

Wrestling with Manhood: Boys, Bullying, and Battering (abridged). Sut Jhally (Director), featuring Sut Jhally and Jackson Katz. Media Education Foundation, 2002 (www.mediaed.org).

Bullying

Bully. Lee Hirsch (Director), 2012.

Clicking with Caution. Four-part DVD. www.nyc.gov/html/nycmg/nyctvod/html/home/cwc.html.

Sexting in America: When Privates Go Public. www.mtv.com/videos/news/483801/sexting-in-america-when-privates-go-public-part-1.jhtml.

Cyberbully. Charles Biname (Director). Lifetime Television, 2011.

Girl Aggression

Finding Kind. Lauren Parsekian (Director). Indieflix, 2010.

Mean Girls (special feature with Rosalind Wiseman, "The Politics of Girl World"). Mark Waters (Director). Paramount Pictures, 2004.

Odd Girl Out. Tom McLoughlin (Director). Lifetime Television, 2005.

Media and Culture

Miss Representation. Jennifer Siebel Newsome (Writer and Director), 2011. www.missrepresentation.org/the-film/.

Codes of Gender. Sut Jhally (Writer and Director). Media Education Foundation, 2009. www.mediaed.org.

Consuming Kids: The Commercialization of Childhood. Adriana Barbaro and Jeremy Ear (Directors). Media Education Foundation, 2008. www.mediaed.org.

Dreamworlds 3: Desire, Sex and Power in Music Video (unabridged). Sut Jhally

(Writer and Director). Media Education Foundation, 2007. www.mediaed. org.

Generation M: Misogyny in Media and Culture. Thomas Keith (Director). Media Education Foundation, 2008. www.mediaed.org.

Hip-Hop: Beyond Beats and Rhymes (abridged). Byron Hurt (Director). Media Education Foundation, 2006. www.mediaed.org.

Killing Us Softly: Advertising's Image of Women, by Jean Kilbourne. Sut Jhally (Director). Media Education Foundation, 2006. www.mediaed.org.

Teenage Paparazzo. Adrien Grenier (Director). Reckless Productions, 2010.

Sexual Harassment

Flirting or Hurting? Sexual Harassment in Schools, based on *Flirting or Hurting? A Teacher's Guide on Student-to-Student Sexual Harassment in Schools (Grades 6–12)* by Nan Stein and Lisa Sjostrom of Wellesley College. www.ket.org/itvvideos/offering/practical/flirtingorhurting.htm.

Overview of Several Promising Research-Based Bullying-Prevention and Character-Education Programs

Bully Busters

Bully Busters was a program developed in 2000 for grades six through eight. In 2003, a Bully Busters program was also developed for kindergarten through fifth grade. Bully Busters focuses on effecting change in the school's social system so that bullying is less likely to occur. The foundation of the program is respect. The program targets bullies, victims, and bystanders and is geared toward educating all school personnel on awareness and interventions with bully perpetration and victimization.

The program focuses more on teacher training than many other programs, which has contributed greatly to its positive results, and it contains several learning modules for teachers. The program includes sections on increasing awareness, recognizing the bully and victims, interventions for bullies and victims, classroom prevention, and coping skills.[1]

Bully-Proofing Your School

Bully-Proofing Your School in Elementary Schools, a whole-school curriculum, was initially developed in 2000 for kindergarten through sixth grade. The Bully-Proofing in Early Childhood program was created in 2005 for bullies and victims aged three to five years old and aims to prevent bullying behaviors from surfacing within the early childhood classes by teaching the students the social skills necessary to avoid victimization. The administrator's Guide to Staff Development includes chapters on identifying and intervening with bullying situations, adopting and adapting the curriculum to meet the needs of individual schools, staff training, prosocial discipline interventions, bus/transportation interventions, and effective parental collaboration techniques.

The teacher's manual offers six lesson plans and materials for kindergarten through first grade, and six lesson plans and corresponding materials for grades two through six. The lessons for kindergarten through first grade focus on social relationships and friendship building. The lessons for grades two through six focus on identifying bullying, classroom rules, and strategies for victims and helpers. The manual concludes with a chapter on maintaining a caring classroom and collaborating with parents. The program also comes with an individualized support workbook that addresses specific cases of perpetration and victimization.[2]

Bullyproof

Bullyproof was developed in 1996 by Nan Stein of Wellesley College and is targeted to students in grades four and five. The guide provides a framework for teachers and students to understand bullying, to identify the differences between bullying and teasing as well as the definition of sexual harassment, and to develop appropriate responses to such behaviors.

The guide contains eleven sequential core lessons for fourth and fifth graders, which are comprised of writing activities, reading assignments, class discussions, role plays, case studies, and homework assignments intended to encourage children to think about the distinctions between teasing and bullying. These activities help children focus on the boundaries between appropriate and inappropriate, and playful and hurtful behavior.[3]

Expect Respect

SafePlace's Expect Respect Program was first developed for use in Austin, Texas, schools in 1988. Expect Respect works with kids and adults in building healthy teen relationships and preventing dating and sexual violence. The program provides counseling and support groups for kindergarten through twelfth grade; classroom presentations on dating violence, sexual assault, sexual harassment, and healthy relationships for grades six through twelve; a summer teen leadership program; and training for school personnel.[4]

The program draws upon research by Nan Stein, who believes that because sexual harassment has been normalized, "a school culture has been created that gives, in effect, permission to proceed, potentially turning schools into practice fields and training grounds for dating/domestic violence and other forms of interpersonal gender violence."[5]

A Cooperative Learning Technique: The Jigsaw Classroom

Elliott Aronson invented the Jigsaw Classroom, which was first implemented in Austin, Texas, in 1971, as a way to help newly desegregated schools manage their newly racially diverse classrooms. Students who participated in a Jigsaw Classroom experienced decreased racial conflicts and increased positive educational outcomes.

To teach a lesson using the jigsaw approach, divide students into five- or six-person jigsaw groups. The groups should be diverse in terms of gender, ethnicity, race, and ability. The day's topic is split into five or six segments. For example, if your class is studying some of the most famous speeches by Abraham Lincoln, segments may include (a) House Divided Speech of 1858, (b) Cooper Union Address of 1860, (c) Farewell Address in Springfield of 1861, (d) First Inaugural Address of 1861, and (e) the Gettysburg Address of 1863. Each student is assigned a different segment to master, and the students may only have direct access to information about their own segment.

The students assigned to a particular segment, such as the Gettysburg Address, can split off from their diverse groups to meet up, essentially forming a team of experts on that segment. They learn everything there is to know about the Gettysburg Address (where it was delivered, the circumstances under which the speech was given, how it was received, and so forth), and they rehearse their presentations about it to one another. Once they have mastered the Gettysburg Address, the experts return to their original diverse groups to teach their topic to the other group members. Each person gets a turn to be the expert on one of the segments. At the end of the lesson, the teacher gives a quiz that covers all segments. If students mistreat or disrespect any member of their jigsaw group, they will not learn that member's expert segment sufficiently to perform well on the quiz. Every piece of the jigsaw is needed to make the whole puzzle.[6]

Olweus Bullying Prevention Program

Dan Olweus is the founder of the Olweus Bullying Prevention Program (OBPP). Many anti-bullying programs are based on the groundbreaking research first conducted by Olweus. The OBPP was initially developed in Norway during the 1980s, where it was very successful and achieved up to 50 percent reductions in bullying. In U.S. schools, the program has yielded reductions closer to 20 percent, and the Olweus team is busy making adjustments to account for the different culture and demographics of American students. One big change is that the Olweus program was traditionally centered on adult interventions, and now it is doing more to empower the students. The OBPP targets elementary and middle school students aged five to fifteen. In recent years, the program has expanded into high schools and is continuing to develop updated print information.

Core components of the program are implemented at the school-wide level, classroom level, individual level, and community level. Some of the school-level components include formation of a Bullying Prevention Coordinating Committee, distribution of an anonymous student questionnaire assessing the nature and prevalence of bullying, training for committee members and staff, development of appropriate positive and negative consequences for students' behavior, and parental involvement. The committee is critical to the success of the Olweus program in American schools.

The classroom-level components include reinforcement of school-wide rules against bullying, holding regular classroom meetings with students to increase knowledge and empathy, and informational meetings with parents. The individual-level components include separate interventions with children who bully and those who are bullied and discussion with parents of all involved students.[7]

Positive Behavioral Interventions and Supports (PBIS)

School-wide positive behavior support (SWPBS) is a term that is interchangeable with PBIS. In both cases, it means a systems approach to establishing the social culture and behavioral supports needed for all children in a school to achieve both social and academic success. The school will identify three to five positive behaviors on which to base expectations. For example, *Be Safe, Be Responsible, Be Respectful.* SWPBS is not a packaged curriculum, but an approach that defines core elements that can be achieved through a variety of strategies. It is targeted to all students in kindergarten through twelfth grade.[8]

There are three tiers in the prevention model. Tier 1, primary prevention, includes school-wide and classroom-wide systems for all students, staff, and settings. Tier 2, secondary prevention, includes systems for students with at-risk behavior and for specialized groups. Tier 3, tertiary prevention, includes individualized interventions, assessments, and supports for high-risk students.[9] PBIS on its own provides a framework for behavioral expectations but works best at bullying prevention when combined with specific lessons on bullying.

Second Step

Second Step is a program targeted to kids in kindergarten through eighth grade. Lessons for kindergarten and first grade focus on skills for learning and listening rules. Lessons for grades two through five focus on empathy, problem solving, and managing strong emotions. Skills are reinforced by five minutes daily practice activities and Home Links. Lessons for grades six through eight are used with an interactive DVD and help students learn the protective skills to make healthy choices and stay engaged in school, even when they are faced with challenges such as substance abuse, bullying, cyberbullying, and peer pressure.

There is a new Second Step Early Learning program for kids aged three through five that is taught through twenty-eight weekly themes, consisting of five- to seven-minute activities to be done throughout the week. The activities build on each other to develop children's self-regulation skills and social-emotional competence.

Steps to Respect

The Steps to Respect program was initially developed in 2001 (updated in 2005) as a full elementary school program with lessons for grades three through five or four through six. Steps to Respect promotes a whole-school approach to bullying by addressing factors at the school, staff, peer-group, individual-child, and family levels. Intervening at multiple levels, they believe, is the most effective way to reduce school bullying. The program is designed to help students feel safe and supported by the adults around them so they can create stronger bonds at school. An evaluation study published in the May–June 2005 issue of *Developmental Psychology* found that there were 25 percent fewer bullying incidents on the playground at the Steps to Respect schools compared to the control group.[10]

In Phase 1, the school establishes a school-wide framework of anti-bullying policies and procedures and determines consequences for bullying. In Phase 2, all school staff members are trained to recognize bullying and receive reports from students. Select staff members are trained to work directly with children involved in bullying incidents, and parents also receive materials about bullying. In Phase 3, students learn and practice bullying-prevention skills, including the three *R*s: *recognize, refuse, and report bullying.* Program support specialists are available to answer questions, help work through problems, and provide strategies for launching or evaluating the program.[11]

Two Examples of Bullying Surveys

A Bullying Survey for Younger Children

The following questions are recommended by Teaching Tolerance in their Bullying Survey for elementary school children:[1]

1. Has anyone ever called you a name?
2. Has anyone ever told you that you can't be friends?
3. Has anyone ever hit, kicked, or pushed you?
4. Has anyone ever threatened you?
5. Was someone mean to you because of how you look?
6. Did you tell anyone about any of these incidents? Why or why not?
7. Have you ever seen someone else being bullied?
8. Have you ever called someone else a name, hit, kicked, pushed, threatened, or been mean to someone?

A Bullying Survey for Older Children

The following survey, provided by Dorothy Espelage, has been administered to many adolescents:[2]

For each of the following questions, choose how many times you did these things or how many times these things happened to you at school in the LAST 30 DAYS.

	Never	1 or 2 times	3 or 4 times	5 or 6 times	7 or more times
I upset other students for the fun of it.	a	b	c	d	e
In a group I teased other students.	a	b	c	d	e
I fought students I could easily beat.	a	b	c	d	e
Other students picked on me.	a	b	c	d	e
I got in a physical fight.	a	b	c	d	e
I spread rumors about other students.	a	b	c	d	e
I started (insti-gated) arguments or conflicts.	a	b	c	d	e
I helped harass other students.	a	b	c	d	e
I hit back when someone hit me first.	a	b	c	d	e
Other students called me "gay."	a	b	c	d	e
I threatened to hurt or hit another student.	a	b	c	d	e

	Never	1 or 2 times	3 or 4 times	5 or 6 times	7 or more times
I got into a physical fight because I was angry.	a	b	c	d	e
I lost my temper for no reason.	a	b	c	d	e
Other students called me names.	a	b	c	d	e
I encouraged people to fight.	a	b	c	d	e
I teased other students.	a	b	c	d	e
I called other students "gay."	a	b	c	d	e
I was mean to someone when I was angry.	a	b	c	d	e
I was angry all day.	a	b	c	d	e
I got hit and pushed by other students.	a	b	c	d	e

Examples of Sexual Harassment Surveys[1]

A Survey to See If YOU Have Been Sexually Harassed by OTHERS: Since the start of school this year, how often have *others* done the following things to you at school when you did not want them to?

	Not Sure	Never	Rarely	Occa- sionally	Often
Made sexual comments, jokes, gestures, or looks.	a	b	c	d	e
How often did boys do this to you?	a	b	c	d	e
How often did girls do this to you?	a	b	c	d	e
Showed, gave, or left you sexual pictures, photographs, illustrations, messages, or notes.	a	b	c	d	e
How often did boys do this to you?	a	b	c	d	e

	Not Sure	Never	Rarely	Occasionally	Often
How often did girls do this to you?	a	b	c	d	e
Wrote sexual messages/graffiti about you on bathroom walls, in locker rooms, and so forth.	a	b	c	d	e
How often did boys do this to you?	a	b	c	d	e
How often did girls do this to you?	a	b	c	d	e
Spread sexual rumors about you.	a	b	c	d	e
How often did boys do this to you?	a	b	c	d	e
How often did girls do this to you?	a	b	c	d	e
Said you were gay or lesbian.	a	b	c	d	e
How often did boys do this to you?	a	b	c	d	e
How often did girls do this to you?	a	b	c	d	e

Remember, we want to know how often, if at all, *others* have done the following things to you at school since the start of the school year?

	Not Sure	Never	Rarely	Occa-sionally	Often
Touched, grabbed, or pinched you in a sexual way.	a	b	c	d	e
How often did boys do this to you?	a	b	c	d	e
How often did girls do this to you?	a	b	c	d	e
Pulled at your clothing in a sexual way.	a	b	c	d	e
How often did boys do this to you?	a	b	c	d	e
How often did girls do this to you?	a	b	c	d	e
Intentionally brushed against you in a sexual way.	a	b	c	d	e
How often did boys do this to you?	a	b	c	d	e
How often did girls do this to you?	a	b	c	d	e
Pulled your clothing off or down.	a	b	c	d	e
How often did boys do this to you?	a	b	c	d	e
How often did girls do this to you?	a	b	c	d	e
Blocked your way or cornered you in a sexual way.	a	b	c	d	e

	Not Sure	Never	Rarely	Occa-sionally	Often
How often did boys do this to you?	a	b	c	d	e
How often did girls do this to you?	a	b	c	d	e
Forced you to kiss him/her.	a	b	c	d	e
How often did boys do this to you?	a	b	c	d	e
How often did girls do this to you?	a	b	c	d	e
Forced you to do something sexual, other than kissing.	a	b	c	d	e
How often did boys do this to you?	a	b	c	d	e
How often did girls do this to you?	a	b	c	d	e
Made you touch their private parts when you did not want to?	a	b	c	d	e
How often did boys do this to you?	a	b	c	d	e
How often did girls do this to you?	a	b	c	d	e

A Survey to See If OTHERS Have Been Sexually Harassed by YOU: Since the beginning of this school year, have you done the following to *other students* at school when they did not want you to?

	Not Sure	Never	Rarely	Occa-sionally	Often
Made sexual comments, jokes, gestures, or looks.	a	b	c	d	e
How often did you do this to boys?	a	b	c	d	e
How often did you do this to girls?	a	b	c	d	e
Showed, gave, or left sexual pictures, photographs, illustrations, messages, or notes.	a	b	c	d	e
How often did you do this to boys?	a	b	c	d	e
How often did you do this to girls?	a	b	c	d	e
Wrote sexual messages/graffiti about them on bathroom walls, in locker rooms, and so forth.	a	b	c	d	e
How often did you do this to boys?	a	b	c	d	e
How often did you do this to girls?	a	b	c	d	e
Spread sexual rumors about them.	a	b	c	d	e
How often did you do this to boys?	a	b	c	d	e
How often did you do this to girls?	a	b	c	d	e

	Not Sure	Never	Rarely	Occa-sionally	Often
Said they were gay or lesbian.	a	b	c	d	e
How often did you do this to boys?	a	b	c	d	e
How often did you do this to girls?	a	b	c	d	e
Touched, grabbed, or pinched them in a sexual way.	a	b	c	d	e
How often did you do this to boys?	a	b	c	d	e
How often did you do this to girls?	a	b	c	d	e
Pulled at their clothing in a sexual way.	a	b	c	d	e
How often did you do this to boys?	a	b	c	d	e
How often did you do this to girls?	a	b	c	d	e
Intentionally brushed against them in a sexual way.	a	b	c	d	e
How often did you do this to boys?	a	b	c	d	e
How often did you do this to girls?	a	b	c	d	e
Pulled their clothing off or down.	a	b	c	d	e
How often did you do this to boys?	a	b	c	d	e

	Not Sure	Never	Rarely	Occa-sionally	Often
How often did you do this to girls?	a	b	c	d	e
Blocked their way or cornered them in a sexual way.	a	b	c	d	e
How often did you do this to boys?	a	b	c	d	e
How often did you do this to girls?	a	b	c	d	e
Forced them to kiss you.	a	b	c	d	e
How often did you do this to boys?	a	b	c	d	e
How often did you do this to girls?	a	b	c	d	e
Forced them to do something sexual, other than kissing.	a	b	c	d	e
How often did you do this to boys?	a	b	c	d	e
How often did you do this to girls?	a	b	c	d	e
Made them touch your private parts when they did not want to?	a	b	c	d	e
How often did you do this to boys?	a	b	c	d	e
How often did you do this to girls?	a	b	c	d	e

Notes

Introduction

1. D. E. Espelage, M. A. Rao, and L. De La Rue, *Current Research on School-Based Bullying: A Social-Ecological Perspective* (Chicago: Univ. of Illinois at Champaign-Urbana, 2011).

2. Ron Astor, interview by author, March 14, 2011.

3. Michael Thompson, interview by author, July 11, 2011.

4. Justin Patchin, interview by author, July 27, 2011.

5. D. E. Espelage and M. K. Holt, "Bullying and Victimization During Early Adolescence: Peer Influences and Psychosocial Correlates," *Journal of Emotional Abuse* 2 (2001): 123–42; J. E. Gruber and S. Fineran, "The Impact of Bullying and Sexual Harassment on Middle and High School Girls," *Violence Against Women* 13 (2007): 627–43.

6. D. Goleman, *Social Intelligence: The New Science of Human Relationships* (New York: Bantam, 2006).

7. M. Lieberman and N. Eisenberger, "Pains and Pleasures of Social Life," *Science* 323 (2009): 890–91; D. D. Price, "Psychological and Neural Mechanisms of the Affective Dimension of Pain," *Science* 288 (2000): 1769–72.

8. C. L. Masten et al., "Neural Correlates of Social Exclusion During Adolescence: Understanding the Distress of Peer Rejection," *Scan* 4 (2009): 143–57.

9. J. Knack, H. L. Gomez, and L. A. Jensen-Campbell, "Bullying and Its Long-Term Health Implications," in *Social Pain: Neuropsychological and Health Implications of Loss and Exclusion,* ed. L. A. Jensen-Campbell and G. MacDonald, 215–36 (Washington, DC: American Psychological Association, 2011).

Chapter 2: The Littlest Jedi

1. Felicia Day, interview by author, June 22, 2011.

2. Tom Kane, interview by author, March 31, 2011.

3. Reprinted with permission from Katie Lucas.

4. James Arnold Taylor, interview by author, March 29, 2011.

5. Term "Littlest Jedi" used with permission of Lucasfilm.

Chapter 3: Our Local Community Response

1. Michael Robey, interview by author, March 1, 2011.
2. Barbara Coloroso, interview by author, February 13, 2011.
3. Trudy Ludwig, interview by author, March 8, 2011.
4. D. Haynie et al., "Bullies, Victims, and Bully/Victims: Distinct Groups of At-Risk Youth," *Journal of Early Adolescence* 21 (2001): 29–49.
5. Ludwig, interview.
6. Rosalind Wiseman, interview by author, April 11, 2011.

Chapter 4: From Geek Girls to Sluts: What Does It Mean to Be a Girl?

1. Lyn Mikel Brown, interview by author, May 21, 2011.
2. L. A. Jackson, J. E. Hunter, and C. N. Hodge, "Physical Attractiveness and Intellectual Competence: A Meta-analytic Review," *Social Psychology Quarterly* 58, no. 2 (1995): 108–22.
3. Brown, interview.
4. Louise, interview by author, December 4, 2011.
5. Carrie Goldman, "Pink Is Not the Enemy," Minnesota Women's Press, February 10, 2012, www.womenspress.com/main.asp?SectionID=124&SubSectionID=684&ArticleID=3988.
6. Peggy Orenstein, interview by author, April 22, 2011.

Chapter 5: Princess Boys and Nonconforming Guys

1. Sarah Buttenwieser, interview by author, March 3, 2011.
2. Cheryl Kilodavis, interview by author, March 3, 2011.
3. J. Freedman, *Easing the Teasing: Helping Your Child Cope with Name-Calling, Ridicule, and Verbal Bullying* (New York: McGraw-Hill, 2002), 128–31.
4. Lyn Mikel Brown, interview by author, December 20, 2011.
5. Jo Paoletti, interview by author, May 2, 2011.
6. J. Paoletti, "The Children's Department," in *Men and Women: Dressing the Part*, ed. C. B. Kidwell and V. Steele. (Washington, DC: Smithsonian Institution Press, 1989).
7. W. Pollack, *Real Boys: Rescuing Our Sons from the Myths of Boyhood* (New York: Random House, 1998).

Chapter 6: Quirky Kids and Kids with Hidden Disabilities

1. C. A. Rose et al., *Bullying and Victimization Among Students in Special Education and General Education Curricula* (unpublished manuscript, 2010).
2. Joslyn Gray, interview by author, February 10, 2011.
3. Woman identified as "Candice," interview by author, March 28, 2011.

4. Coloroso, interview.

5. Mother identified as "Janice," interview by author, December 15, 2010.

6. Mother identified as "Janice," interview by author, February 16, 2011.

7. Mother identified as "Francine," interview by author, March 15, 2011.

8. J. Van Cleave and M. M. Davis, "Bullying and Peer Victimization Among Children with Special Health Care Needs," *Pediatrics* 118 (2006): 1212–19; K. Kumpulainen, E. Rasanen, and K. Puura, "Psychiatric Disorders and the Use of Mental Health Services Among Children Involved in Bullying," *Aggressive Behavior* 27 (2001): 102–10.

Chapter 7: Kids with Different Appearances or Physical Disabilities

1. Mother identified as "Paula," interview by author, March 13, 2011.

2. Coloroso, interview.

3. A. Sourander et al., "What Is the Early Adulthood Outcome of Boys Who Bully or Are Bullied in Childhood?" The Finnish 'From a Boy to a Man' Study, *Pediatrics* 120 (2007): 397–404.

4. D. E. Espelage and S. M. Swearer, ed. *Bullying in North American Schools.* 2nd ed. (New York: Routledge, 2011), 299.

Chapter 8: Gay, Lesbian, Transgender, and Bisexual Students

1. S. D. James, "When Words Can Kill: 'That's So Gay,'" ABC News, 2009, abcnews.go.com/Health/MindMoodNews/story?id=7328091&page=1.

2. K. Brooks, "Bullied Greensburg Student Takes His Own Life," WXIN-TV, Fox 59, September 13, 2010, www.fox59.com/news/wxin-greensburg-student-suicide-091310,0,1101685.story.

3. B. Alexander, "The Bullying of Seth Walsh: Requiem for a Small-Town Boy," Time U.S., October 2, 2010, www.time.com/time/nation/article/0,8599,2023083,00.html.

4. ABC Local News, "Parents: Bullies Drove 13-Year-Old to Suicide," KTRK-TV/DT, September 29, 2010, abclocal.go.com/ktrk/story?section=news/local&id=7695982.

5. Man identified as "Josh," interview by author, May 23, 2011.

6. K. Rigby, "Peer Victimization at School and the Health of Secondary School Students," *British Journal of Educational Psychology* 69 (1999): 95–104.

7. Pollack, *Real Boys*, 211.

8. N. Way, *Deep Secrets: Boys' Friendships and the Crisis of Connection* (Cambridge, MA: Harvard Univ. Press, 2011), 220.

9. D. Savage and T. Miller, *It Gets Better: Coming Out, Overcoming Bullying, and Creating a Life Worth Living* (New York: Penguin, 2011), 8.

10. Pollack, *Real Boys*, 23–24.

11. D. Kindlon and M. Thompson, *Raising Cain: Protecting the Emotional Life of Boys* (New York: Ballantine, 1999), 81.

12. Blogger who identifies himself publicly as "Bedford Hope," interview by author, June 16, 2011.

13. Way, *Deep Secrets*, 280.

14. Young woman identified as "Olivia," interview by author, December 4, 2011.

15. Kesha Burch-Sims, interview by author, March 24, 2011.

16. Kilodavis, interview.

Chapter 9: Victims of Cyberbullying, Sexting, and Sexual Harassment

1. Anne Collier, interview by author, June 9, 2011.

2. Young woman identified as "Meg," interview by author, March 12, 2011.

3. N. L. Kerr and J. M. Levine, "The Detection of Social Exclusion: Evolution and Beyond," *Group Dynamics: Theory, Research and Practice* 12 (2008): 39–52; J. Spoor and K. D. Williams, "The Evolution of an Ostracism Detection System," in *The Evolution of the Social Mind: Evolutionary Psychology and Social Cognition*, ed. J. P. Forgas, M. Hselton, and W. von Hippel (New York: Psychology Press, 2007), 279–92.

4. E. D. Wesselmann, D. Bagg, and K. D. Williams, " 'I Feel Your Pain': The Effects of Observing Ostracism on the Ostracism Detection System," *Journal of Experimental Social Psychology* 45 (2009): 1308–11.

5. R. Faris and D. Felmlee, "Network Centrality, Gender Segregation, and Aggression," *Journal of the American Sociological Association* 76 (2011): 1.

6. Collier, interview.

7. Sheri Bauman, interview by author, July 22, 2011.

8. Patchin, interview.

9. Eric Witherspoon, interview by author, December 13, 2011.

10. Taken from written statement provided by Eric Witherspoon.

11. ABC News interview with Andrea Canning, "Rebecca Black: 'Don't Think I'm the Worst Singer,' " March 18, 2011, abcnews.go.com/GMA/video/ rebecca-black-dont-think-im-worst-singer-13164800.

12. ABC News *Nightline,* "Rebecca Black, YouTube Sensation Turned Award-Winning Pop Star, Talks About Growing Fame and Harassment," abcnews.go.com/Entertainment/rebecca-black-youtube-sensation-turned-award-winning-pop/story?id=14264051.

13. Young woman identified as "Carla," interview by author, December 13, 2011.

14. W. Hu, "Legal Debate Swirls Over Charges in a Student's Suicide," *New York Times,* October 1, 2010, www.nytimes.com/2010/10/02/nyregion/02suicide.html.

15. Collier, interview.

16. Equal Rights Advocates, "What Is Sexual Harassment?" www.equalrights
.org/publications/kyr/shschool.asp.

Chapter 10: The Harmful Effects of Bullying
on the Brain

1. D. Goleman, *Social Intelligence: The New Science of Human Relationships* (New York: Bantam, 2006).

2. S. Graham, and J. Juvonen, "Self-Blame and Peer Victimization in Middle School: An Attributional Analysis," *Developmental Psychology* 34 (1998):
587–99.

3. B. Coloroso, *The Bully, the Bullied, and the Bystander: From Preschool
to High School—How Parents and Teachers Can Help Break the Cycle of Violence* (New York: HarperCollins, 2008), 14.

4. C. Boyle, " 'Bullied' Staten Island Teen Kills Self," *NY Daily News,* January 3, 2012, www.nydailynews.com/new-york/staten-island-teen-kills-jumping-
front-bus-family-cites-bullies-article-1.1000243; ABC News, January 4, 2012,
"Staten Island Teen Bullied Before Taking Her Life," abcnews.go.com/US/staten-
island-teen-bullied-suicide-family/story?id=15287910#.TwnBq9WOeD0.

5. N. McGee and T. Moss, "Girl Was 'Teased and Taunted,' Family Says,"
News-Gazette, November 14, 2011, www.news-gazette.com/news/courts-police
-and-fire/2011-11-14/girl-was-teased-and-taunted-family-says.html.

6. S. D. James, "Gay Buffalo Teen Commits Suicide on Eve of National
Bullying Summit," ABC News, September 21, 2011, abcnews.go.com/Health/
gay-buffalo-teen-commits-suicide-eve-national-bullying/story?id=14571861#
.TvNVQ9WOeD1.

7. CBS News, April 7, 2009, "Parents Sue School After Son's Suicide," www
.cbsnews.com/stories/2009/04/07/earlyshow/main4925059.shtml?tag=currentV
ideoInfo;videoMetaInfo; L. Franks, "Life and Death at Suicide High," *Daily
Beast,* May 30, 2010, www.thedailybeast.com/articles/2010/03/31/life-and-death
-at-suicide-high.html.

8. L. Crimaldi, "DA: School Knew of Brutal Bullying of Phoebe Prince,"
BostonHerald, March 29, 2010, news.bostonherald.com/news/regional/view.bg
?articleid=1243175&srvc=home&position=active.

9. CBS News, March 29, 2010, "Cyberbullying Continued After Teen's
Death," www.cbsnews.com/stories/2010/03/29/earlyshow/main6343077.shtml;
A. Perkus and E. Van Sciver, "NY Suicide Prompts Cyber-Bullying Awareness," Wayland Student Press Network, March 31, 2010, waylandstudentpress
.com/2010/03/31/ny-suicide-prompts-cyber-bullying-awareness/.

10. Man identified as "Scott," written interview.

11. Sourander et al., "Early Adulthood Outcome."

12. D. A. Roth, M. E. Coles, and R. G. Heimberg, "The Relationship Between Memories for Childhood Teasing and Anxiety and Depression in Adulthood," *Journal of Anxiety Disorders* 16 (2002): 149–64.

13. Young woman identified as "Raya," interview by author, May 6, 2011.

14. G. Gladstone, G. Parker, and G. Mahli, "Do Bullied Children Become Anxious and Depressed Adults? A Cross-Sectional Investigation of the Correlates of Bullying and Anxious Depression," *Journal of Nervous and Mental Disease* 194 (2006): 201–8.

15. Burch-Sims, interview.

16. Sourander et al., "Early Adulthood Outcome."

17. Kumpulainen, Rasanen, and Puura, "Psychiatric Disorders"; S. M. Swearer et al., "Psychosocial Correlates in Bullying and Victimization: The Relationship Between Depression, Anxiety, and Bully/Victim Status," *Journal of Emotional Abuse* 2 (2001): 95–121.

18. Laura Hanish, interview by author, March 11, 2011; J. Connolly et al., "Dating Experiences of Bullies in Early Adolescence," *Child Maltreatment* 5 (2000): 299–310.

19. Michele Borba, interview by author, April 1, 2011.

20. Workplace Bullying Institute, "Results of the 2010 WBI U.S. Workplace Bullying Survey," www.workplacebullying.org/wbiresearch/2010-wbi-national-survey/.

Chapter 11: Create a Home Environment That Produces Neither Bullies nor Victims

1. D. Shriberg, "The Critical Role of Families in Combating Bullying and Promoting Wellness," Presentation to the Evanston/Skokie PTA Council, November, 2011.

2. Annie Fox, interview by author, March 15, 2011.

3. Mother identified as "Darla," interview by author, April 8, 2011.

4. J. M. Twenge and W. K. Campbell, *The Narcissism Epidemic: Living in the Age of Entitlement* (New York: Free Press/Simon & Schuster, 2009).

5. L. Gottlieb, "How to Land Your Kid in Therapy," *Atlantic*, 2011, www.theatlantic.com/magazine/archive/2011/07/how-to-land-your-kid-in-therapy/8555/.

6. M. Thompson, L. Cohen, and C. O'Neill Grace, *Best Friends, Worst Enemies: Understanding the Social Lives of Children* (New York: Ballantine, 2001), 109.

7. Thompson, Cohen, and O'Neill Grace, *Best Friends*, 111.

8. Michael Thompson, interview by author, July 11, 2011.

9. Young woman identified as "Deanna," interview by author, December 4, 2011.

10. Girl identified as "Cassandra," interview by author, December 13, 2011.

11. L. M. Brown, L. Lamb, and M. Tappan, *Packaging Boyhood: Saving Our Sons from Superheroes, Slackers, and Other Media Stereotypes* (New York: St. Martin's, 2006), 293.

12. S. D. James, "Gay Teen Jonah Mowry Says Bullying Made Him Stronger," ABC News, December 5, 2011, abcnews.go.com/blogs/health/2011/12/05/gay-teen-jonah-mowry-says-bullying-made-him-stronger/.

13. Girl identified as "Kyra," interview by author, March 22, 2011.

14. Fox, interview.

15. Jodee Blanco, interview by author, February 7, 2011.

16. Girl identified as Shahala, interview by author, December 4, 2011.

17. Victoria Stilwell, interview by author, June 30, 2011.

Chapter 12: Set Out Family Guidelines for Responsible Uses of Technology, Media, and Music

1. Patchin, interview.

2. Kilodavis, interview.

3. Collier, interview.

4. Kilodavis, interview.

5. Fox, interview.

6. C. Maag, "A Hoax Turned Fatal Draws Anger but No Charges," *New York Times,* November 28, 2007, www.nytimes.com/2007/11/28/us/28hoax.html?_r=1&oref=slogin.

7. Net Cetera, printed pamphlet for parents, ftc.gov/bcp/edu/pubs/consumer/tech/tec04.pdf.

8. Patchin, interview.

9. Patchin, interview.

10. Michele Ybarra, interview by author, August 22, 2011.

11. Technology contract reprinted with permission of Rosalind Wiseman on April 11, 2011.

12. S. Hinduja and J. W. Patchin, eds., *Cyberbullying Prevention and Response: Expert Perspectives* (New York: Routledge, 2012), 135.

13. Wiseman, interview.

14. C. Monnot, "The Female Pop Singer and the 'Apprentice' Girl," *Journal of Children and Media* 4, no. 3 (2010): 283–97.

15. Keith Robinson, interview by author, August 1, 2011.

16. Will Crawford, interview by author, August 3, 2011.

17. Jerry Pope, interview by author, August 1, 2011.

18. ABC News, December 6, 2011, "Lady Gaga Takes Anti-Bullying to White House," abcnews.go.com/WNT/video/lady-gaga-takes-anti-bullying-white-house-15100813.

19. Lyn Mikel Brown, interview by author, December 19, 2011.

20. S. Davis and C. Nixon, "Youth Voice Research Project: Victimization and Strategies," 2010, www.youthvoiceproject.com/YVPMarch2010.pdf.

21. Pope, interview.

22. Jim Margalus, interview by author, July 10, 2011.

23. Al Yellon, interview by author, July 14, 2011.

24. Hinduja and Patchin, *Cyberbullying Prevention*, 136.

25. Hinduja and Patchin, *Cyberbullying Prevention*, 134.

26. Hinduja and Patchin, *Cyberbullying Prevention*, 153.

27. Hinduja and Patchin, *Cyberbullying Prevention*, 142.

28. Rachel Simmons, interview by author, August 31, 2011.

29. Bauman, interview.

30. Hinduja and Patchin, *Cyberbullying Prevention*, 142.

31. Hinduja and Patchin, *Cyberbullying Prevention*, 137.

32. Hinduja and Patchin, *Cyberbullying Prevention*, 139.

33. Simmons, interview.

34. Bauman, interview; Patchin, interview; Ybarra, interview.

35. J. Hoffman, "A Girl's Nude Photo, and Altered Lives," *New York Times*, 2011, www.nytimes.com/2011/03/27/us/27sexting.html?_r=2.

Chapter 13: Changing Our Cultural Attitudes Toward Aggression and Cruelty

1. Chase Masterson, interview by author, April 4, 2011.

2. Stan Davis, interview by author, April 1, 2011.

3. The Girl Scouts survey was conducted with the research firm TRU and consisted of a national sample of 1,141 girls ages eleven to seventeen. The survey took place April 6–26, 2011. The facts reported are taken from GSGCNWI press releases and were confirmed by Girl Scouts GCNWI CEO, Maria Wynne.

4. Maria Wynne, interview by author, October 20, 2011.

5. "Monster High & Kind Campaign: The Shockumentary," animated YouTube video, 3:28, posted by MonsterHigh on October 3, 2011, http://youtube.com/watch?v=JKeNh6xgKTg.

6. Lauren Parsekian and Molly Stroud, interview by author, June 28, 2011.

7. R. Simmons, *Odd Girl Out: The Hidden Culture of Aggression in Girls* (New York: Harcourt, 2003), 3.

8. Girl identified as "Kyra," interview by author, March 22, 2011.

9. Simmons, interview.

10. Fox, interview.

11. Rosalind Wiseman, interview by author, July 19, 2011.

12. Brown, Lamb, and Tappan, *Packaging Boyhood*, 1.

13. R. Clark, "Michael Cole Writes Homophobic Slur on Twitter," eWrestling News.com, March 26, 2011, www.ewrestlingnews.com/headlines/Michael_Cole _Writes_Homophobic_Slur_On_Twitte.php.

Chapter 14: Calling on Toy Retailers to Eliminate Gender-Based Marketing

1. Paoletti, interview.

2. Ashley Eckstein, interview by author, March 29, 2011.

3. Brown, Lamb, and Tappan, *Packaging Boyhood*, 271.

4. Eckstein, interview.

5. Paoletti, interview.

6. Hanish, interview; L. D. Hanish et al., "Girls, Boys, and Bullying in Preschool," in Espelage and Swearer, eds., *Bullying in North American Schools*.

7. Paoletti, interview.

8. Max Adler, interview by author, June 24, 2011.

9. Jerry Pope, interview.

10. Lyn Mikel Brown, interview by author, May 21, 2011.

11. R. D. Konigsberg, "Lego Friends for Girls: Have They Stooped to Stereotype?," *Time*, January 2, 2012, ideas.time.com/2012/01/02/lego-friends-for-girls-have-they-stooped-to-stereotype/.

12. B. S. Richards, "Lego's Listening, but They're Not Quite Hearing Us," Spark Summit, December 21, 2011, www.sparksummit.com/2011/12/21/3675/.

13. C. Goldman, "Dear Lego, I Have a Girl," ChicagoNow.com, December 22, 2011, www.chicagonow.com/portrait-of-an-adoption/2011/12/dear-lego-i-have-a-girl/.

14. Orenstein quoted research from Lise Eliot, author of *Pink Brain, Blue Brain*.

15. P. Orenstein, "Should the World of Toys Be Gender-Free?" *New York Times,* December 29, 2011, www.nytimes.com/2011/12/30/opinion/does-stripping-gen der-from-toys-really-make-sense.html?_r=1&scp=2&sq=peggy%20 orenstein&st=cse.

Chapter 15: Stop Marketing Makeup and Sexy Clothes to Children

1. ABC Action News, 2011, "Geo-Girl Pre-Teen Make-up Line Debuts in Walmart Stores," www.abcactionnews.com/dpp/news/local_news/geo-girl-pre-teen-make-up-line-debuts-in-walmart-stores.

2. A. Vanallen, V. Weber, and S. Kunin, "Are Tweens Too Young for Makeup?" ABC News, January 27, 2011, abcnews.go.com/US/tweens-young-makeup/story?id=12777008.

3. American Psychological Association, *Sexualization of Girls,* 2007, www .apa.org/pi/women/programs/girls/report.aspx.

4. Vanallen, Weber, and Kunin, "Tweens Too Young?"

5. P. Orenstein, *Cinderella Ate My Daughter: Dispatches from the Front Lines of the New Girlie-Girl Culture* (New York: HarperCollins, 2011), 84–85.

6. Orenstein, interview.

7. A. Canning, M. Pflum, and K. Hagan, *Bikini Waxing for Tweens! Have Spas Gone Too Far?* ABC News, 2008, abcnews.go.com/GMA/BeautySecrets/story?id=4881675&page=1.

8. Vanallen, Weber, and Kunin, "Tweens Too Young?"

9. V. Rao, "Too Young? Preteen Girls Get Leg, Bikini Waxes," Today Style, 2008, today.msnbc.msn.com/id/26182276/ns/today-style/t/too-young-preteen-girls-get-leg-bikini-waxes/.

10. N. Park, "Child Pageants Bad for Mental Health," *Sydney Morning Herald,* May 25, 2011, news.smh.com.au/breaking-news-national/child-pageants-bad-for-mental-health-20110525-1f430.html.

11. R. Juzwiak, "The Mother of *Toddlers & Tiaras'* Eden Wood: 'We're Not Weirdos; We're Not Freaks,'" TV Guide.com, June 14, 2011, www.tvguide.com/News/Toddlers-Tiaras-Eden-Wood-1034237.aspx.

12. Brown, interview.

13. Brown, interview.

14. H. Moss, "Skechers' Shape-Ups for Girls Called Out by Internet," *Huffington Post,* July 10, 2011, www.huffingtonpost.com/2011/05/10/skechers-shape-ups-for-girls_n_859781.html.

15. American Psychological Association, *Sexualization of Girls.*

16. D. E. Levin and J. Kilbourne, *So Sexy So Soon: The New Sexualized Childhood and What Parents Can Do to Protect Their Kids* (New York: Ballantine, 2008), 56–57.

17. T. Shipman, "High Street Shops to Ban Padded Bras and 'Sexually Suggestive' Clothing for Young Girls," *Daily Mail,* 2011, www.dailymail.co.uk/news/article-1394123/High-street-shops-ban-clothes-sexualise-little-girls.html.

18. Jennifer Stuller, interview by author, August 22, 2011.

19. Jean Kilbourne, interview by author, June 27, 2011.

20. S. L. Smith and C. A. Cook, *Gender Stereotypes: An Analysis of Popular Films and TV* (Los Angeles: Geena Davis Institute on Gender in Media, 2008), www.thegeenadavisinstitute.org/downloads/GDIGM_Gender_Stereotypes.pdf.

21. Jennifer Siebel Newsom, "Miss Representation," www.missrepresentation.org/the-film/.

22. blog.pigtailpals.com.

23. Melissa Wardy, interview by author, July 15, 2011.

24. L. M. Alphonse, "Epic T-Shirt Fail: 'I'm Too Pretty to Do My Homework, So My Brother Has to Do It for Me,'" Shine from Yahoo!, August 31, 2011, shine.

yahoo.com/parenting/epic-t-shirt-fail-quot-im-too-pretty-to-do-my-home work-so-my-brother-has-to-do-it-for-me-quot-2537106.html.

25. Madeline di Nonno, interview by author, June 20, 2011.

26. Smith and Cook, *Gender Stereotypes*.

27. S. L. Smith and M. Choueiti, "Gender Disparity on Screen and Behind the Camera in Family Films"; executive report (Los Angeles: Geena Davis Institute on Gender in Media, 2010), www.thegeenadavisinstitute.org/downloads/Full Study_GenderDisparityFamilyFilms.pdf.

28. Recommendations based on the research (Los Angeles: Geena Davis Institute on Gender in Media), www.seejane.org/research.php.

Chapter 16: Reassess the Role of Schools in Character Education

1. Dorothy Espelage, interview by author, February 15, 2011.

2. Robey, interview.

3. Astor, interview.

4. W. Hu, "Bullying Law Puts New Jersey Schools on Spot," *New York Times,* August 30, 2011, www.nytimes.com/2011/08/31/nyregion/bullying-law-puts-new-jersey-schools-on-spot.html?emc=eta1.

5. Michael Kelly, interview by author, January 13, 2011.

6. Borba, interview.

7. Zachary Herrmann, written interview by author, July 26, 2011.

8. Davis, interview.

9. Collier, interview.

10. Stan Davis, interview by author, July 21, 2011.

11. Man identified as "Roberto," interview by author, August 19, 2011.

12. William Porter, interview by author, August 4, 2011.

13. Brown, interview.

Chapter 17: Social and Emotional Learning

1. *CASEL: Expanding Social and Emotional Learning Nationwide: Let's Go! An Overview* (Washington, DC: CASEL Forum, April 13–14, 2011).

2. Rosalind Wisemen, interview by author, April 11, 2011.

3. John Gottman, interview by author, April 18, 2011.

4. J. Gottman, *Raising an Emotionally Intelligent Child: The Heart of Parenting* (New York: Simon & Schuster, 1997), 69–109. Used with permission of John Gottman.

5. Christina Sung Aie Choi, interview by author, April 21, 2011.

6. Choi, interview.

7. "National Mix It Up at Lunch Day," Teaching Tolerance, www.tolerance.org/mix-it-up.

Chapter 18: Responding to the Bully

1. Hanish, interview.

2. Kumpulainen, Rasanen, and Puura, "Psychiatric Disorders"; Haynie et al., "Bullies, Victims, and Bully/Victims"; S. M. Swearer et al., "Psychosocial Correlates in Bullying and Victimization: The Relationship Between Depression, Anxiety, and Bully/Victim Status," *Journal of Emotional Abuse* 2 (2001): 95–121.

3. B. Vossekuil et al., *The Final Report and Findings of the Safe School Initiative: Implications for the Prevention of School Attacks in the United States* (Washington, DC: U.S. Secret Service and U.S. Department of Education, 2002).

4. Man identified as "Arthur," interview by author, July 9, 2011.

5. Espelage, interview.

6. Kelly, interview.

7. Susan Limber, interview by author, August 3, 2011.

8. S. P. Limber, "Implementation of the Olweus Bullying Prevention Program in American Schools: Lessons Learned from the Field, in Espelage and Swearer, ed. *Bullying in North American Schools.* 303.

9. David Shriberg, interview by author, January 11, 2012.

10. From *Confessions of a Former Bully* by Trudy Ludwig, with illustrations by Beth Adams, text copyright © 2010 by Trudy Ludwig, used by permission of Tricycle Press, an imprint of Random House Children's Books, a division of Random House, Inc.

11. Coloroso, interview.

12. R. Hamilton, "I Was a Bully," *Words by Ross,* November 18, 2010, word smiff.blogspot.com/2010/11/i-was-bully.html.

13. Ludwig, interview.

14. Kate Ellison, interview by author, May 20, 2011.

Chapter 19: Responding to the Victim

1. Stan Davis, interview by author, April 1, 2011.

2. Young woman identified as "Josie," interview by author, December 4, 2011.

3. Thompson, interview.

4. Coloroso, *Bully, the Bullied, and the Bystander,* 14.

5. Davis and Nixon, "Youth Voice Research."

6. Davis, interview.

7. Davis and Nixon, "Youth Voice Research."

8. Davis and Nixon, "Youth Voice Research."

9. Davis and Nixon, "Youth Voice Research."

10. Davis and Nixon, "Youth Voice Research."

11. Davis and Nixon, "Youth Voice Research."

12. Jodee Blanco, interview by author, February 7, 2011.

13. Wes Shockley, interview by author, March 17, 2011.

14. Techniques and descriptions provided to author by Wes Shockley in written form on Friday, January 13, 2012, and confirmed during author's phone call with Wes Shockley on January 15, 2012.

15. Stilwell, interview.

Chapter 20: Restorative Justice

1. Brenda Morrison, interview by author, July 22, 2011.

2. Arika Barton and Susan Trieschmann, interview by author, February 24, 2011.

3. Morrison, interview.

Chapter 21: Strategies That Ease the Negative Effects of Taunting

1. Coloroso, *Bully, the Bullied, and the Bystander,* 110.

2. Judy Freedman, interview by author, December 13, 2010; J. Freedman, *Easing the Teasing: Helping Your Child Cope with Name-Calling, Ridicule, and Verbal Bullying* (New York: McGraw-Hill, 2002), 101–39.

3. D. G. Perry, J. C. Williard, and L. Perry, "Peers' Perceptions of Consequences That Victimized Children Provide Aggressors," *Child Development* 61 (1990): 1289–1309.

4. Young woman identified as "Carla," interview.

5. Davis, interview.

6. Bauman, interview.

7. Davis, interview.

8. Freedman, *Easing the Teasing,* 109.

9. Davis, interview.

10. James Arnold Taylor, interview by author, March 29, 2011.

11. Freedman, *Easing the Teasing,* 136.

Chapter 22: Creating Witnesses and Allies out of Bystanders

1. Justin Roberts, interview by author, January 12, 2012.

2. P. O'Connell, D. Pepler, and W. Craig, "Peer Involvement in Bullying: Insights and Challenges for Intervention," *Journal of Adolescence* 22, no. 4 (1999): 437–52; D. L. Hawkins, D. J. Pepler, and W. M. Craig, "Naturalistic Observations of Peer Interventions in Bullying," *Social Development* 10 (2001): 512–27.

3. Hinduja and Patchin, *Cyberbullying Prevention,* 98.

4. Davis and Nixon, "Youth Voice Research."

5. Coloroso, *Bully, the Bullied, and the Bystander,* 134; Ludwig, *Confessions of a Former Bully,* 31–32.

6. Davis and Nixon, "Youth Voice Research."

7. Davis and Nixon, "Youth Voice Research."

8. Davis, interview.

9. Coloroso, interview; Coloroso, *Bully, the Bullied, and the Bystander,* 159–161.

10. Davis, interview.

11. Collier, interview.

12. www.cartoonnetwork.com/promos/stopbullying/index.html.

13. Burch-Sims, interview.

14. Thompson, interview.

Chapter 23: Cybersupporting Instead of Cyberbullying: A Real-Life Happy Ending

1. Adler, interview; Dan Savage, It Gets Better project.

2. J. Branch, "Two Straight Athletes Combat Homophobia," *New York Times,* May 13, 2011, www.nytimes.com/2011/05/14/sports/two-straight-ath letes-combat-homophobia.html?pagewanted=all.

3. Ben Cohen, interview by author, July 8, 2011.

4. Collier, interview.

Appendix A: Overview of Several Promising Research-Based Bullying-Prevention and Character-Education Programs

1. Espelage, interview; A. M. Horne et al., "Bully Busters: A Resource for School and Parents to Prevent and Respond to Bullying," in Espelage and Swearer, ed. *Bullying in North American Schools.*

2. Porter, interview; A. Plog et al., "Bully-Proofing Your School: Overview of the Program, Outcome Research, and Questions That Remain About How Best to Implement Effective Bullying Prevention in Schools," in Espelage and Swearer, eds., *Bullying in North American Schools.*

3. L. Sjostrom and N. Stein, *Bullyproof: A Teacher's Guide on Teasing and Bullying for Use with Fourth and Fifth Grade Students* (Wellesley, MA: Wellesley College, 1996); D. Espelage and S. Swearer, *Bullying in American Schools: A Social-Ecological Perspective on Prevention and Intervention* (Mahwah, NJ: Lawrence Erlbaum, 2004), 327–50.

4. B. Ball and B. Rosenbluth, *Expect Respect—Program Overview: A School-Based Program for Preventing Teen Dating Violence and Promoting Safe*

and Healthy Relationships (Austin, TX: SafePlace, 2008), www.safeplace.org/document.doc?id=27.

5. N. Stein, *Classrooms and Courtrooms: Facing Sexual Harassment in K–12 Schools* (New York: Teachers College Press, 1999), 11.

6. E. Aronson et al., *The Jigsaw Classroom* (Beverly Hills, CA: Sage, 1978), www.jigsaw.org/.

7. Limber, interview; Limber, "Implementation of the Olweus Bullying Prevention Program," in Espelage and Swearer, eds., *Bullying in North American Schools.*

8. Positive Behavioral Interventions and Supports, handouts and PowerPoints, 2010 PBIS National Forum at Chicago, 2010, www.pbis.org/presentations/chicago_forum_10.aspx.

9. Evanston/Skokie District 65, 2010, *Evanston/Skokie District 65 Guide on Bullying.*

10. K. S. Frey et al., "Reducing Playground Bullying and Supporting Beliefs: An Experimental Trial of the Steps to Respect Program," *Developmental Psychology* 41, no. 3 (2005): 479–91.

11. Committee for Children, "Steps to Respect: A Bullying Prevention Program" (Seattle: Committee for Children, 2001); S. M. Low et al., "Design and Analysis of Randomized Controlled Trial of Steps to Respect," in Espelage and Swearer, eds., *Bullying in North American Schools.*

Appendix B: Two Examples of Bullying Surveys

1. A Bullying Survey for Early Grades by Teaching Tolerance, www.tolerance.org/activity/bullying-survey.

2. Surveys provided by Dorothy Espelage; D. L. Espelage, M. K. Holt, and R. R. Henkel, "Examination of Peer-Group Contextual Effects on Aggression During Early Adolescence," *Child Development* 74 (2003): 205–20; D. L. Espelage and M. K. Holt, eds. "Bullying and Victimization During Early Adolescence: Peer Influences and Psychosocial Correlates," *Journal of Emotional Abuse* 2 (2011): 123–42.

Appendix C: Examples of Sexual Harassment Surveys

1. Surveys provided by Dorothy Espelage; D. L. Espelage, K. C. Basile, and M. E. Hamburger, "Bullying Perpetration and Subsequent Sexual Violence Perpetration Among Middle School Students: Shared and Unique Risk Factors," *Journal of Adolescent Health* 50 (2012): 60–65.

Index